"Roxanne Dunbar-Ortiz is clearly a memoirist of great skills and even greater heart. She's a force of nature on the page and off."
— Dave Eggers, author of *A Heartbreaking Work of Staggering Genius*

"American foreign policy today is being shaped by veterans of the savage Washington-backed Contra war of the 1980s. In the third volume of her extraordinary memoir, Dunbar-Ortiz recounts the secret history of that intervention, as well as her own courageous solidarity with the embattled Nicaraguan revolution."
— Mike Davis, author of *City of Quartz* and *Ecology of Fear*

"Here is the real life of a brilliant activist, the personal woes and conflicts, the roles of friendship, character and gender, as well as the big issues and shining moments; and here is a rousing account of the 1980s, so relevant and so seldom discussed. Yet the 1980s seem very close these days, as a right-wing administration once again sponsors torture, war, and other crimes in the name of freedom—and as Latin America once again is on fire with liberation movements. Of particular importance is Dunbar-Ortiz's exploration of the gray zones between the indigenous Miskitus in Nicaragua and the Sandinistas. An important book, and a gripping one."
— Rebecca Solnit, author of *Hope in the Dark* and *River of Shadows*

"This third volume of Roxanne Dunbar-Ortiz's important memoir combines deep self-reflection with an extraordinary political overview of times that are mostly forgotten because the current owners of history have succeeded in erasing them from our collective consciousness. 'History itself is the issue,' this author writes, and goes on to expose and deconstruct that which she has so courageously lived. From a quarter-century of international indigenous rights work to a run-in with Oliver North and a narrow escape from death on a sabotaged Mexico–Managua flight, Dunbar-Ortiz's story is an exciting and sobering read that holds valuable lessons for today's ongoing struggles for justice."
— Margaret Randall, author of *When I Look Into the Mirror and See You: Women, Terror and Resistance*

"This is an impressive, astounding, and truthful historical document. Every American should read it to understand the shady and dubious role played in Central America by the men who are forging US foreign policy in the world today. A passionate and engaged protagonist of historical times, Roxanne Dunbar-Ortiz tells a story that is moving, profoundly human, and enlightening."

— Gioconda Belli, author of *The Country Under My Skin*

"Terrorism was planted in the Western Hemisphere, or Indian Country, when the first immigrant stole in the name of greed, racism, or on the basis of a political or religious system that placed themselves above all living beings, placed males above females in power—then strove to keep in place this tenuous and terrible system with laws, with gun power. This book is the story of a particular rupture, in Central America, at the heart of the Americas. Roxanne Dunbar-Ortiz speaks on behalf of justice. It's never simple. And there is no clean, perfect ending. What is sure here is the brilliant, fearless storytelling by Dunbar-Ortiz of the devastation wreaked by a ruthless corrupt power. What is sure is the ongoing drama of the story: it entangles all of us."

— Joy Harjo, Mvskoke Nation poet and musician

"September 11, 1973—the date of the CIA-sponsored coup against the government of Salvador Allende in Chile—marks the beginning of a long period of conservative hegemony in the Americas, though the aftermath of September 11, 2001, has witnessed in Latin America at least a gradual shift to the left. In that context, it is urgent to take a new look at the revolutionary upsurge from the 1960s through the 1980s. Roxanne Dunbar-Ortiz was a North American activist personally involved in the revolutionary process, above all in Central America. Her memoir, which deals with the Contra war against the Nicaraguan revolution, is an essential book in this regard, and at the same an engrossing, eminently readable example of the feminist idea that 'the personal is the political.'"

—John Beverley, University of Pittsburgh, author of
Testimonio: On the Politics of Truth

"This is a comprehensive and powerful account of the development of the Contra war of the 1980s, which destroyed many lives and changed the course of Central American history. . . All the gears of Reagan-era political manipulation are exposed here, including the Iran-Contra scandal, and the countless ways in which Reagan's propaganda machine created monstrous lies about the situation of the Miskitu people during the Sandinista Revolution. . . Vividly written with the authoritative voice of a fearless witness, this book is a required reading for anyone interested in the truth."
                    — Daisy Zamora, poet, author of *Riverbed of Memory*

"Roxanne Dunbar-Ortiz's new book . . . captures a messy snapshot of our country and her own life. A living embodiment of the philosophy 'the personal is political,' she navigates a dense narrative river through her early, youthful enthusiasm for social change, moving upstream toward a hard-edged and realistic perception of the undertows of political waters. Along the route she spares no politician—Left or Right—who has pushed antipopulist agendas or pushed indigenous people around. Dunbar-Ortiz takes every political betrayal, accommodation and broken treaty personally; yet always she reveals an unbowed human spirit—a major ingredient in victory."
                    — Jewelle Gomez, author of *The Gilda Stories*

"Rarely do the personal and the political blend so seamlessly as Roxanne Dunbar-Ortiz recounts her tireless efforts to oppose US imperialism during and after Nicaragua's Contra war of the 1980s. [Her] life and work in this period foreshadow today's struggles over issues as diverse as terrorism, governmental press manipulation, engaged scholarship, activism, alcoholism, and even identity politics. This captivating blend of personal memoir and political/intellectual history could not be more timely."
                    — Baron Pineda, author of *Shipwrecked Identities:*
                    Navigating Race on the Mosquito Coast

"To academics, history is an exercise in juxtaposing public facts to create a believable narrative. To the activist struggling within those facts, history is the personal memory of the suffering of the ordinary folks who have been condemned by their history to be, at best, merely a footnote in those facts. As a scholar, she told their story. As an activist, she told her own. In combination, Dunbar-Ortiz has produced some formidable historical memoirs, which end up being autobiographical people's histories. In *Red Dirt: Growing Up Okie*, by describing her upbringing in rural Oklahoma, she made her readers understand what life was like to the repressed, often off-white, sharecroppers (she herself is part Native American). In *Outlaw Woman: A Memoir of the War Years, 1960–75,* she made us feel what it was like to be an independent woman who became a human rights standard bearer at the UN. Now, in *Blood on the Border*, she makes us live through the horrors of Reagan's bloody war against the first decent government in Central America, while at the same time bringing to life the ordeal of the northeastern Nicaraguan tribes caught between Oliver North's vicious and illegal crusade and the ill-conceived nationalism of the Sandinistas, who refused to give those tribes autonomy. In the process, Dunbar-Ortiz, a ferocious feminist who spent years in Nicaragua living through that schizophrenic situation, makes us experience the rise and fall of the anti-war, leftist and especially the women's liberation movements, here at home and its consequences abroad."

— John Gerassi, author of *The Great Fear in Latin America*

"What can I say but **thank you,** Roxanne, for keeping such detailed memories of a time of turmoil and growth of indigenous people to the south. As an early founder of the feminist movement, Roxanne assumed a position in the forefront of international nation building, the realm of male domination, to just basically get the job done. And what a job she did!"

— Madonna Gilbert Thunderhawk, Lakota activist and
AIM leader at Alcatraz and Wounded Knee

Blood on the Border

Blood on the Border

A Memoir of the Contra War

ROXANNE DUNBAR-ORTIZ

SOUTH END PRESS
Cambridge, MA

Library of Congress Cataloging-in-Publication Data
Dunbar-Ortiz, Roxanne.
Blood on the Border: A Memoir of the Contra War. p. cm.
Includes bibliographical references and index.
ISBN 0-89608-742-5 (pbk. : alk. paper)
Library of Congress Control Number: 2005934779

ISBN: 0-89608-742-5 (pbk.: alk. paper)

Printed in Canada by union labor on acid-free, recycled paper.
09 08 07 06 05   1 2 3 4 5

Text design and composition: Hiatt & Dragon, San Francisco

South End Press
7 Brookline Street, Suite 1
Cambridge, MA 02139
www.southendpress.org
southend@southendpress.org

To three great women:
Chockie Cottier, Dr. Mirna Cunningham,
and Maya Miller, for support and love;

To Indigenous Peoples in the struggle for
self-determination;

And in memory of all the casualties of
the Contra war.

Contents

Acknowledgments

The Contra war, Nicaragua, and the Miskitu Indians—front page news two decades ago—are nearly forgotten, even by many who were aware of them at the time, and they are almost unknown to a new generation. Thanks to the entire editorial collective at South End Press for believing in this book. Special thanks go to South End Press editor Jill Petty for her patience, support, and intelligence, and to Jocelyn Burrell and Loie Hayes for careful readings. My old comrade Steve Hiatt has, as usual, done a beautiful and scrupulous job of sculpting the text. It was a pleasure to work with all concerned.

Professor Baron Pineda and Margaret Randall generously read earlier drafts of the book and provided profound insights and suggestions. Sidni Lamb served as a memory bank for names of colleagues who worked with Miskitu refugees in Honduras. I owe gratitude to my sister in the struggle, Chockie Cottier, a true Lakota warrior. Dr. Mirna Cunningham, Miskitu leader par excellence, gave focus to my passion, and remains an important advocate for indigenous peoples' rights in Central America and the world. Maya Miller was sister, confidant, and angel. I thank them.

A note on the spelling and pronunciation of *Miskitu*: Pronounced mis-kit-u, with the emphasis on the first syllable, it is most often spelled in the Spanish forms *Miskito* for the masculine and *Miskita* for the feminine; or sometimes as *Miskitu*. *Miskitu* is the spelling used in the Miskitu language and is the spelling I use in this book. However, I have not changed quotes from other sources using the Spanish versions. Older texts use the British spelling, *Mosquito*, for the people and their language, and *Mosquitia* or *Mosquito Coast* for the region. In keeping with modern usage, I have employed *Miskitia* for the region.

Roxanne Dunbar-Ortiz
San Francisco, August 2005

There is at the head of this great continent a very powerful country, very rich, very warlike, and capable of anything . . . the United States seems destined to plague and torment the continent in the name of freedom.

— Simón Bolívar, 1829

The United States will never leave Nicaragua alone.

— William Walker, US president of Nicaragua, 1856–57

I helped in the raping of half a dozen Central American republics for the benefit of Wall Street. The record of racketeering is long. I helped purify Nicaragua for the international banking house of Brown Brothers in 1909–1912.

— Major General Smedley Butler, US Marine Corps

The United States cannot, therefore, fail to view with deep concern any serious threat to stability and constitutional government in Nicaragua tending toward anarchy and jeopardizing American interests, especially if such state of affairs is contributed to or brought about by outside influence or by any foreign power.

— President Calvin Coolidge, addressing Congress in 1927

Somoza may be a son of a bitch, but he's our son of a bitch.

— President Franklin Delano Roosevelt, 1939

I believe one inevitable outcome of a rejection of this aid would be that it would remove all pressure on the Sandinistas to change. And if no constraints are put on the Sandinistas, I believe the brutality and abuse they already aim at their own country and their neighbors may well be magnified a thousandfold.

— President Ronald Reagan, April 15, 1985

Prologue

The first time I remember hearing about Somoza, Sandino, and Nicaragua was in early 1960 when I was twenty-one years old and new to San Francisco, having just moved there from Oklahoma. All that year, I worked at Remington Rand while establishing residency requirements to avoid paying out-of-state tuition for college. I processed sales, rental, and repair orders for typewriters and adding machines, serving all the company's outlets in the greater Bay Area. It was a small office in a hulking downtown warehouse where assembly, repairs, and stocking were the main functions. The UNIVAC computer, said to be our future god, dominated the main-floor showroom just below the mezzanine where our workspace was located.

Four of us "girls" worked as order clerks under the supervision of a very handsome and elegant Chinese American man about twice our age—by far the kindest boss I'd ever had in my five years of blue- and pink-collared wage-slave jobs.

One of the "girls," Sonia, was Nicaraguan.

Meeting Sonia jogged my memory of the late 1940s pop song "Managua, Nicaragua," which played on the radio when I was a kid in rural Oklahoma. Guy Lombardo and His Royal Canadians, then a favorite band across the flat stretches of North America, recorded the song:

Managua, Nicaragua, is a beautiful town
You buy a hacienda for a few pesos down

1

You give it to the lady you are tryin' to win
But her papa doesn't let you come in. . .

Managua, Nicaragua, what a wonderful spot
There's coffee and bananas and a temperature hot
So take a trip and on a ship go sailing away
Across the agua to Managua, Nicaragua,
Olé,
Olé, olé
Across the agua to Managua, Nicaragua, olé.

With this song my only source of information about Nicaragua, it was little wonder Sonia took it upon herself to reeducate me.

I could not figure out why I didn't even know where Nicaragua was located. I was good at geography and history and wasn't ignorant of world politics, having spent a year at Oklahoma University and having been friends with Palestinians, Jordanians, and Syrians during the 1957 Suez crisis. I even knew about the CIA and its overthrow of Iran's premier Mohammad Mossadeq only a few years earlier. African decolonization was in the news, and I had read Vera Micheles Dean's *The Nature of the Non-Western World*, an anti-imperialist book. I recently had learned something about Southeast Asia and the People's Republic of China from the Kennedy–Nixon presidential debates. Thanks to my engineer husband's co-worker at Bechtel, who was from the Philippines, I had heard all about the US occupation and continued control of his country for the past half-century. I knew—from a Cuban friend at Oklahoma University—every detail about the recent Cuban revolution that overthrew the dictator Batista.

But I was vague about the rest of Spain's former Latin American empire. I had never even heard of El Salvador, Honduras, Guatemala, Nicaragua, Costa Rica, or Panama (wasn't that a canal somewhere?). Two decades later, during the Carter/Reagan/Bush decade of fomenting a civil war in Nicaragua and quelling insurgency against repressive regimes in others, national polls revealed that the overwhelming majority of US citizens, even highly educated professionals, did not know on what continent or even in what hemisphere Nicaragua was located. Even at the University of California, Berkeley, where there was a significant Sandinista solidarity movement, a poll revealed that more than half the students questioned thought Nicaragua was a country in Africa. I empathized with them, but I feared their/our ignorance.

On my first day of work, Sonia told me that the Nicaraguan population of San Francisco was second only to that of Managua, Nicaragua's capital, and that Nicaraguans made up the majority of the Spanish-speaking community of San Francisco. She also told me that Nicaragua was important for more than a pop song and bananas—this was before I'd heard the term "banana republics" in reference to the Central American countries, although she assumed I already had. I looked up Nicaragua in my atlas when I got home, too embarrassed to ask Sonia where it was.

Sonia told me a story about a 1920s civil war in Nicaragua provoked by the United States. Augusto César Sandino, a dissident member of the Nicaraguan parliament, formed a guerrilla army to drive out the occupying US Marines, along with the North American companies they were there to protect—Standard Fruit, the banana company; Wrigley's, the chewing gum company; Pine-Sol; and several companies harvesting sassafras, which was used to make root beer and other products. I knew the products but had no idea where they originated. In retaliation, the Marines bombed villages in the remote northeast of the country where the companies operated. Sandino led a peasant army that eventually triumphed, forcing the Marines and the companies to withdraw. But the game was not over. In 1934, Sandino was assassinated and the Somoza family regime installed.

Only after Sonia had told me quite a lot about Nicaragua and its great beauty—the volcanoes, the inland sea, the beaches, the tropical birds and fruit—did I dream of going there someday. I never saw Sonia again after I left Remington Rand to continue my education at San Francisco State College.

I went on to get my undergraduate degree in history at San Francisco State and then to doctoral work in European history at the University of California, Berkeley. Following three months in Mexico, I moved to UCLA to work on a doctorate in history, specializing in Latin America. Except for the 1954 CIA-organized coup in Guatemala and the Cuban Revolution in 1959, Central America and the Caribbean were rarely discussed, and there were no seminars or courses on the region. The indigenous peoples were called *campesinos*, peasants.

I barely noticed news of the cataclysmic earthquake that destroyed much of Managua and took twenty thousand Nicaraguan lives just before Christmas in 1972. I would not learn for several years more that the outpouring of relief aid that flowed into Nicaragua was shoveled by Somoza into his own private accounts. Beginning in 1977, I did start paying attention to the Nicaraguan revolution that would bring the Sandinistas to power in 1979 and to the beginning of the US military and economic campaign to overthrow them, with which I soon became obsessed.

Those of us who had been activists against the Vietnam War thought that perhaps we had seen the end of such military interventions. The mid-1970s had seemed a peculiarly hopeful time. The United States had been forced to abandon the Vietnam War, and the 1960s social and cultural revolution had pressured government officials into responding to demands from women, Native Americans, Blacks, Latinos, prisoners, the poor, the disabled, children, and elders. From the United Nations came international human rights agreements that provided the framework for social transformation, and the official Decade for Women and Decade to Combat Racism were launched worldwide with great fanfare, programs that brought me into international human rights work. President Richard Nixon, who had continued the war in Vietnam for six years, was forced to resign in 1974, and the CIA and FBI were castigated by Congress for spying on US citizens.

In California, where I lived, Jerry Brown was elected governor in 1974 and was reelected in 1978. He appointed Tom Hayden and other New Leftists to government positions, reflecting the credibility that radicals had gained. Brown also appointed four liberal judges to the California Supreme Court, making the chief justice a woman, Rose Bird.

In San Francisco, my city, a left-leaning populist, George Moscone, was elected mayor, and Harvey Milk became the first openly gay activist to be elected to the Board of Supervisors. Across the bay in Oakland, the grassroots infrastructure built by the Black Panther Party brought radical African Americans into local office and helped to elect Ron Dellums, an African American and self-described socialist, to Congress.

Nationally, the Democratic Party candidate, Jimmy Carter, was elected president in 1976 and appointed civil rights leader Andrew Young as ambassador to the United Nations. Carter even appointed a human rights specialist, Patricia Derrian, as a State Department special envoy. In lobbying to bring the issue of broken Indian treaties into the United Nations, we found that even though Ambassador Young opposed the idea of our taking the issue to the UN, he treated us with respect, and we made gains. I was tapped to serve on National Endowment for the Humanities panels to recommend funding for project proposals.

In Africa, the former Portuguese colonies of Angola, Mozambique, and Guinea-Bissau won their independence, as did Zimbabwe. The southern African armed liberation movements (the African National Congress, Pan-African Congress, and Southwest Africa Peoples Organization), and the Palestine Liberation Organization gained observer status in the UN, legitimizing their claims to political leadership and strengthening the claims of other armed national liberation struggles around the world. Though the Cold War had not ended by any means, détente between the United States and the USSR was policy, and the worldwide antinuclear movement was huge and fused a wide range of cultural and political movements. John Lennon, Yoko Ono, and other countercultural icons mobilized millions of young people to the cause of peace and humanitarianism. The environmental movement took off: Jane Fonda's prescient film *The China Syndrome*, followed by an actual meltdown at the Three Mile Island nuclear plant in 1979, strengthened the already large antinuclear movement and halted the expansion of nuclear-powered energy. These were all liberalizing reforms, not revolutionary, but they provided ample space for those of us on the left to organize for more radical changes.

But first appearances are deceptive. The seeds for the counterrevolution that was to follow were being planted. The political space that had been created by the 1960s movements began to contract even before Reagan's right-wing hardliners assumed power in 1981. Although I was not aware of it at the time, in 1974 when I joined the American Indian Movement, its leadership and grassroots base were already in disarray—co-opted, jailed, killed, exiled, burned out, and wracked by internal conflict, as were the other internal liberation movements. Soon, the Native movement would have to organize not only against repression, but also against ninety-eight proposals in the US Congress to terminate the Native American land base and treaties. To make things worse, the Carter administration's energy policy included an assault on Native resources in the West as the administration declared the western intermountain area a "national sacrifice zone," free for open-pit and surface coal and uranium mining.

In San Francisco, two bizarre cults dominated the news and formed a sort of parody—a tragic parody—of the former mass movements, a kind of hideous coda for the end of an era. One was the Symbionese Liberation Army, a tiny cult led by an African American man, Cinque, an alcoholic ex-con who mesmerized a dozen or so inexperienced young women and men. Armed with weapons and a cartoon version of leftist demands, their first act was to assassinate Dr. Marcus Foster, the reformist African American superintendent of the Oakland school system. Soon after, they gained notoriety by kidnapping nineteen-year-old newspaper heiress Patty Hearst.

A parallel cult was much larger and more mainstream, but no less insidious. Jim Jones's Peoples Temple attracted thousands, a majority of them African Americans. Jones employed the rhetoric of the civil rights movement and anti-imperialism. No demonstration was complete without the arrival of busloads of enthusiastic troops from Peoples Temple, Reverend Jones himself often the main speaker. Liberal politicians—local, state, and national—courted favor with the Reverend. Foundation and private donor funds poured in to support his experimental farm in the jungles of Guyana. In 1978, when suspicions arose about the informed consent of the participants, Jones led the entire community into mass suicide, with bullets to the heads of those who resisted drinking the poison-laced Kool-Aid. *terrible waste*

The collapse of the mass movement that became apparent in the late 1970s cannot be attributed solely to government policies and repression, although the assassination and imprisonment of consensus-building leaders, the discrediting and co-optation of activists, and the fear and paranoia generated by COINTELPRO—the FBI program to "neutralize" antiwar and liberation leaders—all took their toll. The winding down of the Vietnam War and the end of the draft removed the galvanizing focus that had previously united disparate groups and interests in a common cause.

The movement's failure to establish long-term, broad-based coalitions then became apparent, and many individuals and groups were left floundering, some then turning to New Age lifestyles or to mainstream electoral politics. Many returned to complete doctoral or law degrees, as I did, becoming activist academics. Some turned to drugs or alcohol. Unlike the Popular Front of the 1930s, anchored by a well-organized Communist Party (which, although still active even in the 1980s, was no longer credible enough to lead a mass movement or to go far beyond New Deal–style electoral politics), no such hegemonic leadership emerged during the Vietnam War years. Activists recognized this weakness at the time, and many of us made great efforts to re-form the existing left parties or to form new political parties, spawning dozens of Marxist-Leninist-Maoist and Trotskyist groups, none of which was able to meet the challenge.

Solidarity with liberation movements in Africa, Asia, and Latin America formed part of the content of the new-party organizations, but also separately as many US activists formed anti-imperialist solidarity groups that supported national liberation movements in Central America, southern Africa, the Philippines, Palestine, East Timor, Western Sahara, and other areas where the United States was intervening or supplying weapons to crush those movements. The environmental movement surged, but became a ritual of civil disobedience and mass arrests in relatively remote locales, requiring the presence of celebrities and widespread media coverage.

The 1960s women's liberation movement that I had been involved in was linked to antiracism and anti-imperialism, but that strand did not survive either, as an issue-orientation emerged outside a radical political analysis of capitalism, imperialism, and racism. As male violence against women skyrocketed, a focus on rape and pornography developed alongside the existing issues of reproductive rights and the Equal Rights Amendment, leading to legislative campaigns and lawsuits.

Meanwhile, the media's flirtation with a revolution ended. Entertainment replaced news, and public and independent broadcasting were defunded under the Reagan administration. In mainstream politics, which a number of activists had entered, doors were slamming shut soon after opening; symptomatically, a right-winger in San Francisco assassinated Mayor Moscone and Supervisor Harvey Milk in 1978, and then was released on parole following a light sentence. Jerry Brown's Supreme Court appointees were either voted out of office or resigned, and Ronald Reagan became president, consolidating this sharp move to the Right both nationally and internationally.

I was living in New York and attending UN meetings when Ronald Reagan won the presidency. December 1980 was a dreary and troubling month and seemed to foreshadow what was to come: the entire leadership of the Salvadoran opposition and four American churchwomen were slaughtered in El Salvador. John Lennon, a youth symbol of peace, was assassinated. Even before the new administration took office, the Reagan transition team threw out the files and staff of the presidential women's commission and padlocked the office door.

Reagan rode to victory on a wave of superpatriotism and Islamaphobia that had been drummed up when Iranian revolutionaries seized US hostages from the embassy in Tehran in 1979 and held them through the end of Carter's term of office in 1981. Reagan's men geared up to implement his campaign promise to overthrow the successful revolutions in Angola, Mozambique, Afghanistan, Grenada, Cuba, and Nicaragua, and aimed to prevent those in Guatemala, El Salvador, and other countries from occurring. The Reagan administration gave the green light to Israel to invade Lebanon, already wracked by years of civil war, to drive out the Arafat and the Palestine Liberation Organization. The Egyptian Muslim Brotherhood, the first of the fanatical and violent Islamist organizations that replaced crushed secularist movements, assassinated Egyptian president Sadat; all over the Middle East, and soon in South Asia, reactionary Islamism gained adherents, just as violent Zionists did in Israel and Christian fundamentalists did in the United States. And John Paul II assumed the papacy intent on reversing the two decades of growing liberation theology that emerged from Vatican II.

The chilly wind of counterrevolution was upon us. The Cold War, US exceptionalism and unilateralism, crusader Christianity, laissez-faire capitalism, and anticommunism solidified into an iron fist.

And it was in that jumble that the Sandinista Revolution, which had triumphed on July 19, 1979, became a prime target.

Nicaragua under the Somozas had been a reliable US ally, but slipped from its grasp as the greediness and ghoulishness of Anastasio Somoza turned pathological and became a gross liability to the United States. A typical drill of Somoza's infamous National Guards gives a sense of the atmosphere under his rule:

"Who is the Guardia?"
"The Guardia is a tiger."
"What does tiger like?"
"Tiger likes blood."
"Whose blood?"
"The blood of the people."

The Somoza regime collapsed in July 1979 when the Sandinista National Liberation Front (FSLN is its acronym in Spanish) surrounded Managua, and President Carter advised Somoza to resign and leave, as he had done with the Shah of Iran a few months before. Somoza's one-man rule had not left much of a state, Somoza having driven the country hundreds of millions of dollars into debt, which the Carter administration forced the Sandinistas to assume, crippling the possibility of improving people's lives. The Sandinistas, however, set about nation-building, stoked by enthusiasm and the ambition to eradicate poverty, disease, and illiteracy, and to introduce poetry writing to every woman, man, and child.

The larger story of US intervention in Nicaragua during the Reagan era is documented in Holly Sklar's 1988 book, *Washington's War on Nicaragua* (South End Press). Sara Diamond documented the consolidation of the Right and its role in the Contra war in *Spiritual Warfare: The Politics of the Christian Right* (South End Press, 1989) and *Roads to Dominion: Right-Wing Movements and Political Power in the United States* (Guilford Press, 1995). Two excellent books tell the story of the development of the FSLN: Matilde Zimmermann's *Sandinista: Carlos Fonseca and the Nicaraguan Revolution* (Duke University Press, 2000) and Gioconda Belli's *The Country under My Skin: A Memoir of Love and War* (Knopf, 2002). My story focuses on a part of that history, an eyewitness account of how the Miskitu people of Nicaragua were used by the United States as tools in its war against the Sandinistas. For scholarly studies of the Miskitus, see Carlos M. Vilas, *State, Class, and Ethnicity in Nicaragua: Capitalist Modernization and Revolutionary Change on the Atlantic Coast* (Rienner, 1989); Charles Hale, *Resistance and Contradiction: Miskitu Indians and the Nicaraguan State, 1894–1987* (Stanford University Press, 1994); my *Miskito Indians of Nicaragua* (Minority Rights Group, London, 1988); and Baron Pineda's *Shipwrecked Identities: Navigating Race on the Mosquito Coast* (Rutgers University Press, 2006).

Nicaragua is a Central American country sandwiched between Honduras to the north and Costa Rica to the south, with the Pacific Ocean forming its western border and the Caribbean Sea its eastern border. The country's capital, Managua, is located in the west, near the Pacific. The region where most of my story takes place is in the northeast. Running 100 miles along the Honduran border from central Nicaragua to the Caribbean, it extends southward down about 150 miles of Caribbean coastline—about 70,000 square miles of territory in all. The entire eastern half of Nicaragua was called the "Mosquito Coast" or "Atlantic Coast" by the British empire that claimed the territory, and was renamed Zelaya when it became a department of Nicaragua in 1892. But it remained an enclave of Anglo-American imperialism in the Caribbean. Webbed with rivers and rapids, this region had few roads and no paved ones, no telephones or electricity. Even in the 1980s travel was still by dugout. It is the home of two distinct indigenous peoples: tens of thousands of Miskitus and thousands of Sumus (there are a few hundred Rama Indians in the southern part of the region). There are a large number of Creoles, mostly in the southern half, but also a sizable community in the main town of the north, Puerto Cabezas ("Creole" is the self-identification of Afro-Caribbeans in Nicaragua). There are also two Garífuno towns near Bluefields, the southernmost habitation of Garífunos in the eastern Caribbean, the majority of whom live in Honduras and Belize. Tens of thousands of mostly poor Spanish-speaking Nicaraguans migrated to the northeastern zone during the era of the Somozas, 1934 to 1979, seizing traditional Miskitu and Sumu Indian lands and waterways.

Following the Sandinista victory in 1979, the Miskitu, Sumu, and Rama indigenous peoples formed MISURASATA and demanded Sandinista acknowledgment and support for self-determination, starting with including the indigenous languages in the popular literacy campaign. These indigenous communities were well aware of the international indigenous movement making such demands. The Sandinistas agreed to the literacy program in the indigenous languages (as well as English for the Creoles), but balked at the political and economic self-determination demanded especially by the Miskitus. The Sandinistas were overwhelmingly Spanish speaking and from the western half of Nicaragua. They were leftist nationalists who embodied the Latin American tunnel vision of anti-(United States) imperialism and anticapitalism and felt threatened by indigenous demands. Eventually the Sandinistas did realize that their revolutionary dogma contained an element of racism in its nationalism, but by then it was too late because the Reagan administration was there to exploit their mistakes.

As avowed Marxists, friendly to Cuba and other socialist regimes, the Sandinistas were perceived, even by the Carter administration of 1977 to 1981, as a movement that the United States could not and would not tolerate. Consequently, the CIA dusted off the war game that had been known, to the extent it was known at the time, as "the secret war in Laos," brewed during the Kennedy administration, a program that used the disaffected Hmong indigenous communities against socialist and nationalist Laos. Even the same old Laos hands were shaken from slumbering retirement to train a new secret army of Miskitus. We anti-interventionists had access to the vast knowledge and experience of former and now dissident CIA officers Phil Agee, John Stockwell, and Ralph McGehee, the latter having actually designed the Laos plan and worked on the ground with the Hmong. The Hmong people had been organized into a CIA proxy army, and then dumped after their usefulness ended. Many had to flee the country, ending up as refugees in the US. I predicted that the United States would do the same with its Nicaraguan indigenous proxies. I cared about the survival of the Sandinista revolution, but cared equally, if not more, for the liberation and self-determination of the indigenous peoples. I knew that an alliance with United States Contra counterinsurgency would backfire on any group that entered into it. I also believed that the Sandinistas could transform themselves into leaders in Latin America promoting the self-determination of the native peoples. Without US intervention, I think they would have achieved that goal they set for themselves in 1981.

As I became increasingly active in exposing the US program, I myself became a target of the anti-Sandinista project. The US government's propaganda machine took enough notice of my work to try to discredit me—spreading rumors about me alternatively as a KGB agent, a Sandinista security agent, a Cuban agent, or an FBI or CIA agent, depending on the constituency the disinformation was designed to address. Nor did they stop with propaganda. At one point, I was detained and threatened by the Honduran military in the Honduran/Nicaraguan border zone, which resulted in my exclusion from the Miskitu refugee camps.

I had published four scholarly books on Native American history and issues between 1977 and 1980. During that same time, I was doing nongovernmental lobbying at the United Nations for indigenous peoples' rights, and in 1980 I moved to New York and began research for a fifth book, *Indians of the Americas: Human Rights and Self-Determination*, which was published in 1984. But, I spent almost every waking moment from 1981 to 1988 either in Central America or on the situation there. At the end of that time, I had lost confidence in academia and scholarly writing, and I began a historical novel on the Contra war and the Miskitus. This was a mind-spinning time for me—the US invaded Panama, the Sandinistas were voted out of power, the Berlin Wall was torn down, Chinese authorities brutally cracked down on protestors in Tiananmen Square in Beijing, the Soviet Union and surrounding socialist states dissolved, apartheid was annulled and Mandela released; in the same period, I experienced personal crises that involved alcoholism, despair, and life-threatening bronchial asthma—fallout from the overwork and attacks I had experienced in the preceding years. I shelved the novel.

I turned instead, in 1992, to writing historical/literary memoir. In 1997, I published *Red Dirt: Growing Up Okie* (Verso), which took my story from my childhood up to the year 1960. I followed *Red Dirt* in 2002 with *Outlaw Woman: Memoir of the War Years, 1960–75*. Now this book, the sequel to those two.

I have a doctorate in history, and I understand the importance and methodologies of discovering and writing history, including oral history. That professionalism is not as important to my writing as is my rural upbringing among storytellers and the time I've spent with the traditional storytellers—actually the historians—of the Native communities whom I have had the good fortune to know over three decades. I think we are becoming increasingly aware that history itself is an issue, often *the* issue: Who owns the history of the United States? Do we accept the history of the Latino and Anglo conquerors or the indigenous peoples in the Western Hemisphere? Whose version of history is valid in Palestine/Israel, in Northern Ireland, in Cyprus, in Kashmir, in Afghanistan, in Sri Lanka, and in hundreds of other situations?

This book alternatively could be called "Living—and Dying—under Reagan's America," or "Site(s) of Shame." The particular site of shame in this book is the northeastern region of Nicaragua, a war zone in the US-sponsored Contra war. Although Nicaragua (and Central America in general) was

a Reagan-era sideshow to that more important Cold War site of shame, Afghanistan, the Central American civil wars resulted in hundreds of thousands
of dead and maimed, with the United States, as usual, propping up oligarchies
by building and financing a war machine against insurgent poor.

Why a memoir? Why do I consider choosing to write an historical memoir to be important? History. That battle over history. I can no longer bear to
write—or to read—texts in which the author is present only behind a maze of
screens, pretending objectivity. History is never the "objective" account found
in academic writing. Nor is history always what happens to someone else. I
write memoir in part to give shape to the important slogan of the sixties, invented by the Student Non-Violent Coordinating Committee and embraced
and elaborated by the women's liberation movement later in that decade: *The
personal is political.*

Along the way, "the personal is political" was lost in the mass media and
dissolved into "truth is in the eye of the beholder" and "everything is equal
and relative."

But I had learned not only the power of storytelling, but also the power of
memoir through reading the memoirs of the most influential political figures
in my own political development: Emma Goldman, Big Bill Haywood, Elizabeth Gurley Flynn, Agnes Smedley, Simone de Beauvoir, Oscar Ameringer,
Malcolm X, Che Guevara, Bobbi Lee (Lee Maracle), Angela Davis, Rigoberta
Menchú, and dozens of others, including those renegade CIA officers Agee,
Stockwell, and McGehee.

I write this memoir recalling this form's influence on me, and the lack of
such works available to me from the crucial rise and fall of the United States
Left, 1930–55, except for a few unhelpful mea culpas. I write that the younger
generation may have access to an earlier generation's political experience and
theory. I write this book to give a human face to the consequences of the
Contra war in the destruction of the Sandinista Revolution, resulting in a
setback for a better future for the indigenous peoples of the world, and for all
peoples struggling for self-determination and a better life.

1

The Road to Nicaragua Runs
Through the Black Hills

What ended up being my road to Nicaragua began when I was "born again" as an American Indian. That thin red line, inherited from my maternal grandmother, was tapped in 1970 when, following the Alcatraz call to "Indians of all Nations," Mad Bear Anderson, the famed Tuscarora traveling diplomat (and merchant seaman by trade), encouraged me to embrace my Native heritage. I finally did so during the siege of Wounded Knee in February 1973, when I was a functioning alcoholic working in a Nevada casino, burnt out, and isolated from the radical movements that had been my family for the previous decade.

I always had known that my mother was part Indian of unspecified heritage, most likely Cherokee, although I grew up in west-central Oklahoma, Southern Cheyenne territory. One relative has fantasized that we were from the Nez Perce of Idaho, who had been forced onto a reservation in southeastern Oklahoma following the defeat of the resistance led by Chief Joseph, but that seems unlikely. It was known that my grandmother's family had left the Tennessee mountains, part of the former homeland of the Cherokee Nation, to settle in Missouri. In any case, my mother was not proud of being part Indian, and it was far from fashionable to be an Indian in Oklahoma when she grew up. I knew about her—and my—Indian ancestry only through whispers by relatives on my father's side of the family and hearing my father's taunts during the nearly daily conflicts between him and my mother. At seventeen, my mother married my father, who was nineteen, an itinerant ranch hand

and farm laborer. My father was of old-settler Scots-Irish heritage on both sides of his family—except for his grandmother, who was said to be Indian or perhaps Mexican. He could have been a prosperous rancher rather than a hired hand but for his own father's devotion to radical politics. Emmett Victor Dunbar, my grandfather, a veterinarian and Oklahoma settler-farmer, was a member of the Oklahoma Socialist Party and the Industrial Workers of the World (the IWW, or "Wobblies"). He named my father Moyer Haywood Pettibone after the Wobbly leaders then on trial in Boise for murdering former Idaho governor Frank Steunenberg, two years after the IWW was founded in 1905.

In the early 1920s, the family was forced to flee rural Canadian County in Oklahoma, my grandfather a victim of KKK violence and the Palmer Raids aimed at the Wobblies and Socialists during the Wilson administration's repression of anyone opposed to World War I. My father defiantly remained in his county in Oklahoma, and there he met my mother, who was then incarcerated in a home for juvenile delinquent girls but allowed visits to a sister who lived in the county. The teenaged couple married and began sharecropping and picking cotton with other migrant laborers. Hard as her life was as the wife of a white sharecropper, at least my mother had escaped the fate of being Indian in an Oklahoma where stray dogs were far better regarded. A red—a socialist—in the closet on my father's side, a red—an Indian—on my mother's, and the red dirt of Oklahoma formed my identity.

The nearby federal Indian boarding school at Concho was in the same basketball class (the smallest towns) as my town, and our teams played each other twice a year. There was always tension in the gym on those nights, and sometimes fights between the Indian boys and the white boys. My older brothers were especially targeted, surely perceived as being half-breeds passing. That, and seeing Indians on skid row in the county seat, El Reno, were my only encounters with Indians growing up. Shame, that is what was instilled in me, the shame of being Indian. I was well aware then, and now, that I was not a citizen of a Native Nation or a member of an Indian family having to survive as Indians. Yet my whispered Indian heritage had always been an important part of my ambivalent identity, even if I had not yet acted on it. I had spent my years at San Francisco State College, UCLA, and after as an activist—against the Vietnam War, in solidarity with African liberation movements, for women's liberation. Toward the end of that period, I was involved in some labor organizing that devolved into clandestine plans that never materialized but led to my arrest, torture under interrogation, and trial in Louisiana. Though I was released on probation, I became depressed, started drinking heavily, and, after my trial in 1972, avoided the movement spotlight. I returned to California and worked under a false name in electronics assembly plants in Silicon Valley and under my own name in Harrah's casino at Lake Tahoe. I know now what I did not know then—that many full-time activists like me, even the movement itself, were collapsing in various ways.

I was thirty-five in 1973, and I was a wreck. I spent my nights working the graveyard shift in the casino, and my days drinking away a history of broken relationships and crushed dreams, personal and political. My only other activity was practicing Tae Kwan Do, which I had first taken up with my women's liberation group in 1968. In fact, I found out about the Wounded Knee standoff when the news preempted my favorite television show, *Kung Fu*.

Wounded Knee and the American Indian Movement (AIM) became the magnet that drew me back to open activism and gave me back my life; for once you become a revolutionary, there is no other possible life, only self-destruction if you try to escape that commitment. On February 27, 1973, on the Pine Ridge Sioux reservation in South Dakota, traditional Oglala Sioux, led by young warriors of the American Indian Movement representing seventy-five Native Nations, seized the Wounded Knee trading post at the iconic site of a US army massacre of unarmed and starving Sioux in 1890 and proclaimed their independence from the United States. For seventy-one days, they held out against federal marshals, the FBI, and units of the National Guard with their tanks, helicopters, and fighter jets. The defenders were prepared to die, and believed that they would be required to do so. But unlike 1890, the whole world was watching the event, as I did, on television.

In August 1973, I came down from the mountain to enter law school at the University of Santa Clara. There, one of the Wounded Knee Legal Defense/Offense Committee (WKLDOC) lawyers recruited me—San José–based attorney John Thorne, who had represented many radicals, including George Jackson and Angela Davis. Work on the committee taught me a great deal about the limitations of the legal system, but it also led me to the American Indian Movement. I entered AIM thinking of myself as an orphan, alienated from the culture as a whole, but also from the left and the women's liberation movement that had consumed my life from 1964 to 1972.

As a member of AIM, I found a new set of friends, mainly Native Americans who had grown up poor, rural, isolated, without running water, indoor plumbing, or electricity, just as I had grown up in rural Oklahoma. In a kind of shorthand language I could never use in the Left and women's movements, I could communicate with my newfound comrades. I remained unnecessarily secretive about my past radical activities, however, often letting others fill in the blanks. One early AIM friend, Robert Mendoza, who was Creek from Oklahoma, recognized my name as a leader in the women's liberation movement in the late 1960s and had seen my picture and an article in *Newsweek*, in which I was quoted as saying that I grew up in Oklahoma and that my father was a cowboy, my mother an Indian. He was impressed to meet me face to face, but I lied and said that the woman in the article wasn't me. When we had become friends, I told him the truth but asked him not to tell anyone else. Later, when my credibility was on the line for supporting the Sandinistas, this fundamental error in judgment would come back to haunt me as I was both red-baited *and* denounced as a fraud pretending to be Native American. I never knew back then where to draw the line between being identified as Indian and being in solidarity with Indian aspirations, and felt more conflict in dealing with non-Indians than with Indians. Non-Indians, unfamiliar with the chaotic conditions produced by warfare, reservation incarceration, and forced assimilation, tended (and still tend) to have a monolithic image of Indians rather than comprehending the complexities and contradictions of Indian life and heritage.

Most of my Native American friends were from families with alcoholic members, and some were alcoholics themselves. AIM itself had strict rules against drinking and using drugs, though they were often broken in daily life. Up to that time, I had feared becoming like my mother, whose drunken violence drove me away from home at age fifteen and ultimately led to her death at age fifty-nine. Being with Indians gave me permission to remain the out-of-control drinker that I had become in the early 1970s. But it also made drinking appear as a political act, as if when drinking I was somehow more authentically Indian than when I was sober.

The American Indian Movement began as a pan-Indian organization that embodied a missionary zeal, with AIM pretty much accepting anyone who claimed to be Indian and accepted its goals of asserting Native rights to their territories and to political sovereignty over them. Anyone who reclaimed Indian roots, especially Chicanos, Indians who had been adopted by white families, and anyone like me with a likely, but not validated, Indian identity was welcome. AIM was an ambitious, populist movement that envisioned cultural, social, and political hegemony in North America—AIM operated in Canada as well—if not the hemisphere. AIM's founders saw themselves as following the tradition of the nineteenth-century pan-Indian resistance to US settlement on their lands and the revered leaders of that resistance, from Tecumseh in the Ohio Valley to Crazy Horse in the Northern Plains.

Although most US citizens, and indeed the rest of the world, view the US War of Independence as the first example of resistance to colonialism, Native Americans know better. They see the United States as imperialist from its founding, the most extensive colonial-settler project in the five-hundred-year history of European expansion; the Declaration of Independence thus did not end a colonialist venture that began in 1607 at Jamestown but merely announced a change of flags. The Treaty of Paris between Britain and France in 1763 that ended the French and Indian War had forbidden European settlement over the Allegheny / Appalachian mountain spine and required the return of settlers already there, since the British preferred profits from the fur trade to more settlements. A few months after the peace treaty took effect in the summer of 1763, a Native confederacy of Ottawa, Anishinaabe (also called Ojibwa, Chippewa), Potawatomi, Huron, Shawnee, and Delaware led by Pontiac, an Ottawa, attacked British military forts in the region. In their search-and-destroy response, the British commander, Lord Jeffrey Amherst, used biological warfare by having his soldiers give out smallpox-infected blankets to Delaware refugees, causing an epidemic. Pontiac's Confederation was soon crushed. The colonies meanwhile balked at implementing provisions of the treaty limiting western settlement, and settlers began filtering into the Ohio Valley (think of the near-mythical Daniel Boone), then called the "Northwest Territory." Gaining free access to western lands was thus one of the colonists' main goals in 1776.

The first land law following the Declaration of Independence from Britain

was the Land Ordinance of 1785, which established a national land system
and the basis for its implementation. This act included maps that extended
the boundaries of the original thirteen colonies/states all the way to the Pacific Ocean. The Northwest Ordinance of 1787 then set forth a plan for white
settlement and colonization. It established a procedure for the creation of
new states in order of military occupation, territorial status, and finally state-
hood, which could be achieved when the number of settlers outnumbered
the indigenous population—a provision that required either the annihilation or forced removal of the original inhabitants. Thus began the long, hard
struggle of a number of Native confederations between the Appalachian/Al-
legheny mountains and the Mississippi River that culminated in their mass,
forced removal to Oklahoma in the 1830s.

The American Indian Movement thus saw itself as an anticolonial movement like other national liberation movements against colonialism around
the world, a movement that began with the onset of European colonialism in
the Americas, and particularly the establishment of the United States.

I began to see my own family history as a contradiction or amalgamation
of those two forces—settlers on Indian lands and resistance by the indigenous
inhabitants. This history had political implications that burned in me, but was
also deeply personal.

I learned to connect the Monroe Doctrine—the early US government's
announced intention of controlling the whole Western Hemisphere—to
Manifest Destiny—the settlers' belief that expansion from the Atlantic to the
Pacific was their destiny, willed by God. Later I began to see how Native resistance in settler expansionism in North America was linked to resistance
to US intervention in Central America, particularly Nicaragua. In the mid
nineteenth century, after half of Mexico had been annexed and gold was discovered in northern California, goldseekers and settlers rushed westward, but
were forced to travel by ship around South America to get there because the
territory between the Missouri River and California was Indian—Lakota and
Cheyenne warriors in the northern plains and Navajo, Apache, and Comanche warriors in the southern plains and deserts, forming a solid wall of resistance to encroachment. It was during this time that a band of mercenaries
from the United States led by William Walker seized control of Nicaragua,
which had only recently become independent from Spain. Walker reintro-

duced African slavery during his presidency (1856–57). Cornelius Vanderbilt, who had been shipping goods and goldseekers from northeastern ports to San Francisco by way of Tierra del Fuego, made deals with the Nicaraguan authorities to transport his cargo through the rivers and lakes of Nicaragua to its west coast, transferring to his ships waiting there and cutting the voyage in half, beginning the quest for a deep-water canal that was finally cut through Colombia, detaching the province of Panama from that country. But the longer-term goal was to gain access to land routes from St. Joseph and Omaha to California, both for wagon trains and eventually railroads. At first, the United States made treaties of "peace and friendship" with the Lakota and Cheyenne, but settlers did not abide by the terms of the treaties and the Plains Indians responded by attacking wagon trains. The federal government sent troops to accompany the settlers, leading to armed engagements between soldiers and Indian fighters.

During the US Civil War, the federal government was distracted from its campaign to gain control of the Plains, although it did remove the Navajos from their territory to a desert prison in 1864 as well as sanctioning massacres of the Cheyenne at Sand Creek and the Sioux in Minnesota. Soon after the end of the Civil War, the federal army's battle-experienced regiments, including Black troops that the Indians called "Buffalo soldiers," invaded Sioux and Cheyenne territory. Even so, the Indians were strong enough to make a treaty with the United States in 1868 that guaranteed their territorial and sovereign rights. Soon after the government broke the treaty, annexed the Black Hills (*Paha Sapa* in Lakota, sacred to the Sioux and the Cheyenne), and signaled that it would be satisfied with nothing less than the complete pacification or eradication of the Plains peoples.

This new round of expansion triggered the rise of a new pan-Indian movement, led by Crazy Horse and Sitting Bull, who took the offensive against the invaders, most notably defeating Colonel George Armstrong Custer and his 7th Cavalry at the Battle of the Little Big Horn. Soon after, Crazy Horse was murdered, and by the end of 1890, after Sitting Bull was assassinated, Custer's old unit took its revenge on a group of starving and freezing Lakota refugees who were trying to reach the Pine Ridge federal Indian agency, killing hundreds of unarmed Indian women, children, and old men at Wounded Knee Creek.

These events were vivid in the memory of Lakota survivors still living, and in the memories of their children and grandchildren, on the Pine Ridge reservation in South Dakota in 1973 when the Lakota at Pine Ridge took their stand at Wounded Knee. In a salute to this heritage of resistance, AIM adopted the slogan "in the spirit of Crazy Horse," and it was no accident that it chose Wounded Knee as the site of its protest, which, thanks to the overreaction of the Nixon administration, became world news and put AIM on the map, bringing thousands of recruits from many Native Nations to its side.

It was my decision to devote myself to the Native struggle that led me to quit law school after just one year and to complete my doctorate in history instead. Back in 1966, I had been advanced to Ph.D. candidacy in history at UCLA, but had abandoned my dissertation after my best friend and sister doctoral student, Audrey Rosenthal, was killed in a plane crash in South Africa, where she had been working clandestinely to help victims of apartheid communicate with their loved ones in exile. Audrey and I had been buddy anti–Vietnam War activists and emerging feminists on campus for three years, but after she was killed in early 1967, I chose the vocation of revolution and went at it nonstop from 1967 until I crashed at Lake Tahoe in 1972.

When I returned to UCLA to finish my doctorate, I had already been researching the history of land tenure in New Mexico—one of the reasons I had enrolled in law school was to learn how to do legal research and study property law—and the UCLA History Department agreed to allow that topic for my dissertation. In 1974, I accepted an appointment in the newly established Native American Studies program at California State University's Hayward campus, a working-class commuter school halfway between Berkeley and San José. On one level, I had really just picked up from where I had left off when I fled academia in 1967, advocating ethnic and women's studies programs in universities. But on another level, my research and writing and teaching were inseparable from my commitment to the American Indian Movement.

I also conducted an all-day seminar on Fridays at D-Q University near Sacramento, where I often stayed for the weekends. D-Q was born of the Alcatraz occupation by "the Indians of all Nations" for eighteen months in 1969–70 and was founded as a North American—including Mexico and Canada—

Indian studies university. By the time I taught there in 1974, D-Q had received California junior college accreditation and was developing a master's degree program. The campus occupied a section of prime Sacramento Valley agricultural land and was a former military storage dump, long abandoned. In place of ceding Alcatraz to the Indian occupants, a deal was struck with the federal government to cede the Sacramento Valley land, with the proviso that it not be used for agricultural purposes, which had everything to do with limiting the water rights so generously granted to California agribusinesses. Right off, D-Q's most obvious potential as an agriculture school, right next door to the University of California's agriculture school at Davis, was unreachable.

Because D-Q faculty members were mostly drawn from the Native American Studies Department at UC Davis, teaching at D-Q gave me the opportunity to connect with a larger circle of Native scholar-activists. Among them was Professor Howard Adams (now deceased), a militant Métis leader from Saskatchewan, Canada. Howard was a Marxist theorist and a specialist on colonization who influenced my own thinking profoundly. His brilliant book *Prison of Grass* was an unusual and effective combination of his own life history as a Métis growing up in poverty and social deprivation with a parallel scholarly history of the birth of the Métis (a new bilingual-bicultural nation combining Cree Indians and French) and their resistance movements, beginning with the uprising led by Louis Riel in 1885. It was the first study to apply colonization and development theory— André Gunder Frank, James Cockcroft, Samir Amin, Pierre Jalée, Pablo Gonzales Casanova, and others had focused on Asia, Africa, and Latin America—to a Native American situation.

Howard's colleague at UC Davis, Jack Forbes, was the primary architect of both D-Q and UC Davis's Native American Studies Department. Jack introduced the term *Native American* for American Indians, although he preferred simply to use *American* to refer to indigenous Americans of the Western Hemisphere and force all other groups to hyphenate. He created a Native American–centered theory of colonization that viewed Chicanos as indigenous Americans. Howard and Jack disagreed about many things, and their personalities and egos often clashed. Howard was a Marxist who saw the reservation land base and resources, along with democratically elected native governments, as essential to a necessary nation-building process, while Jack embraced a utopian view of a pan-Indian America with no boundaries.

Jack Forbes and Howard Adams thus established the terms of a theoretical debate that would consume the American Indian Movement, and soon the international project of indigenous peoples. A pervasive theme of Cold War anticommunism also tinged the debate, with some Native American leaders condemning Marxism as a "white man's theory" despite Native Marxists' support for Indian self-determination. Both Jack and Howard influenced my own views. I had by that time considered myself a Marxist for over a decade, though not an orthodox Marxist; rather, I found the use of Marxist analysis indispensable—that is, considering the political economy of any given historical or current situation, along with cultural and social factors.

I remained connected to the Wounded Knee Legal Defense/Offense Committee after leaving law school to finish my doctorate in 1974. The committee attracted Native American and progressive non-Native attorneys and law students from all over the country who worked on the case without pay. John Thorne invited me to serve as an expert witness at a federal district court hearing in December in Lincoln, Nebraska, the purpose of which was to win dismissal of the charges against the Wounded Knee participants. Along with John, attorney Larry Leventhal, and Sioux lawyer-activist and bestselling author (*God Is Red; Custer Died for Your Sins*) Vine Deloria Jr., were in charge of the defense team.

The defense attorneys were able to turn the proceedings in Lincoln away from deciding the defendants' guilt or innocence and into a decision based on the 1868 Fort Laramie Treaty of Peace and Friendship between the Sioux and the US government. That treaty sought to end the war that had alternately simmered and raged on the Northern Plains ever since President Jefferson had "purchased" the French-claimed territory that had been Sioux land (the Louisiana Purchase) in 1803. On both sides of the Missouri River lay the ancestral and contemporary home of the Lakota and Dakota peoples of the bison ("The Great Sioux Nation," as the United States dubbed their homeland, based on the 1868 treaty). In the treaty, the Sioux relinquished about half their hunting grounds and ceded rights-of-way for US transcontinental roads and rail lines. The US government assumed the obligation to control its citizens and prevent their incursions into Sioux territory; the Sioux likewise agreed to prevent attacks against settlers and travelers on the US side. This agreement was soon violated by the incursion of the US 7th Cavalry under the command of Major George Armstrong Custer. Goldseekers and squatters overran the sacred site, an invasion that was temporarily halted by Custer's "last stand" in July 1876. Between 1876 and 1890—when the 7th Cavalry's revenge massacre of civilians at Wounded Knee occurred—the United States annexed the Black Hills, Congress ended its treaty-making power with Native nations, the US Major Crimes Act removed police jurisdiction from Native control, and Native lands were subjected to allotment, breaking down contiguous Indian territories into Bantustan-type fragments, with the loss of 90 million acres of Indian land. The colonization of North American native nations and communities was completed, and this framework remained static until the liberation movements of the 1960s shook up the status quo and created new realities.

At the Lincoln hearing, the defense team asked the court to strike down the constitutionality of the Major Crimes Act based on the continuing validity of the Fort Laramie Treaty and to release all the Sioux and non-Sioux defendants who had been charged with various crimes and misdemeanors stemming from the 1973 siege of Wounded Knee. In the end, Judge Warren Urbom refused to find in favor of the treaty claim, arguing that the US Supreme Court had already pronounced that treaty-making was a power of Congress and not for the courts to decide (that is, treaties are "political" rather than "judicial" documents under the Constitution's separation of powers clause). However, the judge did recommend that the claimants address their issues to international juridical authorities rather than domestic US ones, citing an intractable conflict of interest on the part of the US government in deciding Indian claims fairly. This was precisely the recommendation that the American Indian Movement had sought. To pursue this strategy, AIM had established the International Indian Treaty Council six months before the Lincoln hearing, but had waited for a green light from the traditional Sioux elders, who wanted to exhaust all possible domestic remedies before taking the case to the international arena.

The impact of the trial was even greater than winning this ruling from the court. Because the courtroom was small with few seats, Indian elders were allowed to fill the twelve-seat jury box, which gave a definite sense that they were sitting in judgment on America. Most of the other seats in the

courtroom were given to the press and occasional celebrities such as Marlon
Brando and Buffy Ste. Marie. The proceedings were broadcast on closed-cir-
cuit television in other rooms of the courthouse. Hundreds of Lakota and
Dakota people came down to Lincoln from the reservation communities,
camped on the outskirts of Lincoln, and were at the courthouse every day. In
the evenings, meetings at the campsite allowed the attorneys to explain what
had happened that day and the collective to decide strategy for the next day,
including which witnesses would be called. John Thorne, Vine Deloria Jr.,
Larry Leventhal, and other lawyers never tried to force their expertise on the
people, and these meetings were amazing examples of Native oratory and
consensus decision-making.

I was there in Lincoln as an expert witness as well as part of the defense
team. The lawyers put me on the stand on five different occasions for a total of four hours of testimony. Historians Wilbur Jacobs, Alvin Josephy, Jr.,
William Laughlin, Raymond DeMallie, Jr., Father Peter Powell, and I provided the history of British and Spanish colonial and US actions and policies
in regard to North American Indians. A number of Sioux and other Native
American legal, anthropological, and linguistic specialists—such as Lakota
anthropologist Dr. Beatrice Medicine and Native attorneys Kirk Kickingbird
and Mario Gonzales—provided expert testimony. The other forty-one expert
witnesses were traditional Lakota and Dakota, along with Anishinaabe AIM
leader Dennis Banks and Muskogee spiritual leader Phillip Deere. Each of
the beautiful names—Crow Dog, Chasing Hawk, Young Bear, Bear Stops, He
Crow, Yellow Bird, Spotted Horse, Looking Cloud, One Star, White Hawk,
Red Shirt, Kills Enemy, Iron Hawk, Thin Elk, Red Owl, Bird Horse, High
Bear, Red Willow, Kills Straight, Bear Runner, Bad Wound, Red Bear—became unforgettable women and men and intimate friends in those two weeks
and after. After the hearing ended, they presented me with a request, which I
took as a command, to find a way to publish the proceedings. For two years I
worked through the 10,000 pages of court transcripts, and in 1977 *The Great
Sioux Nation: Sitting in Judgment on America* was published, my first book. It
was presented as the primary document at the Indians of the Americas Conference held at the United Nations in Geneva in September 1977. It sold well
during the following three years while in print, and all the royalties went to
support the International Indian Treaty Council office in New York.

There was a dark side to those two idyllic weeks in Lincoln: there is always a dark side when one is a drinking alcoholic, and that I was. Chuck, my travel companion and then boyfriend, was from a prominent traditional Lakota family at the Rosebud Sioux reservation and a truly beautiful human being, but an alcoholic who often raged and struck out in violence while drunk. I would not return to my hotel room until 9 or 10 p.m. each night after long strategy meetings. There I would find Chuck entertaining a crowd of heavy-drinking Lakota brothers, charging drinks to my room bill (the court had to pay my lodging, travel, and per diem, but not my bar bills). Of course, I joined in the drinking, usually blacking out and awakening with a terrible hangover, but sober, to go to court the next day.

When the hearing was over, just before Christmas, Chuck and I took the train to visit his mother in western Nebraska, and to spend Christmas with his siblings and father in Denver. His mother, a beautiful Lakota woman, was also an alcoholic, remarried to a blue-collar white man, also alcoholic, who blasted his own head off with a shotgun a month later. Chuck's father—a traditional Lakota man who spoke little English—we found on Denver's skid row, where he lived on the streets and in shelters. We took him to a nearby fast-food joint to sober him up before taking him to his daughter's home for Christmas dinner, where all of us proceeded to pass out drinking before the day was over.

I think it was the effect of this atmosphere that I began to visualize a future I did not want, and that brought back painful memories of my mother drinking, albeit alone, in that same desperate way. It would be six months more of that kind of "partying" with my Chuck before I saw the light of day. After one night of drinking, he knocked me down on the pavement and stomped on me until I was a bruised and bleeding pulp.

However, after the Lincoln hearing in late 1974 until I quit drinking in August 1975, I remained in San José and devoted my nonteaching time to the local AIM chapter. With all those activities, my primary interests clearly lay outside academia. My first year teaching and directing Native American Studies at Cal State Hayward—before I quit drinking—was tumultuous and often dangerous. Drinking, reckless driving, and barroom brawls punctuated very hard organizing work. Nearly every weekend the D-Q campus was the site of conferences or parties or ceremonies or powwows, and I stayed over in the creaky dormitory. It was hardly the life of an ordinary university professor even in those unusual times.

Soon our San José AIM chapter was presented with a challenge when Navajo assembly line workers supported by AIM seized and occupied the Fairchild electronics assembly plant in Shiprock in the Navajo Nation, February 25 to March 3, 1975. Fairchild had established an assembly plant in the Navajo Nation to take advantage of a harebrained Nixon administration scheme. Termed "red capitalism," this plan offered large corporations tax breaks to locate on Indian land, with the federal government using Indian trust funds to pay for infrastructure development as well as three-month training salaries for local Indians. Fairchild Camera and Electronics, having grown fat on military contracts during the Vietnam War, took up the offer and moved into a specially designed and constructed factory at Shiprock, in the New Mexico part of the Navajo Nation. Problems arose, however, when Fairchild engaged in the nasty practice of sacking the "free" trainees after their three months of work had expired and hiring another batch—and of course using outsiders, who were mostly white, as supervisors. This revolving door meant that no Navajo would ever advance beyond the minimum wage, receive any substantive job training, or get job tenure beyond three months. Not surprisingly, the Navajos wanted to form a trade union—the Navajo Nation already had a strong United Mine Workers Union local as well as the Operating Engineers and Chemical Workers unions on the reservation—but the company's policies made it hard for the union to get a foothold in the plant.

Our AIM chapter decided to hold a demonstration at Fairchild headquarters in Silicon Valley and to ask the workers there to support their Navajo brothers and sisters. In my dreams, I believed that this action might lead to the unionization of the Silicon Valley electronics industry, a project I'd worked on in 1972 and 1973, when I was an employee, first at Fairchild, then at another assembly plant. We had a rude surprise when our small AIM contingent arrived at Fairchild at noon one day only to find police snipers lining the roof of the plant building and tactical squads swarming the place in riot gear. No workers came out of the plant to support the demonstration, and we ourselves were pretty terrified and retreated. The next day, the Fairchild occupation on the Navajo reservation ended because the company announced that it was moving the Navajo plant to Taiwan, where it would pay workers fifteen cents an hour, illustrating the aptness of the term *footloose industry*.

Though we did not succeed, the planning, flyer-making, and discussions did galvanize our small chapter and led to links with Bay Area trade unions. Our next project was to challenge the construction of a Holiday Inn in downtown San José after an Ohlone Indian burial site was discovered during excavation, one of a number of such actions taking place all over the state of California. The courts halted construction, and Governor Jerry Brown supported legislation that created the California Indian Heritage Commission and laws controlling the investigation of burial sites found in any California construction project.

In early 1975, a small group of AIM warriors—Leonard Peltier, Dino Butler, and others, along with strong Indian women Anna Mae Aquash and Nilak Butler—had scored spectacular successes in supporting militant seizures in Indian country that put AIM back in the headlines. They had joined the Navajo workers occupying the Fairchild plant, and earlier in February had joined Menominees in Wisconsin in seizing a Catholic abbey to publicize their demand for renewed federal acknowledgment, which the tribe had lost in the government's "termination" policy during the Eisenhower era. In March, the AIM group was invited to set up camp at the Jumping Bull compound on the Pine Ridge Sioux reservation in Oglala, South Dakota, near the site of the Wounded Knee siege two years earlier. They came to support Dennis Banks during his trial and to protect Banks and the extended Jumping Bull family from attacks by the vicious "goon squad" made up of Sioux—propped up by the FBI and the Bureau of Indian Affairs police—who supported the corrupt tribal chairman, Richard Wilson. These FBI-friendly Sioux literally named themselves "Guardians of the Oglala Nation," the acronym of which was GOON.

During those cold winter months of 1975, a damper was put on the enthusiastic momentum that was leading AIM out of courtrooms and back to what AIM did best—agitate and organize. Douglass Durham, who was Dennis Banks's bodyguard and had been at Wounded Knee two years earlier, was exposed as an FBI informer, a charge to which he admitted; he then disappeared, reappearing later on the lecture circuit to condemn AIM. Naturally, this revelation created a great deal of fear and internal distrust. By the time of the national AIM conference, June 6–18, 1975, outside Farmington, New

Mexico, the paranoia seemed almost palpable. Even Anna Mae Aquash was being questioned as an FBI plant, a charge that seemed utterly absurd to me, and I feared that all women would be mistrusted, as often happened in male-dominated organizations.

Then, on June 26, 1975, eight days after the AIM conference ended, FBI agents entered the Jumping Bull family property where AIM had its encampment. A firefight broke out, leaving one AIM man (Joe Kills Right) and two FBI special agents dead. The other encamped AIM warriors escaped and went underground (Robert Redford later produced an excellent feature documentary about the FBI's incursion, *Incident at Oglala*). The historian in me immediately noticed that the date, June 26, 1975, was the ninety-ninth anniversary of Custer's defeat at the Battle of the Little Big Horn. I could not help wondering if this was yet another payback for a defeat that still festered in the US imperial memory.

For weeks the shootout was a national news story, dominating television, radio, and newspapers, which portrayed the American Indian Movement as a terrorist organization and the FBI agents as sweet, innocent family men. The FBI spokesperson described bunkers, trenches, and other installations on the Jumping Bull compound in vivid detail, using military terminology. Our AIM chapter geared up to try to counter the propaganda locally. But we had little information, since no one back in South Dakota wanted to talk on the telephone. The chapter decided that Fern Eastman, a Sioux from the Sisseton reservation, and I should go back to Pine Ridge and try to find out what happened.

Two days after the incident, we flew to Rapid City, South Dakota, and rented a car. We had to sign a document promising that we would not enter the Pine Ridge reservation, but of course we did just that. First, we visited a number of Lakota families in Rapid City, who told us that the AIM warriors at Jumping Bull had been an important presence in putting a brake on GOON squad and FBI violence on the reservation. The reservation itself was a tinderbox: that year, the reservation homicide rate was the highest per capita of any political unit in the United States as the GOON squad tied to Sioux chairman Richard Wilson attempted to eradicate the American Indian Movement from the area. Some of the people we spoke with believed that the FBI intended to murder AIM leader Dennis Banks, who was living with the

Jumping Bull family during his trial nearby, with the intention of making it appear to be a firefight rather than an assassination. Others thought that the armed assault was a more generalized act of terror against AIM, with the goal of expelling the organization and its supporters from the reservation. They warned us that the roads to the Jumping Bull property were blocked and that it was unlikely that we would be able to get in.

To our surprise, we drove directly to Oglala and then to Jumping Bull without seeing any sign of the authorities, federal or local. Since the Jumping Bull property was most often called a "ranch," I was expecting to find a Texas-style spread and was surprised to find instead a weather-beaten one-room shack and a lean-to chicken house that looked very much like the sharecropper cabins of my early childhood. Down the hill by the creek were the remnants of the AIM camp. Although yellow crime-scene tape surrounded the house and the camp, they seemed to be unguarded.

We had brought newspaper photographs of the alleged bunkers and trenches to see if we could find them. The "trench" was actually a dip that had been dug into the ground, black with oil, where decrepit vehicles were maintained—a feature of every poor rural homestead. The "bunkers" turned out to be flimsy chicken coops. We walked around the small house and noted that all the walls were dotted and splintered with bullet holes, but that the shell casings had been removed. We entered the house with some trepidation, expecting FBI men armed with M-16s waiting inside. After shoving the squeaky door open, we waited for voices or gunfire but heard only silence. Inside, everything—the few chairs, a table, sofa, some mattresses, and dishes—was smashed or torn to pieces. Peaceful sunlight streamed in through the bullet holes.

Fern said, "Oh, no," and I jumped. She beckoned me to the wall where she was staring at a photograph featuring a young Indian man proudly posing in his dress military uniform, of World War II vintage. The glass frame was shattered. Fern said, "Look, look at what the feds did." I looked more closely and saw that there was a bullet hole between the eyes of the Indian in the picture. Fern was not one to cry, but she cried, and I cried, not knowing exactly why this had given her such anguish.

On our return trip, Fern explained the peculiar colonial relationship between Native Americans and the military that emerged during World War II, in which Native Americans volunteered in large numbers, much larger proportionately than their numbers in the general population (including Native women in the auxiliary services). Following several generations of enforced government-boarding-school education from first grade through high school, Native American young people were accustomed to military-style discipline, along with strong doses of patriotic indoctrination. The military was also a way out of desperately impoverished and marginal lives on the reservations. Particularly for the Native peoples who had fought longest and hardest during the nineteenth century against US dominance—the Plains peoples and the Navajos—the military tapped into a warrior oral tradition. Families took enormous pride in their fallen war heroes, and in nearly every home the framed photographs—such as the one we found that day—filled a prominent space in the living room.

Another item—the US flag presented to the mother or widow of the dead soldier—was also considered sacred. When the news spread about the intentional shooting of the soldier's picture at the Jumping Bull house the mothers and widows of local Sioux war dead organized a delegation to Washington, D.C., where they deposited those formerly sacred flags at the gate of the White House.

Five months later, Dennis Banks, Leonard Peltier, and the other militants were captured. The following month, Anna Mae Aquash's body was found on the side of the road on the Pine Ridge reservation. She had been shot execution style. After Dino Butler and Bob Robideau were acquitted of killing the FBI agents, Leonard Peltier was charged and found guilty and sentenced to two consecutive ninety-nine-year terms in federal prison, where he remains as of this writing.

My personal and political life seemed restored by the end of 1975. In August, I entered a recovery program for alcoholism and was clean and sober for the first time in three years. I moved to San Francisco, where the AIM chapters had consolidated, and I was elected a member of the San Francisco Bay Area AIM Council as well as to the board of the American Indian Center. I was working on my first book. I had won tenure at my university. As part of this work, I became a part of a group of like-minded Indians, including Robert Mendoza and others, in San Francisco. We linked up with a Native Marxist study group we learned about in Vancouver, British Columbia, led by Ray and Lee Bobb (now Lee Maracle). Members of the group had recently toured the People's Republic of China and were enthusiastic about Mao's teachings and the Cultural Revolution. Lee had just published a memoir she called *Bobbi Lee*, a classic story of a Native woman coming of age in the 1960s, and had become a celebrity. Our goal was to apply Marxian analysis and national liberation theory to the history of colonization of Native Americans in North America, and to figure out a strategy of decolonization. Over the period of nearly two years that we worked together, Robert and I drove to Vancouver for meetings, and we sponsored speaking engagements for Lee in the San Francisco area. Robert and I met once or twice a week with a half-dozen other Native Marxists in the Bay Area, studying Mao and the Chinese revolution. We regularly exchanged reports between our group and the Vancouver one. Robert and I had been elected to the Board of Directors of both the local AIM chapter and the American Indian Center, but soon our AIM group was dissolved along with others. We resigned from the board of the American Indian Center, and the Marxist Study group became our refuge.

And on top of everything else, I fell in love with someone I considered the love of my life, my destiny.

I had been married twice, first in Oklahoma to a fellow student at Oklahoma University at age eighteen. We moved to San Francisco in 1960, where my daughter, Michelle, was born in 1962. Her father won custody when I left a year later, and she was raised by her father and stepmother while I became a roving political activist. I later married a fellow graduate student at UCLA, ending that marriage in 1969. I then intended to remain solitary, yet I married Simon Ortiz after a nine-month relationship.

Simon was a full-time writer and poet from the Acoma Indian Pueblo in New Mexico, and Harper & Row had just published his first collection of poems, *Going for the Rain*. We met in San Francisco in November 1975. He was doing readings, and I went to one; he stayed with me for two weeks; and then I drove to Acoma to spend Christmas with him and his family. While there, I met his two children and their mothers. He decided to move to San Francisco to live with me, and joined our Native Marxist group. We were immediately immersed in local Indian activities, including our campaign around the extradition hearing of Dennis Banks, one of the founders of AIM, who was a fugitive from trumped-up felony charges in South Dakota. Banks had gone underground following threats by the then state attorney general (later governor and US congressman), William Janklow. The long hearing in the San Francisco Federal Building was a gathering place for Indians demonstrating every day. The trial of Patty Hearst was taking place at the same time in a nearby courtroom, however, and the press was obsessed with it and paid little attention to the trial of Dennis Banks. After a federal judge ordered his extradition, California Democratic governor Jerry Brown refused to extradite, giving Dennis asylum.

During one of the trips to Vancouver, our Marxist study groups had been joined by Jimmie Durham, who was in Vancouver for the United Nations Habitat conference. He spent hours telling us about the work of the International Indian Treaty Council (IITC), of which he was a director. The Treaty Council had been established a year after Wounded Knee, in 1974, when the American Indian Movement invited Native peoples from the entire hemisphere and from the Pacific islands and Australia to a gathering. Thousands of native representatives, including intensely radicalized Mapuche Indian exiles from Pinochet's Chile, met and discussed their common issues for a week, deciding to take the 1848 Sioux treaty with the United States to the United Nations or perhaps to the International Court of Justice at The Hague. Jimmie, a Cherokee artist and writer who had lived in Geneva, Switzerland, introduced the idea to the Sioux warriors and elders in the aftermath of the Wounded Knee siege. During the 1960s era of decolonization of Africa and Asia, the UN offices in Geneva were a center for national liberation movements. Jimmie had become friends with national liberation leaders like Amilcar Cabral, and as they took power in their newly independent countries, they did not forget Jimmie's work on behalf of Native Americans in the United States. Jimmie had developed the idea for IITC in the context of the United Nations' Decade to Combat Racism, which began in 1973 and focused on the implementation of the International Convention on the Elimination of All Forms of Racial Discrimination (CERD). The Decade grew out of the campaign by the African states at the UN to end the illegal South African apartheid regime. However, the agenda for the Decade included several categories of racism, including discrimination against indigenous peoples, migrant workers, and peoples under occupation. The latter was an indirect but clear reference to Palestinians trapped under Israeli occupation following the 1967 Six-Day War.

In June 1976, Simon went to Chinle, in the Navajo Nation, to teach at Navajo Community College (now Diné College), and I went to the third International Indian Treaty Council meeting in the Sisseton Sioux reservation in southeastern South Dakota, on the banks of the Missouri River. It was my first IITC meeting and smaller than the first two, because the FBI had determined that we were dangerous and, to scare people away from coming, had set up roadblocks and checkpoints and lined the hills around our campground with snipers. FBI agents had also filled up the two small motels near the reservation, so we all had to camp. I had been promised a motel room along with other invited "experts," but I ended up sleeping in a small schoolhouse on the floor with many others, including Russell Means. I had rented a car at the airport, and Russell drafted me to drive him around, not going anywhere in particular, rather to talk. I had not met him before, and as we drove and talked I was impressed with his brilliant mind and his dedication to the movement.

Despite the constant presence of the FBI and the likelihood of a raid, the meeting went on. Jimmie had brought in a representative of the Zimbabwe African National Union (ZANU, one of Zimbabwe's national liberation movements) and a representative of the Puerto Rican Socialist Party, which favored independence from the United States. I spent most of the time with a working group led by Jimmie hammering out a manifesto, "Red Paper," that was approved by the participants. The "Red Paper" reiterated and strengthened the "Declaration of Continuing Independence" from the first International Indian Treaty Council at Standing Rock Indian Country in June 1974. It had claimed sovereignty for the Indian nations, and viewed the history of the United States as colonialist and expressed unity and solidarity with other national liberation movements, particularly for the independence of Puerto Rico. It directed the Treaty Council to approach the United Nations for recognition:

We recognize that there is only one color of Mankind in the world who are not represented in the United Nations; that is the indigenous Redman of the Western Hemisphere. We recognize this lack of representation in the

United Nations comes from the genocidal policies of the colonial power of the United States.

This conference directs the Treaty Council to open negotiations with the government of the United States through its Department of State. We seek these negotiations in order to establish diplomatic relations with the United States. When these diplomatic relations have been established, the first order of business shall be to deal with US violations of treaties with Native Indian Nations, and violations of the rights of those Native Indian Nations who have refused to sign treaties with the United States.

After the conference I spent the rest of the summer with Simon in Arizona and New Mexico, and we married in Grants, New Mexico, in July. We had a dream, a feasible one it seemed, to move to New Mexico and to start a literary/political journal, perhaps a cultural center or a Treaty Council office for the Southwest. We would buy land near Acoma, and I would teach at one of the universities.

Jimmie met with Simon and me in the fall of 1976, telling us about the international conference he was organizing to take place at the United Nations headquarters in Geneva the following year. By then the IITC would be officially acknowledged as a nongovernmental organization (NGO) with consultative status to the Economic and Social Council of the United Nations. He proposed that we set up a West Coast office of the organization and publish a monthly newsletter. He would send a young Comanche, Paul Smith, from the New York office to be the full-time administrator, and we put our plans for New Mexico on hold. The IITC and the *Treaty Council News* thus became the centerpiece of my political life.

Paul, Simon, and I immersed ourselves in organizing for the Indians of the Americas conference that was scheduled for September 1977. Besides publishing the *Treaty Council News* to publicize the conference, we organized a successful benefit to raise funds. I was delighted and comfortable in my old 1960s role of making newsletters and flyers, and organizing events. In June, the IITC met for five days at the Standing Rock Sioux reservation to elect official delegates to the conference. We drove to South Dakota, hauling bundles of the newsletter and copies of documents. Everyone camped out, and we met inside a large tent. By then I'd participated in dozens of camp meetings on Indian land, but none as significant and exciting as this one, which was devoted to selecting delegates and planning for the first international conference on Native Americans.

From South Dakota, Simon and I drove to New Mexico to visit his family, and attended the meeting of the National Congress of American Indians (NCAI) in Albuquerque in order to inform the gathered Indians about the conference and to write a report for the newsletter. The contrast between the Standing Rock encampment and the NCAI meeting in a sleek hotel, with all the delegates in western business attire and too much expense-account drinking at the bars, led me to write an essay that became quite popular—"Two Conferences," which was published in *Treaty Council News*. I then flew to join Simon and his son, Raho, in Anchorage, Alaska, for a conference of Native writers and poets. I brought copies of the newsletter and information on the upcoming conference at the United Nations.

The international conference on Indians of the Americas was organized by UN-affiliated NGOs, thanks to Jimmie Durham's relationship with them, and took place at the UN offices in Geneva, where the UN Human Rights Center was located. The event dazzled the international community and press (without receiving a line in the US press), and was even embraced by the citizens of Geneva, who normally ignored UN events. A local angle helped rivet local interest: In the early 1920s, the Iroquois leader Deskeheh had been sent by the Six Nations of the Iroquois in North America to approach the newly established League of Nations for recognition and membership. Although Deskeheh never achieved that goal, his presence for several years in Geneva became the stuff of legend known to every schoolchild. Conference delegates included Deskeheh's descendants, and Geneva officials rolled out the red carpet for us with a formal reception and museum exhibit.

In Geneva we met also political exiles from South American military regimes. Mario Ibarra, a Chilean militant who had been detained, tortured, and imprisoned after the 1973 military coup, had been allowed to leave a Chilean prison for what turned out to be permanent exile in Geneva, arriving just before the conference. For several years after the conference, Mario was often the only person in Geneva representing Indigenous issues on a day-to-day basis during the periods between the human rights meetings in which at first just a few of us participated. Within the UN Human Rights Center, we also had our very own mole in Augusto Willemsen-Díaz, an international law specialist from Guatemala who had already clocked two decades as a UN human rights officer. In the early 1970s, Augusto had convinced an Ecuadoran diplomat to propose a UN study of Indigenous peoples, which Augusto then began writing—a project that continued for years until Native Americans arrived in 1977 to assume responsibility for their own liberation. During the following decade before he retired, Augusto transferred his vast knowledge of UN/NGO workings to us, and some of us, including me, trained others, and that is how our numbers multiplied and we became an unlikely force within the UN's immense bureaucracy and influential among its many member states.

The 1977 Geneva conference appeared to be a triumph for the International Indian Treaty Council and the American Indian Movement. But behind the scenes it was crisis-ridden. Jimmie Durham, the brilliant magician who had made it all happen, chose the occasion of the Geneva conference as his moment to exit the international stage, leaving a letter asking me to assume the duties he would not be around to attend to. He had problems with Russell Means that I had not been aware of, a trajectory in Russell's thinking and behavior that continued on an erratic path. Jimmie had planned for a delegation from the conference to visit some African states and also meet with African liberation movements. Russell insisted that he wanted to meet with the Ugandan dictator, Idi Amin, and Jimmie refused to include that as part of the tour, canceling it altogether and leaving, reasoning that granting Russell's demand would discredit him and the Treaty Council in the eyes of progressive African leaders.

Being one of a quickly assembled group of volunteers, I knew no more than the others, which was nothing and no one. Only Jimmie held the metaphorical keys to the secrets of the United Nations. The notes I had taken when he briefed me in New York were hopelessly confused. I did not speak French, the language of Geneva and the UN workers, and in which Jimmie was fluent. But together, Paul Smith, Fern Eastman, Chockie Cottier, Bill Means, Winona LaDuke, and I, along with the other NGOs and local supporters, carried off the feat, a spectacular event.

I didn't realize during those years from 1975 to 1978 that my ideal existence was fragile and had begun disintegrating almost from the beginning. First the Native Marxist study groups fell apart. Robert and his wife moved to her Passamaquoddy community in Maine, and our group stopped meeting. Lee and Ray Bobb split up and their Vancouver group stopped meeting as well. And a few months after moving to San Francisco to live with me, Simon began disappearing and drinking. He was an alcoholic and had come out of a bad bout of drinking and hospitalization when we met (recounted in his amazing prose-poem, *From Sand Creek*). He was a binge drinker, and when he fell off the wagon, he migrated to skid row and often ended up in jail. In between the drinking bouts, he was on edge. I don't believe the term had even been invented yet, but I became a co-dependent and our relationship deteriorated accordingly. During the two years we lived together, I saw the rough times as exceptions and thought Simon would succeed in quitting (as he has since done). As a child of an alcoholic, I fell easily into patterns of denial and caretaking. After spending Christmas 1977 at Acoma, Simon and I returned to San Francisco; and there he left me.

And just as I had come to center my life on working with the Treaty Council, that connection too was broken.

2

Starting Over and Finding the Sandinista Revolution

After the 1977 Geneva conference, the World Peace Council (WPC), one of the main sponsors, asked me to be the US co-coordinator with Jack O'Dell, a veteran African American civil rights activist and writer, for their upcoming conference on racism in Basel in May 1978, in preparation for the United Nations Conference on Racism to be held that August. I agreed and began work when I returned to San Francisco. In February, I attended the planning meeting of all the coordinators from around the world—a dozen or so—in Basel, during which we planned the plenary, panels, and workshops.

I was excited that the WPC intended to highlight the situation of Indians in the United States, and I got busy organizing the delegates from the western United States, while Jack O'Dell did the same in the eastern half. Harry Bridges of the International Longshore and Warehouse Union (ILWU) in San Francisco volunteered to sponsor two African American longshoremen. I recruited Wendell Chino, a descendant of Geronimo, who was president of the Mescalero Apaches of New Mexico, and Sid Welch, Mojave and member of our San Francisco AIM chapter.

Roberto Vargas and Alejandro Murguía, founders of the Mission Cultural Center and leading supporters of Nicaragua's Sandinistas, joined the delegation, since the Sandinistas needed international support and were not well known in UN/NGO circles. This would be an opportunity for them to make contact with important activists from around the world. Both Alejandro and

Roberto were poets and leaders of a vibrant cultural movement in the Bay Area. At the Basel conference, they put on a poetry reading and spread the word about their revolution—one that few at the time thought would ever triumph.

Murguía is Chicano, married to a Nicaraguan, and Vargas is Nicaraguan. San Francisco then had a population of over 50,000 Nicaraguan immigrants and their descendants, many of them from families that had supported Sandino and had fled Nicaragua after the Somoza family took power in the early 1930s. The San Francisco Sandinista group that sprang from this population was small, but they thought big. One of their first public actions was to seize the Nicaraguan consulate, expelling the consul and his secretary. They held it for the day, then withdrew peacefully with no arrests. I happened to be working that day in the Treaty Council office in the Flood Building at Powell and Market, which was on the floor below the Nicaraguan consulate. When I heard the racket, I walked upstairs and saw the small band wearing black-and-red scarves over their faces. Even so, I recognized Roberto and Alejandro.

During that time, I learned about the Sandinista movement and their long struggle against the Somoza regime. In one of their most spectacular actions, the Sandinistas took corporate executives hostage at a party in December 1974 and demanded as ransom the release of their political prisoners, safe passage out of the country, and a million dollars in cash, which they won. Soon after that, Carlos Fonseca, the FSLN's founder and leader, was killed in combat, and they spent the next several years reorganizing. Then the masses rose up against Somoza and changed the political equation in the country. In January 1978, Pedro Joaquín Chamorro Cardenal, publisher and editor of the independent daily La Prensa and the leader of an opposition alliance campaigning for the removal of President Anastasio Somoza Debayle, was assassinated, gunned down on his way to work in Managua. At his funeral, thousands of people followed the coffin from the hospital to the Chamorro home, taking turns carrying it. Some 30,000 people rioted in Managua, setting cars afire and attacking buildings owned by Somoza. Nicaragua's trade unions called for a general strike. In the rest of the country, there were uprisings, particularly in places where National Guardsmen had massacred peasant farmers during the previous three years of counterinsurgency operations.

The most amazing story was about an unarmed uprising, one that surprised even the Sandinistas, in Monimbó, the Indian district of Masaya, which was crushed by Somoza's National Guard. Somoza responded to all resistance with increased bombing and massacres, imposing martial law and censorship. The Somocistas also carried out seven armed attacks on *La Prensa*, now under the management of Chamorro's widow, Violeta. As a feminist, another event caught my attention. To commemorate International Women's Day, March 8, 1978, the young feminist Nicaraguan lawyer, Nora Astorga, wooed a high official of Somoza's National Guard into her bedroom, where two Sandinista friends sprang out of the closet and killed him. Nora disappeared, and soon posters of her appeared all over San Francisco's Spanish-speaking Mission district, Nora dressed as a guerrilla, rifle on her shoulder. Meanwhile, the celebrity former wife of the Rolling Stones' Mick Jagger, Nicaragua-born Bianca, now living in New York, turned up as a supporter of Nicaraguan refugees. Yet it was not until a US citizen was killed that the US public reacted with demands that their government do something. On June 20, 1979, a Somoza National Guardsman shot to death execution-style ABC News correspondent Bill Stewart. His cameraman managed to capture the event on film, which was then smuggled out of the country and shown on the US nightly news. A month later, President Carter told Somoza he should leave Nicaragua, and the Sandinistas, who had surrounded Managua, took power on July 19, 1979.

After the Basel conference, I stayed in New York for the summer, then took a job offer at the University of New Mexico for two years, with Nicaragua always in the back of my mind, wondering about Roberto and Alejandro, who had left soon after the Basel conference for the Southern Front to join the Sandinista guerrilla war against Somoza.

That summer of 1978 in New York, I found out that Jimmie Durham was back running the IITC office, which I took as good news. I went to visit him soon after arriving. The office door was open; Jimmie's desk was, as usual, piled with documents, books, and papers, his feet propped on the pile. I sensed tension right away when he gazed up at me with hard blue eyes. He took his feet off the desk and shuffled papers for a few minutes, ignoring me as I stood in the doorway. He crushed a cigarette in the ashtray and lit a fresh one, and, without turning his head to me or asking me to come in and sit down, said, "What is it you want?"

"I'm here for the summer—I'm participating in a National Endowment for the Humanities seminar at the CUNY Graduate School, led by Eleanor Leacock."

Perhaps I said this to impress Jimmie. Leacock, now deceased, was one of the few Marxist anthropologists and had written a long and brilliant introductory essay to a new edition of Frederick Engels' *The Family, Private Property, and the State.* I added that I hoped to help out in the IITC office during the summer, as he had urged me to do.

"Better to take over, right?" he growled. I thought he was joking and laughed.

"It's not funny, Roxanne. Your behavior is unacceptable, and you are not welcome in this office."

"What behavior?"

"The World Peace Council conference. Who gave you permission to be an organizer?"

"They invited me, and I told you about it."

"We have nothing to discuss. Now, if you'll excuse me, I'm busy," he said.

I left, stunned, too stunned to be upset, until I was on a bus headed back to the apartment I was subletting, when I burst into tears.

At that time, Jimmie was understandably paranoid about many people, having been targeted by a congressional committee investigation of the American Indian Movement (which had been given the status of a "domestic terrorist organization"). I was one of the people he had become suspicious of, and I learned a few months later that he had circulated a letter suggesting that I might be an FBI informer. Later I would learn about a long letter he circulated accusing Dan Bomberry and Jose Barreiro, both then associated with the main North American Native newspaper, *Akwasasne Notes*, of being FBI or CIA agents sent to destroy the IITC.

Jimmie's letter about me was sent out after I had seen him briefly the month before when I was in New York and spent the night at his apartment, as I had on several occasions. For the first time, he had indicated an interest in me sexually, an interest I did not share, but I responded anyway since I considered him a close friend and comrade. He had a reputation for having many lovers since he and his wife had divorced several years before; however, he was unable to perform with me and seemed to resent me for it. Whether this was a factor in his new hostility toward me, I had no way of knowing, but I suspected that it was. This is an old story, not only between male bosses and female employees, but also in social movements, in which as a woman, you're damned if you respond to a comrade's overtures and damned if you don't; which of course goes on all the time but is particularly destructive given the fragile nature of movement organizations.

I wanted to continue learning about the United Nations, so I took up an offer from the Afro-Asian Peoples Solidarity Organization (AAPSO) for me to represent it at United Nations meetings in New York. AAPSO was based in Cairo and was a product of the Non-Aligned Nations Movement, which had been founded in 1955 at the Asian-African Conference in Bandung, Indonesia, when twenty-nine former colonies decided to coalesce as nonaligned nations. The movement was initially led by men like Nasser of Egypt, Nehru of India, and Soekarno of Indonesia, who created the concept of solidarity of the "Third World"—the Western capitalist states being the First World and the socialist bloc the Second World.

The emergence of Third World solidarity paralleled the African American civil rights movement in the United States. Black Americans were embraced by Third World countries as heroes for fighting US imperialism from within. In turn, Black civil rights and nationalist leaders like Paul Robeson, Bayard Rustin, W.E.B. DuBois, Adam Clayton Powell, Martin Luther King Jr., and above all Malcolm X, saw their movement as a part of Third World liberation. On the radical edge of the civil rights movement, activists viewed their struggle as part of the international movement against white supremacy and US imperialism. Reflecting the influence of this movement, Muhammad Ali famously explained his refusal to be drafted during the Vietnam War with the remark, "No Viet Cong ever called me nigger."

The Second World socialist bloc, particularly after Che Guevara brought Cuba and other Latin American progressives into the nonaligned movement, supported Third World liberation. The Cubans established OAASPAL (the Organization of African, Asian, and Latin American Peoples), a sister organization to AAPSO with a touch of competitiveness. AAPSO focused on economic development issues, while OAASPAL and its journal *Tricontinental*, founded by Che, openly expressed solidarity with armed national liberation movements, particularly Vietnam. A fanatical Islamic faction that disagreed with Egypt's negotiations with Israel had assassinated AAPSO's beloved founder, a well-known intellectual and former Egyptian minister of culture, Youssef El-Sebai. The new secretary-general, Nouri Abdul Razzak, was a member of the Iraqi Communist Party and was engaged in establishing an international development research center in Baghdad until Saddam Hussein began rounding up and publicly executing Communist Party members. Nouri and other Iraqi communists dared not return home.

My goal in representing AAPSO was to bring the indigenous issue firmly in alliance with the nonaligned movement. I worked especially to educate the non-Western member states of the United Nations about indigenous conditions and aspirations. AAPSO's journal, *Development and Socioeconomic Progress*, published my research on development in Native American land bases (reservations). This "Group of 77," as the Third World states are still known in the UN today, would vote on any proposal we might make, and they made up the majority of UN member states. The radical wing of that grouping included the liberation movements that held observer status in the United Nations: the African National Congress (ANC, South Africa), Pan-African Congress (PAC, South Africa), Southwest Africa Peoples Organization (SWAPO, Namibia), and the Palestine Liberation Organization (PLO).

Most US citizens, unlike other of the world's peoples, are aware only of the Security Council of the United Nations, in which the US, UK, France, China, and Russia (the USSR up to 1990), as the only permanent members, hold veto power over any decision of the fifteen-member council. But the Security Council deals (usually badly, thanks to the permanent members' veto power) only with armed-conflict situations. I learned about the inner workings of UN departments and councils on human rights, disarmament, decolonization, and humanitarianism. My experiences at the UN were both eye-opening and inspiring. For the first time in my life as a political radical, I began grappling with and seeking out realities, rather than romanticized versions of anti-imperialism. I struggled to implement Gramsci's dictum: pessimism of the mind, optimism of the will. I witnessed plenty to be pessimistic about, but also achievements in struggles over significant issues, particularly on the part of some Asian, African, and Latin American states and national liberation movement attempts to avoid becoming pawns in the Cold War and to find their own independent, nonaligned road.

My initial experience inside AAPSO was at its conference in Colombo, Sri Lanka, in June 1978. I was the only US citizen in attendance, and as far as I could tell, the only one in the whole country. I was not the only woman, as I had feared I might be, given that I had met only men in AAPSO. Although not numerous, the women delegates, particularly the Sri Lankan committee members, were solid and committed leaders. The head of the Cyprus delegation was a remarkable woman, Elli Mozora, an architect by profession, with whom I would work over the next several years. One of the refreshing aspects of the AAPSO meeting, so different from the UN meetings whose diplomatic language and behavior often annoyed me, was the openness of debate and the expression of differences, often quite heated, both in public and in behind-the-scenes meetings.

The Sri Lankan civil war between the minority Tamils (Hindu, Christian, and Muslim) and the majority Sinhalese (Buddhist) was still five years away, but the future of Sri Lanka and the Third World as a whole was already visible in 1978. The Sri Lankan government was deeply in debt to the World Bank. Bankers at the lending agencies were already insisting that countries in debt restructure their economies to enable the "free market" to determine economic priorities. Countries were thus forced to privatize public services or cut them drastically. Days after our conference ended in 1978, riots broke out in Colombo over the government's selling off the public transport system. Over the next several years, I saw global neoliberalism as it took shape in the Third World, and I witnessed its ugly—often bloody—results. Governments like Sri Lanka, facing threatening bankers on one hand and angry mobs of their own people on the other, chose a third way out, using ethnic conflict to redirect the masses from class struggle, so that the governments could do the bidding of the World Bank and the International Monetary Fund. Thus began Sri Lanka's scapegoating of the Tamils and the Tamils' fierce resistance to violent attacks on members of their community.

My trip to Sri Lanka included stopovers both ways in Moscow, since the Soviet AAPSO committee provided Aeroflot tickets for the delegates. Aeroflot had weekly flights from New York to Moscow and back, and weekly flights from Moscow to Sri Lanka, but they were days apart from each other, so luckily I had a week to spend in Moscow. Tair Tairov, an Uzbeki who taught international law at Moscow University, greeted me at my hotel. He and I had both been on the World Peace Council preparatory committee for the May conference on racism in Basel, and had met several times during the preparations. I felt quite at home in that faraway place where I understood not a word of the language.

A cheerful young Russian woman was assigned to show me around and translate. She took me to all the typical tourist attractions: the Bolshoi ballet, parks and museums, around the famous subway system, Lenin's tomb, the World War II memorial, and the space museum. Before I left for Sri Lanka, my guide asked what I would like to do with my time on return and I requested a visit to Patrice Lumumba University, the international institution for African, Asian, and Latin American students. I had met the president of Patrice Lumumba University at the Basel conference on racism, and he had invited me to visit. The university's medical school was renowned and honored by the World Health Organization, and I was interested in their adaptation of indigenous medical practices. I was surprised to find that a full-day reception had been organized for me. Every few minutes it seemed that either a champagne or vodka toast was required, which, as a recovering alcoholic, I was forced to decline, to the confusion of my hosts.

At the Sri Lanka meeting, I found that most of the African and Asian delegates had graduated from Patrice Lumumba, and their common language was Russian. Later, when I told this story in the United States, often the reaction was horror, as if speaking Russian as a common language at an international meeting was somehow worse than speaking the French, English, Portuguese, or Dutch of the various colonizers. That reaction made clear to me how anticommunism in the United States found an emotional home in the mental structures of racism.

From 1978 to 1980, I administered the Native American Studies program at the University of New Mexico in Albuquerque (UNM). Phil Reno, whom I knew only through letters, was the person who drew me there. Phil was a brilliant development economist associated with Monthly Review

Press. He had written me after he read my doctoral dissertation on New Mexico land tenure, and we corresponded regularly. Phil lived in Farmington, New Mexico, one of the border towns just off the Navajo Indian reservation. He taught economic development at the Navajo Community College branch in Shiprock, mentoring hundreds of young Navajos. Phil, a Coloradan, had been a member of the Communist Party in the 1930s and through World War II, at which time he was expelled from the party without ever being told why. Nevertheless, the FBI pursued and blacklisted him, getting him fired from the University of Colorado and assuring that he would never again be appointed to a university teaching position. Phil and a group of his young Native and non-Native apprentices persuaded me to apply for the directorship of the Native American Studies Program at UNM.

During those two years, I set up a research institute, the Institute for Native American Development, and organized a major conference inviting everyone, Indian and non-Indian, who was working on the problems of Native economic development. The institute published books and reports on reservation economic development and even a book of poetry and stories, *Fight Back*, which Simon Ortiz wrote about working in the uranium mines. I edited and wrote the introduction to two other books published by the institute while I was there: *Economic Development in American Indian Reservations* and *American Indian Resources and Development*. Phil and I established a seminar-training program with course credit from the university for Native American development officials and brought in UN development experts to teach. In the process, we developed close relations with the All Indian Pueblo Council, as well as with the Navajo Nation. All the while, I was rewriting my dissertation into a book that was published as *Roots of Resistance: History of Land Tenure in New Mexico, 1680–1980*. The latter year, 1980, was a significant year for the Pueblo Indians of New Mexico, marking the tricentennial of the Pueblo revolt in 1680 against Spanish colonial rule, a revolt that succeeded in restoring Pueblo independence until 1692, when the Spanish reconquered the area. For the first time the Pueblos publicly were commemorating the revolt, and the All Indian Pueblo Council endorsed *Roots of Resistance* as a part of the commemoration.

During my first year at University of New Mexico, Phil had persuaded a Navajo former student at Shiprock, Larry Emerson, to take the position of assistant director of the Native American Studies Center. Larry brought the best out in everyone, and Larry and I worked as a team establishing the institute and organizing the conference. Never before or since have I worked so well with another human being. Like his older sister, Gloria, Larry was a gifted artist, writer, and mentor to younger Navajos. Only thirty years old, Larry was wise beyond his years. But he resigned at the end of the first year when an accident led him to rethink the direction of his life.

Larry drove home in his pickup truck to Shiprock every weekend—straight north from Albuquerque to Farmington, New Mexico, on the Navajo border. Inside the Navajo Nation, alcohol could not be bought or sold, so the five-mile strip of state highway between Farmington and the Navajo Nation line that Larry had to cross on his way home to Shiprock was banked on both sides by shabby bars. Young Navajos, including Larry, protested the border towns' exploitation of Navajos, but to no avail—during one demonstration at Gallup, another border town, a Navajo youth leader was shot and killed by police. On one of his trips home in the spring of 1979, a woman suddenly stepped in front of Larry's pickup. Although he was driving below the speed limit, he was unable to swerve or stop before hitting and killing her. He clearly was not at fault, and was not even cited by police. The dead woman was obviously a Navajo, though, and Larry would need to make restitution to the family in the Navajo way. However, she carried no identification. Fingerprints revealed no identity. No Navajos came forward to claim the body or file a missing-persons report. Larry called and asked to take off a week to find the family, but they were not to be found. He was distressed that he could not carry out his responsibility to make restitution, but something far greater in this case terrified him. He explained to me that it was impossible for a Navajo to get lost. Every Navajo has family or clan members with obligations to her or him. This woman had none. More important: there must be other lost Navajos. For Larry this was urgent, a sign of something more ominous even than the dreadful "long walk" and imprisonment of Navajos in a military concentration camp in the 1860s. I tried to argue with him and convince him that this was a unique case, but he would not listen. He resigned and returned to Shiprock to work with his people, which he has continued to do since that time.

I missed Larry the second year I was at UNM, and there was no one who could replace him. Simon moved back to New Mexico, and I hired him to teach a course. We were able to become friends and colleagues, and I still was part of his family.

I continued doing UN work on indigenous issues as best I could from New Mexico during the two years I was there, often traveling to the UN in New York, and twice to Geneva during that time. I agreed with Jimmie Durham's approach to international work and thought it essential that the emerging indigenous peoples' movement find its home and support in the circle of progressive national liberation movements and nations that were grouped in the Non-Aligned Nations Movement. Jimmie had left the IITC for good, and without him at the helm Russell Means and his followers sought headlines rather than doing day-to-day international work. For example, the IITC became involved in the Iranian hostage crisis of 1979, and took up the Palestinian issue as its own, not making clear what these activities had to do with indigenous peoples. Then, after the onset of the Iran–Iraq war in 1980, they became close to an Iraqi Baathist representative in New York. I spent a lot of time in the IITC office on my trips to New York. But I was frustrated because I felt that the international indigenous issue was getting lost in the midst of headline chasing—or worse, in the absence of IITC, being managed by the Scandinavian countries, Canada, and the Carter administration through their government-funded indigenous organizations.

In 1980, I left the University of New Mexico to accept a National Endowment for the Humanities research grant to research and write a book on Native Americans on the international stage, and moved to New York. Fortunately, Ted Jojola from Isleta Pueblo took over for me at UNM. He had just received his doctorate from the East-West Institute of the University of Hawaii and specialized in development planning. I intended to return to UNM the following year and looked forward to working with Ted.

As a representative of AAPSO, I was a member of the international NGO organizing committee for the UN Mid-Decade Women's Conference that took place in Copenhagen in July 1980. Elli Mozora and I headed the AAPSO delegation to the conference. The UN Decade for Women had been declared in 1975. This initiative owed everything to the mass women's liberation movement that burst forth from the 1960s' antiracist, antiwar, anti-imperi-alist movements in the United States and rapidly spread around the world through movement connections and literature. It was a truly autonomous, international mass movement that shook the very premises of existing social orders, and I had been involved in it from the beginning and on the front line. The initial Decade of the Woman conference in Mexico in 1975 had not been a success in terms of broad international participation. However, by the time of the Copenhagen conference five years later, a great deal of organizing had brought thousands of women from all parts of the world. North Atlantic white women still far outnumbered others, but they no longer dominated politically. Our NGO organizing committee made sure that the program fo-cused on Africa, Asia, and Latin America, particularly highlighting the libera-tion movements, Nicaragua's recent success among them.

The most dramatic event of the conference for me and for many others was the appearance of Leila Khaled, the Palestinian guerrilla who highjacked an Israeli El Al airliner in 1970 and became a hero to women leftists all over the world. Although captured and imprisoned, she was later released in a prisoner exchange. Her co-highjacker, Patricio Arguello, was killed during the security operation. He was a Nicaraguan Sandinista, still revered to this day, one of several Sandinistas who were trained by the Palestinians. When Khaled arrived, surrounded by the press, at our conference center, everything stopped and masses of women greeted her with flowers and applause. I was among them, but I caught sight of a group of US feminists—Bella Abzug, Gloria Steinem, Robin Morgan, and others—who were poker-faced and not applauding, physically and politically sidelined at the conference. In fact, looking around, I saw that I was one of only a handful of US women in the greeting crowd.

After returning from Copenhagen, I moved into a summer sublet near the UN where the television received the new twenty-four-hour news channel, Ted Turner's CNN. CNN was a time-consuming dreamworld for me, a news junkie. Because of CNN, I followed the Democratic primary contest much more closely than I would have otherwise, especially because Ted Kennedy's challenge to incumbent Jimmy Carter dominated the news. Kennedy was be-ing red-baited for proposing "socialized" medicine, that is, a Canadian-style national health care system. How laughable this seemed when I was working

for truly revolutionary change every day. Here was Ted Ke
for trying to make a small (though positive) tweak in the
and here was I, studying US economic, political, and cultural domination in
order to help construct an anti-imperialist program.

I did some thinking that summer, for the first time in years free of organizing and teaching. The prospects for revolution in 1980 were not what they had been in 1968. I was now forty-two years old. After years of work, there was still no revolution within the United States on the horizon. What I discovered living in New York in 1980 was that the world was in a far more serious mess than I had understood. I had been prepared to spend the rest of my life in New Mexico, working locally, venturing out to UN meetings and to secure resources for projects with the Pueblo and Navajo Indians, assisting in the construction of a liberated zone through both fierce resistance and parallel institution building, Native nation building, while others were doing the same in other parts of the country. My year in New York killed that dream, revealing it as an illusion, or perhaps it deluded me into underestimating the long-term effects of local organizing. I returned to New Mexico several times from New York, including a trip to organize a conference with a Ford Foundation grant I had secured to form a Native American Scholars Association. But I began to realize that I would have to choose to continue the international work or devote myself to local issues and national Native issues.

In the background to that year, the Soviet intervention in Afghanistan and the Iranian hostage crisis became the perfect fodder for the former governor of California—my archenemy from that time—Ronald Reagan, and for his fundamentalist Protestant backers. Under their pressure, Carter retreated ever closer to their positions.

Then came a series of disturbing events that seemed to me like death knells. The first was an actual death, the assassination of Allard Lowenstein by one of his former disciples. Lowenstein was one of the activist lawyers in the southern civil rights movement of the early 1960s. He moved on to international human rights work and had led the US government delegations to the UN Human Rights Commission meetings during the Carter administration. I had not met him but was planning to try to set up a meeting with him that summer. However, he was shot and killed in his Manhattan office just after returning from the 1980 Human Rights Commission meeting in Geneva in March. For me, this tragedy foreshadowed the death of liberalism. The disillusioned disciple who shot Allard Lowenstein was murdering a lie, the lie of liberalism that the United States was redeemable, which was the hallmark of Lowenstein's bouncy optimism.

In September 1980, Iraq invaded Iran. In this brutal eight-year war, Saddam Hussein served as the West's proxy to overthrow the Iranian Islamic government, an effort that was ultimately unsuccessful. For the war industry, it was an opportune occasion to test the latest weapons, and, as it turned out in 1991, to become familiar with Iraq's military capability. Once again, the Kurdish communities that straddled the Iran–Iraq border were devastated, even before Iraq used chemical weapons on several villages in 1988. (In the leadup to the 1991 and 2003 US invasions of Iraq, this chemical attack on the Kurds was used by both Bush administrations as an example of Saddam Hussein's atrocities; however, I was in Geneva in 1988 and observed the Reagan administration's refusal to allow an investigation of Iraqi war crimes, much to the disgust of the exiled Iraqi Kurdish exiles present.) It seemed a repeat of eight years earlier, when the Nixon-Kissinger team fomented hostilities between Iran and Iraq, that time with the Shah of Iran serving as US proxy. Kissinger, when queried about his schemes, famously remarked that foreign policy was not social work, while the Shah drove Iraqi Kurds back into Iraq to be slaughtered by a regime that considered them traitors.

Another setback indicated the future direction of the United Nations: the defeat of proposals for a New International Economic Order (NIEO). A 1974 United Nations resolution contained a Declaration and Program of Action of a New International Economic Order, which was subsequently adopted by UNESCO in 1976. In response to the momentum generated by this declaration, Robert McNamara, then president of the World Bank, initiated the establishment of the Independent Commission on International Economic Issues, with Willy Brandt, the former prime minister of Germany, serving as chairman. In 1979, the commission issued a persuasive 300-page report in favor of the NIEO, which was published in many languages and in English as *North-South: A Program for Survival*. Often referred to as "the Brandt Report," it called for the radical transformation of the world economic order, with massive transfer of technology and development financing from the "North" (the industrialized states) to the "South" (former European colonies and other nonindustrialized states). The 1980 UN Special Session on Development was in part convened to respond to that report. It was an enormous event, attended by heads of state from all over the world. The Carter administration, however, sent a low-level delegation to announce its refusal to accept the terms of the discussion and to generally disrupt the proceedings. It was not the first such behavior I had observed: the Carter administration had boycotted the UN Conference on Racism in 1978. But this conference was even more significant, given the popularity and prestige of the Brandt Report, and the US attitude came as a surprise to many. Without US political and economic support the NIEO project was doomed.

A large and well-organized parallel nongovernmental conference was held at the Waldorf-Astoria Hotel, only a few blocks from UN headquarters. Our large AAPSO delegation worked in teams and covered all the meetings, governmental and nongovernmental, sharing information at late-night meetings in preparation for the next day. After a few days, violent demonstrations materialized outside the Waldorf-Astoria and made their way inside. The demonstrators were a group of Jamaican thugs who had been wreaking havoc in Kingston opposing the Jamaican socialist prime minister Michael Manley's outspoken leadership of campaign for the New International Economic Order. Most people assumed that the demonstration was a Carter administration CIA operation with the goal of regime replacement in Jamaica (a goal that was soon achieved).

It was also at the Special Session on Development that I heard the first rumors of a counterrevolution against the Sandinistas in Nicaragua, who had been in power for only a year. I picked up a flyer that announced an anti-Sandinista meeting at the UN auditorium, a space that required a government's request for its use. It turned out that the Canadian government had made the request on behalf of the National Indian Brotherhood, a Canadian government–funded Native organization in Canada. The theme was what the speaker termed "Sandinista genocide" against the Miskitu Indians in northeastern Nicaragua. I knew little about the Miskitu situation in Nicaragua: three Miskitu professionals had attended the 1977 Geneva conference on Indians of the Americas, two years before Somoza was overthrown, but they had avoided talking about Somoza or the Sandinistas.

After listening to the Canadian Indians tell their horror stories about Sandinista crimes against the Miskitu people, I introduced myself to the speakers—Chief George Manuel and Marie Marule—and invited them to lunch in order to figure out what they were up to. I quickly realized that they did not know much about the situation and had been reading from a script. That is when I knew everything would change for the burgeoning international indigenous movement, and that my own life would be redirected. I could not bear to see the United States overthrow another popular government or crush it by war, as it had done in Greece, Guatemala, Iran, Indonesia, Brazil, Vietnam, Laos, and Chile, and was attempting to do in Angola, Mozambique, and Cuba, as well as providing counterinsurgency support in South Africa, El Salvador, Guatemala again, Western Sahara, and East Timor. And I realized that the US might well destroy the new international indigenous movement in its attempt to use the movement for its own ends.

Soon after I encountered the lobby against the Sandinistas at the UN, I met with Roberto Vargas, who was posted in the Nicaraguan embassy in Washington, D.C. He put me in touch with Alejandro Bendeña in the Nicaraguan mission to the UN. Bendeña had grown up in the United States and had a Ph.D. in history from Harvard. He was well aware of the Miskitu situation and introduced me to a young Stanford anthropology graduate student who was in New York visiting his mother. Philippe Bourgois knew everything there was to know about the Sandinistas' relations with the Miskitus in the eastern half of Nicaragua, and it was not good news. Philippe had spent several months in the Miskitu zone. He dismissed the allegations of massacres and genocide as propaganda, but warned that the Miskitus could be the Achilles' heel of the revolution. This was where the United States would aim if it tried to destabilize the Sandinista government, a platform being openly touted by the Reagan presidential campaign.

Bill Means, Russell's younger brother, was now in charge of the Treaty Council office and had invited Bendeña to the annual Treaty Council meeting that summer. The tie between the Sandinistas and the American Indian Movement that had been created after the 1973 siege of Wounded Knee was now revived. AIM leaders recalled that the cofounder of the FSLN, Carlos Fonseca, had written a letter of support to the AIM warriors under attack by the US military, so the rumblings from a remote corner of Nicaragua involving a few hundred Christianized Indian communities controlled by missionaries didn't count for much in AIM's big picture. My first reaction was that the CIA was up to its old tricks, fashioned in Vietnam and Laos, when they armed the mountain tribes, a strategy that had a devastating impact on the Hmong people in Southeast Asia and would soon force the Miskitus to pay a same high price.

The realization that I could not return to the University of New Mexico or remain in academia anywhere came to me in a decisive moment one day in the fall of 1980. I was in Washington, D.C., for a week-long meeting of an eight-member humanities panel selected by the National Endowment for the Humanities (NEH). I had been serving on such panels for NEH during my two years at UNM, and I always looked forward to them. We were not paid, except for expenses, but it was a prestigious gig, and we were put up together at an elegant hotel. It was hard work, reading a hundred or so long applications before the meeting, but I always felt that I had accomplished something important by supporting proposals that leaned left. I was politically more radical than any other panelists, but I was persuasive and usually my chosen projects were approved, a couple of them becoming quite famous—the film *The Ballad of Gregorio Cortez* and the sympathetic documentary *Seeing Red*, about US Communist Party members. There weren't any Native American proposals among the ones I reviewed, but there were a number of anthropological and archeological ones by non-Natives that I was able to persuade others to reject or to change to include Native voices. But, on the third day of the panel, the last I would serve on, I was standing with the other panelists at the ornate doors of the elevators in the government building that housed the NEH, and I became hyper-aware of the others, the setting, and myself. The question "What am I doing here?" pounded in my head.

3

Desaparecidos

Ronald Reagan was elected US president by a landslide right in the middle of the 1980 UN General Assembly session. Although all the polls had predicted the outcome of the election, my friends at the UN seemed surprised, as if there was no way such a terrible nightmare could become reality. His victory did not bode well for the UN since Reagan had railed on the campaign trail against "world government," playing to his right-wing and evangelical followers, and most likely really believing what he said.

Following the election I felt a strange euphoria—not happiness, but a fighting spirit welling up within me, a sense that now the adversary was clear, and that the true face of the US ruling class would now be revealed. As a part of his campaign platform, Ronald Reagan had vowed to remove the "godless, communistic" Sandinistas from power in Nicaragua. I draw a line here, I repeated to myself. Here I stand, and across that line is the destruction of Nicaragua, further weakening of the UN, increased brinkmanship and terrorism in response, possibly even nuclear war. I vowed that I would do all in my power to help prevent the overthrow of the Sandinistas, one part of the larger picture that I could possibly affect.

In early 1980, ominously, Reagan had announced his bid for the presidency in the backwoods town of Philadelphia, Mississippi, in Neshoba County. In doing so, he and his wealthy corporate backers signaled their intention to restructure white supremacy in the United States. Neshoba County was where civil rights workers James Chaney, Andrew Goodman, and Mickey Schwerner were murdered in the summer of 1964. (Reagan was equally obvious about his debt to white supremacists following his reelection in 1984, when he traveled to the Kolmeshohe Military Cemetery near Bitburg to honor the Nazi war dead.) The civil rights movement had forced white supremacy into euphemisms and symbols—hoisting the Confederate flag became "free speech" and "states' rights," while "equal rights and responsibilities" became code words for their policies against welfare recipients, inner-city youth, and Native American sovereignty; and "right to work" meant that trade unions were the enemy.

At the time of Reagan's election, I was so disillusioned with the Carter administration that I hardly cared who was elected. But my life—and the world—was changed in unimaginable ways by Reagan's victory. My friends from other countries felt the change more sharply and quickly than I did. On Election Day I arrived first at a Brazilian restaurant in Midtown Manhattan to meet a British friend for dinner. It was a small and crowded upstairs space filled with music, laughter, loud conversations in Portuguese, the wonderful aroma of food blending meats and codfish, spices, and sauces. Although I had been there many times, I was never comfortable in those days being a woman sitting alone. I took a window table overlooking 45th Street and the restaurant's neon sign flashing off and on. It was rush hour in Midtown, and the sidewalks were jammed with men and women toting lookalike briefcases, the women all dressed up but wearing frayed Nikes and carrying their high heels in Bergdorf and Bloomingdale's shopping bags. The men had loosened their ties. For a half-hour I scanned and separated the faces of the men, hoping to spot Roger walking from the United Nations building a few blocks away. Roger Plant was a visiting lecturer at Columbia University's Human Rights Institute. I had gotten to know him well enough after a dozen United Nations meetings over three years to know it was unusual for him to be tardy.

Suddenly Roger appeared and folded his bony six-foot-three frame into the chair across from me. He apologized for being late and said that he had been walking through the Manhattan streets half-crazed. He was perspiring even though the evening was autumn chilly. Roger's pinkish skin had turned nearly red, and he seemed to breathe with difficulty. His usually calm, diplomatic

eyes were furtive, shifting, not focused on me or on anything el.
asked in Portuguese if Roger wanted a drink and he answered 1
in Portuguese—an ethnologist, he was fluent in most languages o.
icas. When the neat Scotch came, he downed it in one gulp.

"What should we do?" Roger asked.

Bewildered, I did not answer. Roger and I had been meeting with Guatemalan exiles and lobbying at the United Nations General Assembly for a resolution condemning the Guatemalan military government for human rights
abuses against the Mayan population and trade unionists. That was why we
were meeting now. Roger was an important player as the author of *Unnatural
Disaster,* a best-selling book on Guatemala.

"Aren't you afraid?" Roger asked, staring into my eyes, trying to read my
face.

"Afraid of what?"

"A first-strike nuclear attack by the Soviets."

I laughed, thinking he was joking, but tears rolled down his now-ashen
face. Roger was in his mid-thirties, but suddenly he appeared old and haggard.
A sharp jolt of panic alerted me to the possibility that something dire had
happened. My first thought was that the United States was bombing Cuba.

"What . . . what is it, what happened?"

"Reagan has won," he said.

"I know that." Although the polls were still open in most of the country,
the results were clear, a landslide for Reagan.

"If you were the Soviets, wouldn't you risk a first strike?" Roger was serious. And I realized, not for the first time, how terribly afraid the rest of the
world was of the United States. I took Roger's trembling hand in both of
mine. His hand was so cold. I comforted him, telling him that the Soviets
were not that trigger-happy and that surely they understood US politics, that
Reagan was not that much different than Carter or any of the others—my
standard US leftist refrain.

The mercenaries of the Central American oligarchies lost no time in seizing the initiative they now held. The night of the election Guatemala's
military and oligarchy danced in the streets, and work began on their genocid-

al project against the majority Mayan population. Within weeks of Reagan's election, the entire leadership of the Salvadoran civilian opposition was assassinated in broad daylight, and four US Roman Catholics, three nuns and a laywoman who were doing work with the poor, were raped and murdered in San Salvador. In the mix somehow was the December assassination of John Lennon, the radicalizing troubadour of the post-Sixties generation.

In the midst of what seemed like a coup d'état by Reagan's transition team that December—for instance, they ransacked Carter's office on women's issues and changed the locks on the door—I accompanied Roger and our Guatemalan exile friends to the annual meeting of the American Anthropological Association in Washington, D.C. My doctorate was in history, so I had never attended an anthropology conference, and I was impressed with this gathering of engaged and enraged anthropologists who denounced Reagan's policies, particularly in Central America. Ralph Nader was the guest speaker in a meeting organized by an activist anthropologist, Shelton Davis, who had shunned academia to run his Anthropology Resource Center in Cambridge, Massachusetts, working on behalf of threatened indigenous peoples. Davis asked all of us at that packed meeting to vow, with him, to refuse to collaborate with the Reagan administration in any way. Yet, a few years later, Davis would close the doors of his resource center, take up the anti-Sandinista banner, and become a high-paid official at the World Bank.

And Davis was not the only one who crossed over. In the following years lobbying at the UN, I learned never to underestimate ambition and career opportunities as motives. I witnessed many human rights activists, especially the US ones, changing their tune during the Reagan administration. Would things have been different under a second Carter administration? It's doubtful. Carter prepared the groundwork for everything attributed to Reagan. He brought the major corporations into the inner circle of his administration. He initiated corporate deregulation of the airlines and ground transportation. Carter had won office by wooing the labor and civil rights movements that had forced radical changes in US policies and laws, but he betrayed every promise he made and was a prime mover in the undoing of those reforms. Worst of all, his born-again Christian sentiments, spouted while in office, opened the door for the Christian right to enter politics.

In late November 1981, my Uzbeki friend, Tair Tairov, arrived representing the World Peace Council during a debate on disarmament issues in the General Assembly. The disarmament superstar British historian E. P. Thompson was scheduled to speak at the Riverside Church, sponsored by the National Council of Churches (also known as "the god box"), and Tair and I went together to hear him. I had expected a dry lecture, but the church was packed that night, standing room only, and Professor Thompson was dramatic and charismatic, the audience reflecting his energy. Afterwards, I ran into one of the organizers and she invited me to come to a smaller meeting with the professor upstairs, where Tair and I joined about forty others. After a few softball questions from the others, Tair introduced himself as Uzbeki and challenged Thompson on a number of his assertions regarding Soviet arms policies. Thompson's face froze and the room became hushed.

Thompson said, "You're an émigré from Russia?"

Tair said, "No, I'm Uzbeki from the Soviet Union."

"So you agree with Soviet policies?"

"Not all, but with the commitment to disarmament, yes. The ways of getting there are disputable."

It was clear that Professor Thompson had never debated a Soviet expert on disarmament face to face, and his previously sunny aura seemed to slip away, leaving a scared and haggard, hollow man. The experience impressed me for what it revealed about the gap in dialogue between peoples. Tair and I walked in the cold November night all the way from the Upper West Side to Midtown discussing how direct discussion between Soviet and US citizens might occur.

From the end of 1980 until the late summer of 1981, I did not have a home and was once again a roving activist. I left my Manhattan apartment after the end of the General Assembly in December, stored my belongings, and flew to San Francisco to spend the Christmas holidays with my daughter, Michelle. My apartment there was sublet, and I stayed with a friend. The day after Christmas I flew to Washington, D.C., to present a paper at the annual meeting of the American Historical Association and stayed through New Year's Day. I spent most of my time in D.C. with Roberto Vargas, my old Nicaraguan poet friend, who was serving as cultural and labor attaché at the Nicaraguan embassy to the United States. He was trying to facilitate my travel to the troubled northeastern Miskitu Indian region of Nicaragua, where across the river border in Honduras the CIA had been organizing anti-Sandinista forces clandestinely even before Reagan took office.

Fortunately—so we mistakenly figured—Julio López, the head of the international office of the FSLN, now a legitimate political party, was visiting the embassy and Roberto invited me to the reception, telling me that this was the one person who could definitely obtain permission for me to travel to northeastern Nicaragua, where foreigners and the press were prohibited. I had visited the embassy many times that week but had not been there for a formal reception. The embassy was housed in a mansion near Dupont Circle, fit for the dictator Somoza. Up a broad, winding mahogany stairway to the grand parlor I walked among the formally attired diplomatic guests, feeling out of place in my corduroy slacks, turtleneck sweater, and boots. Huge tables topped with white tablecloths were laden with every imaginable example of Nicaraguan cuisine, delicious and beautifully presented. Then I noticed that the young women and men in crisp server's attire were daughters and sons of the Nicaraguan embassy staff that I had met before. Roberto found me and whispered that he and everyone else in the embassy, including the ambassador, had been cooking all day. I was touched by the generosity of this make-do event.

But my conversation with Julio López did not go well. His response to my rap about the international indigenous movement, international law, and autonomy was, "There are only Nicaraguans in Nicaragua." This was the standard Latin American answer. Finally, Roberto convinced me to join the delegation of San Francisco labor leaders he had organized to visit Nicaragua in May, telling me that he was sure he could get me out to the coast once we were in Managua, if I could stay over after the delegation.

I had a month before the UN Commission on Human Rights would begin in Geneva, which I would attend for AAPSO as part of the work on the book I was writing on international human rights and indigenous peoples. I decided to spend it in Cuernavaca, Mexico, at one of the many language schools to brush up my rusty oral Spanish.

In early January 1981, I returned to Mexico after a thirteen-year absence. Why had I stayed away for such a long time, after having made it my second home during the mid-1960s? I had loved Mexico. Then I stopped going in mid-1968, as if separating from my Mexican husband at that time barred me from entering his homeland. I went there to study Spanish, but I benefited far beyond that, meeting hundreds of Mexicans and North Americans involved in Central American solidarity work, poised to resist the Reagan onslaught. Cuernavaca became my stopping-off point for trips to Central America for the following eight years.

I had participated in United Nations meetings at the UN European headquarters in Geneva on three occasions before I returned in February 1981 for the six-week meeting of the United Nations Commission on Human Rights, the most important annual event in the human rights field. Everyone doing human rights work feared the Reagan administration's threats to dismantle human rights programs, withdraw from UNESCO, and perhaps even leave the United Nations altogether. On the other hand, many of us found it hard to imagine how the UN could be destabilized any more than it had been already under the Carter administration. I had monitored the General Assembly meetings in the fall and witnessed US support for Saddam Hussein's aggression against Iran and its insistence on recognizing Pol Pot and the Khmer Rouge in defiance of Vietnam's intervention that overthrew that regime. Yet, despite longtime US domination of the United Nations, the distant drums of the marginalized right wing against "global governance" had not echoed in US administrations until Reagan. From 1981 on, the UN came under tremendous pressure as those previously marginalized right-wingers assumed positions of power and influence.

I knew I was in for a rough first experience at the February 1981 Commission on Human Rights, but I was not prepared for what—for whom—I encountered there: ghosts of the disappeared, *los desaparecidos*. I met their relatives—mothers, husbands, wives, children, brothers, sisters, friends, and colleagues of the disappeared, often themselves having been tortured, many of them forced into lives of exile. I spent hours in the circle of people who would gather each day around members of the Madres de Plaza de Mayo, the group that mothers of the disappeared in Argentina had begun two years earlier with their silent vigils in the plaza in front of the presidential palace. Others who spoke for the disappeared were from Chile, Brazil, Bolivia, Uruguay, and Paraguay—the military regimes that had formed the infamous "Operation Condor," a sort of Latin American gestapo designed by its US creators to neutralize democratic oppositions, using torture and death as the tools of control. The regimes found that the easiest way to neutralize their opponents was simply to make them disappear, dumping bodies into mass graves or into the ocean depths. This brilliant solution to the problems of political conflict was already being applied in El Salvador, Guatemala, and Honduras, and Argentine torturers would soon be subcontracted by the Reagan administration to train former Nicaraguan National Guards in their techniques in preparation for the Contra war against the Sandinistas.

I had read the reports, knew the numbers of disappeared, attended rallies condemning US complicity. But meeting face to face with torture victims who had managed to survive and escape and talking with the families of the dead and disappeared were things I was not emotionally prepared for.

The Serpentine Lounge next to the conference room where the Commission met was full of these wounded and traumatized people. I saw them and for the first time I fully realized that the UN human rights organizations were a matter of life and death, and not simply talk and bureaucracy. I realized that other governments took human rights accusations seriously, even though the United States did everything in its considerable power to prevent the US public from knowing about human rights proceedings. The Carter administration had tried to undermine the Commission by turning it into a forum on the alleged repression of Soviet Jews and Soviet dissidents, particularly calling for the freedom of the banned physicist, Andrei Sakharov, whose wife, Elena Bonner, epitomized the US government's version of human rights.

The Reagan people were even worse. The head of the US delegation to the Commission was Richard Schifter, a corporate lawyer with the influential Washington, D.C., firm of Kampelman, Shriver, and Hoffman. Schifter struck me as an obnoxious and arrogant loudmouth who knew nothing about international human rights law and could care even less: his role was to discredit human rights concerns, not to participate in the proceedings.

Schifter reflected that strategy of the Reagan administration when the Geneva Democrats Abroad chapter hosted him for a two-hour lunch meeting. My friend Lorraine Ruffing, who was active in the chapter, invited me to go as her guest. I took notes on his rambling talk and afterwards typed them up and distributed the anonymous document widely, causing quite a stir, especially among the African delegates. Schifter had confided to his all-white, US-citizens-only luncheon audience that "Africa has no interest in human rights, only in their own issues." Of course, among "their own issues" was the apartheid regime in South Africa, for which the proposed solution of the US government was "constructive engagement," that is, investment in and support for the regime.

Schifter had begun his talk by stating that "the UN Human Rights Commission exists for one purpose: to investigate human rights infringements by rightist forces in Latin America." But he went on to call the Commission's investigations of Latin American atrocities "a narrow focus" and then tried to persuade us to follow what he described as the much better US policy of "gentle nudging" of the rightists toward an end to killing. Of course, Schifter did not acknowledge how those "rightist" forces in Latin America had come to power and who had trained their militaries in the fine art of "interrogation" and counterinsurgency; nor did he mention the US-sponsored military coups or the fact that these officers learned their skills at the infamous US School of the Americas, then located in the Panama Canal Zone.

Another main target of the Commission, Schifter argued, was the state of Israel. He launched into a history of the Commission and Eleanor Roosevelt's role in its initiation and her solid support for the partition of Palestine and the establishment of Israel, arguing that the Commission had strayed far from its historical roots, as evidenced by its condemnation of Israel for its occupation of Palestinian territory and blocking the establishment of a Palestinian state. Schifter named three nations as "sincere countries that don't act in their own interests" regarding human rights—Denmark, the Netherlands, and Norway—without noting that they too had voted in favor of the resolutions that condemned human rights abuses by Israel, the apartheid regime, and the Latin American dictatorships. He made it clear that the Reagan administration was considering withdrawing from the Commission, and even the United Nations itself.

Schifter warned that Reagan's newly appointed ambassador to the United Nations, Dr. Jeane Kirkpatrick, "will be in policy-making more than any other UN representative." Kirkpatrick was especially known for her vehement hatred for the Sandinista government in Nicaragua. Schifter took off in that direction, arguing that the Sandinista Ministry of Interior (headed by one of the FSLN's founders, Tomás Borge) was "controlled by communists," and that the FMLN opposition to the military-controlled regime in El Salvador was communist. Schifter echoed Kirkpatrick's refrain that "once a country is in the Soviet orbit, it is lost for good." He argued that "Salvador's problems are endemic to Salvador and no one outside is to blame, yet the US is kindly taking responsibility to help build infrastructure and to stabilize El Salvador, while the Soviets exploit the endemic situation." Finally, regarding Central America, Schifter said that it was irrelevant, that the real concern of the US was Mexico and the possibility of a communist takeover there.

Schifter ended his diatribe by alleging that Southeast Asia "has proved that the domino theory is correct, and were the trend lines of the 1970s to continue, the United States would not survive." He was referring to the Vietnamese victory over the United States as having emboldened liberation movements all over the non-Western world. Instead, the Reagan administration would take over the Carter administration's program for "constructive engagement," forging human rights into a hammer rather than leaving the Commission, and accompany those methods with pumped-up paramilitary counterinsurgency along with the usual bribes and threats to ensure good behavior as defined by Washington. What I appreciated about Schifter's unvarnished presentation was that he revealed the real outlook of the United States government, rather than the human face usually presented for public consumption.

In the 1970s, international nongovernmental organizations had gained a considerable voice in the UN human rights field, and we were allowed to make multiple fifteen-minute statements as well as present written statements produced and translated by UN services. During the Reagan years, all those NGO privileges were swept away on the grounds of "budgetary considerations." What happened to the money? UN dues are calculated according to member states' gross national product, meaning that the United States is assessed the highest dues, around 40 percent of the UN budget at the time. The Reagan administration began withholding payments, and earmarking the payments it did make for particular purposes, never human rights.

However, at the 1981 meeting, each NGO with UN consultative status was still allotted fifteen minutes of speaking time on each of a dozen agenda items. It was the first occasion for me to address member states of the United Nations. I spoke on behalf of AAPSO under several items. For most items, I read statements that AAPSO had prepared on apartheid, Israeli occupation, the Cyprus question, peace, development as human rights issues, and so forth. But AAPSO also allowed me to speak on the indigenous issue, during which I blasted the United States as racist and imperialist. Schifter was not listening to what anyone said, but many people from all parts of the world shook my hand and commented on my courage.

The Commission of 1981 was the first and last one that I participated in while sober—I did not attend the 1982 session when I was still abstaining. But I did function in an altered mental state even in 1981, which I now realize was the first sign that I was headed back to drinking. That winter in Geneva I suffered bronchitis that left me with a hacking cough. Someone recommended codeine-based cough pills, which, like nearly all drugs in Switzerland, could be bought without a prescription. I kept taking the pills after the cough was gone for the duration of the Commission session. I quit the habit after leaving Geneva in mid-March, but the breach should have signaled me to return to counseling, as I had learned in recovery that I should do. Testing, just testing, that is the addict's twisted thinking that paves the way for returning to the comfortable altered state that the brain has become rewired to demand.

I had made close friends in Geneva over the four years of meetings I had attended there. A few lived in Geneva permanently, but others came from various parts of the world for UN meetings. I stayed with Lorraine Ruffing, who had a doctorate in economics from Columbia University and worked for the UN. Lorraine had written her dissertation on Navajo economic development and had, like me, adopted Phil Reno as a mentor. Lorraine and her family lived in an old three-story stone farmhouse outside a small French town quite a way across the Swiss border to the south, and I commuted with them daily.

Many of the Geneva-based NGO activists who had helped with the 1977 conference were now close friends, especially those at the international office of the Women's International League for Peace and Freedom (WILPF). Edith Ballantyne, a native of Czechoslovakia and naturalized Canadian, was president of the WILPF for many years. She had been the prime mover behind our 1977 Indian conference and became one of the most important mentors of my life. Edith had encyclopedic knowledge of weapons of mass destruction—how they worked, how much they cost, military budgets for every country, the new generations of weapons as they developed—and was the most important nongovernmental lobbyist at the disarmament division of the UN, which was also based in Geneva. Her office assistant, Lee Weingarten, was the daughter of German immigrants to the US, and a permanent resident of Geneva. There were other international workers and citizens of Geneva who had been involved in organizing the 1977 conference and were always willing to be of help—Jacqueline Dupoys, Isabelle Schulte, Louis Necker, Rene Fuerst, Sidni Lamb, and Mario Ibarra. In the early 1980s, Prexy Nesbitt, an African American activist, then Ester Prieto, from Paraguay, as officers of the World Council of Churches, provided small but important grants for my work.

At the 1981 Commission, I also met the recently appointed California Supreme Court justice, Frank Newman. I had heard Frank speak in 1977, when he was still dean of the University of California's Boalt School of Law. It had been at a United Nations Association forum, the audience filled with elderly retired diplomats and their spouses, plus a few perky law school students. During the question-and-answer period, I made a pompous statement about the 1977 Indians of the Americas Conference, and Frank drew a blank on it but graciously acknowledged the information. I had noticed the news of his appointment by Governor Jerry Brown to the state Supreme Court, joining two other radical Brown appointees, Rose Bird and Cruz Reynosa, former lawyers for César Chávez's United Farm Workers. (Judges Bird and Reynosa were voted out of office after Republicans took control of the state in 1983, and Frank resigned and returned to Boalt rather than stand for the election.) Despite his new high-status position, Frank attended the Commission in 1981, as he had done for two decades. I introduced myself to him as the rude questioner at his lecture four years earlier, and he actually remembered my question, but not at all negatively. Frank Newman was a big-hearted person if there ever was one, and we spent many hours talking during those six weeks and continued the conversation until his death in 1996.

The intense six weeks of work at the Commission on Human Rights convinced me that, flawed as it was, the United Nations was the only institutional barrier to total imperialist domination. It was clear that the Soviet Union, although a bogeyman justifying US militarism and dominance, lacked the power and will to control the world, compared to the United States. The UN was the only recourse for the peoples of the Third World and for the oppressed within the empire. I could not forget the *desaparecidos*.

4

A Revolution Is Not a Dinner Party

Journal: *May Day 1981. Cuernavaca, Mexico. I await my fellow travelers, the trade union delegation to go to Nicaragua. Today is May Day. How do I explain to my compañeros Mexicanos why May Day is not a holiday in the United States where it originated? They know about the Haymarket martyrs of Chicago, but workers in the United States do not. That alone should be enough to cause them to revolt. If they only knew what they do not know, were not told. I tell my Mexican friends that my grandfather was a Wobbly in Oklahoma and that 20 percent of the state's population voted Socialist in five presidential elections, but that no one there remembers. They keep asking me: "¿Por qué no hay fiestas para recordar los martires?" Why are there not festivals for your martyrs? My answers do not seem to satisfy. Then I realize they do not believe me, do not want this to be true. Somehow it explains all too clearly why and what United States imperialism is. Mira, diga, escucha, vamos a ver. Now it is the hour I love most. Dusk. Especially in Mexico where the second day of the day begins.*

I was a member of a San Francisco labor delegation to Nicaragua, organized and led by Roberto Vargas. Our five-day program took us to shop floors, docks, warehouses, construction sites, sugar and coffee fields, and mills. We met with dozens of labor organizers and officials and hundreds of ordinary workers. Everyone we talked to asked us to return and force the US government to reinstate the wheat shipments to Nicaragua that had been cut in the final days of the Carter administration. Their slogan was simple: *Pan con dignidad*, bread with dignity.

Roberto chose each of us eight members of the San Francisco trade union delegation because we had supported his solidarity work in San Francisco during the 1970s, but some of us had not met each other before. The delegation included the president of the San Francisco trade union council, two longshoremen from the famous Harry Bridges San Francisco local of the ILWU, the head of the local Service Employees International Union—the membership of which, at that time, was more than half Nicaraguan—and the lone woman besides me, representing a Communications Workers local. I was representing my university local of the United Professors of California (a year later, this radical union would be fiercely attacked, leading to its being voted out as the bargaining agent for state university professors; such unions were the target of the right wing, greatly buttressed by Reagan's firing of the civilian air traffic controllers in the summer of 1981).

Walter "Chombo" Ferretti was our host, along with the Sandinista Trade Union Confederation (CST) in Nicaragua. Chombo was a great hero of the revolution, having been commander of the final successful urban battles resisting Somoza's Guardia. At twenty years old in 1970, he had moved from Nicaragua to San Francisco and worked as a cook at the Mark Hopkins Hotel until he returned to join the Sandinista guerrilla army in 1977. He was an active member of the culinary workers' union and had persuaded the San Francisco union members and leaders to support the Sandinista struggle. Now he was commander of the national police. He was generous and humble and, as the first Sandinista guerrilla commander I met, exactly as I had imagined, and hoped, he would be.

In the following several days we visited factories and other Managua work places, large and small, talking to workers. Most were enthusiastic about the revolution, while some were dissatisfied but seemed unafraid to complain openly. We drove to a town in the northern highlands toward the Honduras border, passing on our journey a two-hundred-truck convoy filled with young Sandinista soldiers armed with Czech rifles and Uzis. A people armed. *El pueblo armada*. Roberto and Chombo told us that former Somoza guardsmen had carried out assassinations and burned crops in the border towns. These killers of the former regime would make up the core of the US-organized Contras, which was already being organized and trained by Argentine military officers in Honduras.

Back in Managua, we met with an anti-Sandinista trade union group that claimed that they were descendants of the original Sandino nationalists but hated the Marxism of the Sandinistas now in power. The Somocistas, it appeared, had gone from not even uttering Sandino's name to appropriating him as their own. But it was true that Sandino was a nationalist and Latin Americanist, an anti-imperialist, but not a Marxist like his contemporary Farabundo Martí in neighboring El Salvador, the hero of the FMLN—the Salvadoran national liberation front. Sandino's program was rooted in his experience working in the banana fields, which were owned by huge US corporations, and seeing his country overrun by US Marines. Oddly enough, the only ideological influence on his development that has been traced is his interest in Rosicrucianism.

A t the US Embassy we met with the Carter-appointed ambassador, Lawrence Pezzulo, who had not yet been replaced. What a weasel! He claimed that he had tried to help the Sandinistas and that the United States had given Nicaragua more aid than any other country, but instead the Sandinistas had brought in thousands of Cuban military advisers who had taken over the telephone company. Pezzulo told us a litany of lies, challenging our delegation to check out each one of them. He claimed that dockworkers in Puerto Corinto were outraged because the Sandinista union was forced on them, throwing this nugget out to the two longshoremen on our delegation. He said that the Sandinistas would have abolished the church if they could have, but they had brought in foreign Marxist Jesuit priests from El Salvador. He predicted that the Sandinistas would not get by with their anti-Americanism, that "we have lots of people on the Atlantic Coast." But then he insisted that there was no threat from the United States to the Sandinistas and that they were just using that claim as propaganda to maintain their political support.

What appeared to provoke Ambassador Pezzulo most was what he called the "stupidity" of the Sandinistas, giving as an example an incident that had happened a month before, an incident that I had found hilarious, and, yes, stupid, but in that endearing Sandinista make-do way that I loved. It seemed that the Sandinistas needed a helicopter for flood rescue work. They contacted a friend in Texas where Bell helicopters were manufactured, and he agreed to purchase one on their behalf. However, the Sandinistas could not afford the shipping costs, which were greater than the cost of the helicopter itself. They came up with the bright idea of flying two pilots to Dallas to pick up the helicopter and fly it back. Of course, the US Air Force forced the helicopter down soon after takeoff, the helicopter was impounded, and the pilots were arrested for a variety of immigration and licensing infractions. For some reason, this incident was the last straw for Pezzulo. He went on to discuss the insurrection in El Salvador, observing that the Salvadorans are "Indians and not very bright, but when pressured, they revert to savagery." All this from Carter's appointed ambassador, soon to be replaced by an even more virulent one representing the new Reagan administration.

No Nicaraguans accompanied us on our visit to the embassy, but when we returned to Roberto and our Sandinista labor hosts, some members of our delegation insisted that we be allowed to investigate the ambassador's charges about the Puerto Corinto workers. We took off for the northwest port to make a surprise visit to the docks, where we found no basis for the ambassador's charges.

I welcomed the drives into the interior of the country, since Nicaragua is majestically beautiful. Plains, valleys, mountains, horizons, smoking volcanoes in every direction, everywhere, just as my old friend Sonia had described it to me two decades before. But Managua was a city in shambles. Residents could not always remember if it had been the 1972 earthquake or Somoza's bombs that had created those craters, wrecked this building, or buckled that street. The two were related, because Somoza pocketed all the disaster aid money sent to Nicaragua in 1972, and nothing was rebuilt except suburban mansions for the rich.

After the delegation left, Roberto and I stayed on. It took two weeks to obtain permission for me to visit the troubled northeast region of the country, the Miskitia, or Atlantic Coast as the locals call it. I moved from the Mercedes Hotel across from the airport to the trade union confederation protocol house, which was near the center of town. There I met more labor representatives and organizers from different parts of the country as they passed through, visiting the capital for this or that meeting or workshop, some of which were held in the hospitality house. I was welcomed to sit in on the meetings, and there were normally at least a half-dozen people around the dinner table every evening, eating the delicious meals cooked by two sisters who were war widows. That experience gave me a very special grounding in the meaning and means of the Sandinista Revolution, one I hung on to over the following terrible years.

From the first minute I set foot on Nicaraguan soil, I felt the energy and dedication of the Sandinista militants. But I also felt something else that I could not at first identify. I had never before been in a place recently wracked by war, and the markedly peaceful ambience in Managua in mid-1981 was deceptive. I noticed some erratic behavior—a lot of drinking, for one thing. As a recovering alcoholic with five years of sobriety at the time, I was acutely aware of signs of alcohol abuse and dependency in many of the people I met. Then there were the tears, sudden tears that could turn into angry outbursts and even fights. It occurred to me that the people I was meeting needed counseling. The one outlet for the traumatic effects of the war, the only outlet acceptable to those hard-working, determined, and rarely rested militants, was poetry. Poetry was in the air and everywhere—workshops and literacy training just for the purpose of being able to write poetry. It was a national obsession, writing poetry. But the contents of the poems were brave, not confessional, meant to bolster weakened spirits. Bravado poems, I called them.

The last thing the Nicaraguan people needed was more violence, more war. But that was what was in store for them. Soon I would understand a little better the effects of living in a war zone, dodging Washington-made bullets and walking gingerly around Claymore land mines, and I would be exhibiting many of the same symptoms I had observed during that spring of 1981.

Thanks to a meeting that Roberto scored for me with Comandante William Ramírez of the Ministry for the Atlantic Coast (INNICA), I finally possessed a three-day pass to travel in the northeastern region. The *comandante* radioed ahead—the only means of communication to Miskitia—to find a room for me in the capital of the region, Puerto Cabezas (now officially named Bilwi, the original Miskitu name for the town), and guides to show me around and translate for me. I flew out on a domestic flight, a decrepit old prop plane with wooden benches on each side of the cabin.

I took the one dusty cab waiting for the flight to the local INNICA office. Two young Miskitu men, Marcelo Zuñiga and Bobby Holmes, were there to meet me. I was hoping to meet with the regional head of INNICA, Francisco Campbell, but he did not receive me at the time. Bobby was a local leader of MISURASATA (acronym in the Miskitu language for Miskitu, Sumu, Rama, Sandinistas All Together). The organization had replaced ALPROMISU (Alliance for Progress of Miskitus and Sumus), which had been founded in 1972. Bobby supported the revolution and had been one of the few Miskitus who had been a Sandinista combatant before they took power. Marcelo was Miskitu and worked for the Atlantic Coast Ministry. He was married to a woman from the US who had arrived in the region as a Peace Corps volunteer before the Sandinistas took power. The two of them had lived in Guatemala, where they worked with the Mayans, but returned following the Sandinista triumph. Marcelo was from Waspám, the capital of the border region along the Río Coco (Wanki in Miskitu) with Honduras, the area where there was the most opposition to the Sandinista regime. On meeting me, he told me what the Miskitus wanted: autonomy, since the Miskitus regarded themselves as a nation.

They took me to a boarding house overlooking the Caribbean, saying they would pick me up early the next morning. My room was tiny, painted bright blue, and spotlessly clean. There was no running water—and, judging from the many candles and lanterns around, the power (generators, not hydroelectric power) was unreliable.

The boarding house where I was lodged was so very Anglo-American. The owner and other business people there spoke a mixture of Spanish and English, but everyone seemed to use English numbers, even the Miskitus. The British had been there for over a century, then the US Marines and North American companies dominated the coast until Somoza was installed. Not many US companies had stayed after the 1930s, but there had been Christian missionaries from the United States—mostly Moravians, but also Southern Baptists, Church of Christ missionaries, and several influential Capuchin-Franciscan friars from Wisconsin.

The elderly woman who owned the house called herself English, although her family had been there for generations and she was considered by the community to be Creole, the all-purpose term for people, whatever their color, whose mother tongue was English (that is, Caribbean-inflected English). She sat me down at the large dining room table and brought a plate of lobster for me to eat—it was lobster season, and I was served lobster for every meal in Puerto Cabezas. She did not sit down at the table with me, but flitted around the room and in and out of the kitchen, talking. I said I had come to visit Miskitu villages, and she said, "Miskitus no good people." She did not like or approve of the Sandinistas and warned me that the Cubans were taking over, something I had heard many times in Managua.

When the Sandinistas had put out the call for volunteer medical personnel and literacy workers, people showed up from all over the world—the *internationalistas,* as they were called. A number of governments also supported programs—the Scandinavian countries, Mexico, and others—but by far the largest number of volunteer doctors came from Cuba, a form of aid the Cuban government had long before initiated and still continues, responding to humanitarian relief calls whatever the country's politics. That first night, dead tired, I fell asleep around 9 p.m. but was awakened by several male voices speaking Spanish, clearly Cuban Spanish, talking about how well they had done and the response of people. Even I conjured up suspicions of the Cubans, until at breakfast when I met them and learned that they were members of a touring salsa band that had performed in the local ballpark the night before.

The next morning, when Marcelo and Bobby picked me up, the first person I sought out was Armando Rojas Smith, one of two Miskitu lawyers. I had met him at the 1977 Indian conference in Geneva, where he, Armstrong Wiggins, and Mildred Levy had been the three Miskitus representing AL-PROMISU, their indigenous organization. Following the detention and release of MISURASATA leaders, Armstrong Wiggins had left Nicaragua for Washington, D.C., to denounce the Sandinistas and was being supported by several US-based Native organizations. Brooklyn Rivera, the current head of

MISURASATA, was rumored to be planning to leave as well. I had met Brooklyn briefly at the Puerto Cabezas airport, but he was leaving town on the plane I arrived on. We agreed to meet in Managua.

Bobby and Marcelo said that they did not trust Armando because he had not openly opposed Somoza, and they did not want to take me to meet him, but I insisted. Armando was surprised and pleased to see me. He accompanied us for lunch at a Chinese restaurant that had only country-western music on the jukebox. I was surprised to find that there were three Chinese restaurants in this small town. It turned out that Chinese men had come to the Atlantic Coast in the late nineteenth century as merchants and had married local Miskitu women, but had maintained their language and customs. We ate fresh lobster, Chinese style.

Armando told me that his law practice had never been better, because now there were laws and the rule of law and litigation was possible, whereas under the Somoza government law was arbitrary. However, he felt that the Sandinistas did not trust him. Armando expressed pessimism, but seemed sincere and dedicated to the Miskitu organization and reluctant to leave his beloved hometown. We walked to the home of Mildred Levy. She was a nurse working with Dr. Mirna Cunningham at the Health Ministry and was more optimistic about the situation, but she was worried as well.

Finally, it was time to meet the regional director of the Atlantic Coast Ministry, Dr. Francisco Campbell, a bright young Creole man. Marcelo told me that Campbell spoke only Spanish and Caribbean English, the latter his mother tongue, but not Miskitu. He had earned a doctorate from Hawaii's East-West Center. His brother, Lumberto, was famed on the coast as the only Sandinista guerrilla commander and was now military commander of the southern half of the Atlantic Coast. But Dr. Campbell was just leaving his office as we arrived, saying that he would talk to me later.

The guys then took me to see Dorotea Wilson, the regional head of the Sandinista government. She was a young Creole woman whom I thought very sensitive and likeable. But I learned that many Miskitus did not trust her or Francisco, or any other Creoles as far as I could tell, unless they were also Moravian pastors. They said it was because they lacked the Miskitu language, but there seemed to be more to their hostility than that. During the long US occupation of Nicaragua, US companies had favored Creoles because they spoke English, and they had served as bosses over the Miskitus in the mines and plantations. To my disappointment, Dr. Cunningham, a Miskitu/Creole medical doctor who was head of the regional health ministry, was away on a speaking tour in the United States and Europe. She was respected and loved by the Miskitu people even though she was a Sandinista because she had doctored the people for years before the revolution and spoke fluent Miskitu.

Enthusiasm for the revolution, which was palpable in the western part of the country, was absent in Puerto Cabezas. The people there had not experienced Somoza's bombing of civilians, nor the rounding up of young men to kill or be killed. In Miskitia, the revolution was a distant rumor. All the Coast people saw was a new batch of Spanish-speaking Nicaraguans arriving with plans, not a good sign; if they had to choose, they preferred the benign neglect of the Somoza dictatorship. But I did meet elderly Miskitus who remembered the US Marines bombing their villages in the late 1920s, trying to dislodge Sandino and his soldiers who were fighting to rid Nicaragua of the Marines and the fruit companies, and everyone appeared to revere Adolfo Cockburn, a Miskitu general in Sandino's army who was assassinated by a US Marine.

There was tension in people's voices as they told me about the government's crackdown on the Indian organization, MISURASATA. Three months before, the most charismatic MISURASATA leader, Steadman Fagoth, had fled to Honduras with three thousand of his followers—mostly young Miskitu men—to form a guerrilla army to fight the Sandinistas. This happened in February 1981, following a shootout between Sandinista police and MISURASATA members in the Miskitu town of Prinzapolka. It was an ugly story, the result of a catastrophic mistake on the part of the Sandinistas, who were spooked by the threats of the incoming Reagan administration.

Steadman Fagoth, claiming to be a gung-ho Sandinista, had been selected by them to represent MISURASATA on the Sandinista-established Council of State, an interim quasi-legislature that was conceived as the building block for a real parliament. Armstrong Wiggins, who was supported by the Moravian church, was given a desk to represent MISURASATA in the Casa de Gobierno, the skeleton of a governing executive. In February 1981, Steadman was heading from Puerto Cabezas to Managua to take the Miskitu "Plan 81" to the council. Among other MISURASATA demands, Plan 81 proposed that

Steadman be appointed a member of the governing executive (JGRN) that had been established by the Sandinistas as an interim body. However, an arrest warrant had been issued for him because of allegations that he was a Somoza agent at the national university in 1978. Steadman countered that he had in fact been a Sandinista plant within the Somoza apparatus. In any case, Steadman was arrested and jailed, while arrest warrants were issued for two dozen other MISURASATA leaders on the Atlantic Coast and for Armstrong Wiggins in Managua. Armstrong was seized at his workplace, the Casa de Gobierno.

To make things worse, a few days later at the Miskitu coastal town of Prinzapolka, during an award ceremony for the successful MISURASATA literacy campaign, four Sandinista police officers (two of them Miskitu and two Spanish-speaking from western Nicaragua) interrupted the ceremony that was taking place in the Moravian church. They called out the name of the Miskitu master of ceremonies, announcing that he was under arrest. He asked them to please wait outside until the ceremony was over, but the police went forward and tried to handcuff him by force. Several fellow MISURASA-TA activists gathered around their leader to try to protect him. Two off-duty Sandinista soldiers, outside drinking, heard the commotion and entered firing their guns. The people fled the church and hit the ground, terrified, surely the first violence of that sort any of them had ever experienced. When the dust settled, six Miskitu men and two non-Miskitus lay dead, four of them police, four of them civilians.

Other arrests followed. Tens of thousands of Miskitus rallied in protest, and in response the government released Steadman and the others. Steadman went straight to the Río Coco and led several thousand young Miskitus across the river border to Honduras, where the US-supported Contra camps awaited their arrival.

It did not help to alleviate tensions that there were so many soldiers in Puerto Cabezas, virtually all of them Spanish-speaking. They did not fit in, and the people did not like their presence. It felt repressive, like an occupation. I wondered why they were not put to work. They seemed to just stand around and move trucks from one spot to another.

I was left to myself before dinner, and I walked around the town, stopping to talk with people. It was Sunday, and evening church services were about to begin. I felt that I was inside a moment of history, those fractions of time that turn up in history texts a century later. I had never felt that way before, and always wondered what it would be like to be inside an important historical moment. I had participated in historic events of the sixties, including key events in the foundation of the women's liberation movement, and I had felt I was a part of making history then, but I never had the feeling of being inside a moment of history, not as I did in that shabby marginal corner of the globe called the Miskitia. I think that in a way it was a personal connection, that I was discovering there a part of my own lost history.

I realized that there were many surprising similarities between Nicaragua and Oklahoma, which are identical in size and population, only three million people. And eastern Nicaragua, the Miskitia, was as sparsely populated as Oklahoma's western half where I was from—just a quarter of a million people in each place. In both places, there are Indians, Blacks, and whites, and complicated loyalties and animosities. But in the Miskitia, unlike Oklahoma, there are also the Chinese, while in Oklahoma the merchants had been Assyrian and German. Even the Norther, that frigid wind that always brought in its wake my worst asthma attacks, blew into the Miskitia, no longer cold but just as deadly, because it carried in its wake malaria-bearing mosquitoes. Western Oklahoma was dry, however, with cycles of drought. It was a dust bowl, and rain was the most precious commodity. The Miskitia, in contrast, was a tropical rain forest. In the season they called dry, rain pounded down only a few hours each day. But during the rainy season, the downpour never ceased for more than an hour, and it hit hard, like giant birds' wings flailing your body. Land turned to water. Trees were uprooted. Placid streams turned into wild rapids. People vanished, and whole villages disappeared. Rain was an enemy. Yet when the rain ceased for an hour in the Miskitia, the dust took over, fine red dust just like in Oklahoma.

Beyond the evocations of my childhood provoked by the ambience—including the very poverty and ruralness of the place—it was the music that enveloped me like a part of my skin, the music of my childhood—country and western and church hymns. Merle Lindsey, Hank Williams, and Bob Wills spilled out of homes and shops; "The Old Rugged Cross" and "Bringing in the Sheaves," traditional evangelical Protestant hymns, wafted out from the churches.

I was jolted out of my reverie by realizing that along with these folkways, some of the least attractive aspects of Oklahoma littered the Miskitia, especially the rabid hatred that accompanied the disease of anticommunism, but the consumerism as well. I found nostalgia for the good old days of access to products from the United States, products that were no longer available. A family I visited complained that they could no longer get toothpaste since the revolution. I noticed a tube in their window and pointed to it. "No, that's Mexican. Ipana is toothpaste." I understood. I recalled how my family considered only Wonder Bread to be bread. My mother baked the best bread in the county, but sold it in town in order to buy Wonder Bread. I expect that we would have said there was no bread had we not had Wonder Bread. And Spam and Vienna sausages were sorely missed in the Miskitia.

My walk took me to The Rock, a saloon overlooking the Caribbean in Puerto Cabezas that sat on the site of the 1961 gathering of the CIA-organized flotilla of fishing boats used to stage the invasion of Cuba at the Bay of Pigs. I went there to ask questions of the old men who were sitting around drinking Victoria, the Nicaraguan beer. When they found I was from the United States, they began reminiscing about the glory days when they drank Falstaff at The Rock. They stared out to sea and longed for Falstaff, or what it represented, and they mumbled about communism taking over. The Miskitus were unhappy with the Sandinistas, but they resented being labeled counterrevolutionary. One woman told me about a meeting in Mexico where a resolution had been passed condemning the Miskitus, and this outraged the Miskitus, who felt that their image in the world was being smeared. I told her that the story was false, or I would have heard about it when I was in Mexico. The Sandinistas were similarly concerned about their image in the world; with good reason, as I was to find out.

Finally, I would go to the border. The Río Coco, "the Wanki," as the Miskitus call it, was the heart of their civilization. The river marked the border between Nicaragua and Honduras, but that had not always been so. Until 1960, when the border was moved to the Río Coco from much farther north, all of the Miskitu nation had been within Nicaragua's border. The change cut the Miskitu population in two, half in Nicaragua, half in Honduras, with the Río Coco now a border rather than the center of the Miskitia.

After studying the case, I concluded that Somoza had just given the area away, probably on US orders, although the dispute was settled in the World Court in an action brought by Honduras. No Miskitus were called to present their opinions or were even aware of the case. After the decision, Somoza's National Guard forced many of those who refused to leave the Honduran side of the river into planned communities south of the Río Coco, organized by the Franciscans.

Marcelo, Bobby, and I left Puerto Cabezas at 9:30 in the morning and arrived in Waspám at 11:30. It rained all the way and there was no windshield in the jeep. We drove on a dirt highway for miles through pine forests and a great deal of clear-cut land, but we saw only three other vehicles. We met with the local ministry official, a Latina, and the Sandinista representative, a Latino, and had a big meal, the last morsel of food or drink that appeared for the rest of the day. I was lodged in a run-down rooming house for transient workers, while the guys stayed in Marcelo's home.

The next morning, Marcelo and Bobby took me to Waspám's town park, where, to my surprise, approximately fifty Miskitus, mostly women, had gathered to hear me talk. I told them about the indigenous international human rights projects. I spoke in Spanish, and Marcelo translated my talk into Miskitu. It would have been preferable for me to speak in English, since the Miskitus distrust Spanish-speakers, but neither of my Miskitu guides spoke English. We talked for over an hour, and although their comments and questions were hostile, at the end they each shook my hand and thanked me. They were worried, and many of their sons had followed Steadman Fagoth into Honduras. They seemed to appreciate that I would come so far to visit them, but also suspicious of my motives, since the Sandinista government had sent me. I assured them that although the government had allowed me to visit, I was not representing the government.

Following the meeting, and, at last, lunch, we drove east along the river through dozens of Miskitu communities. We stopped in Wasla to tell the town leaders that we would be back so they could set up a meeting, and we drove on to Kum, where we arrived unannounced. The bridge from the road to the town was out, and we had to park the vehicle and walk across a log above some very scary rapids and rocks way below.

Darkness fell and fireflies swarmed around me—I had not seen fireflies, "lightnin' bugs" we called them, since growing up in Oklahoma. There was no electricity and no large meeting place. Yet about a hundred villagers gathered, standing outside, to hear me speak. It was the first time Bobby and Marcelo had gone into these communities since Steadman Fagoth fled across to Honduras with most of the young men. These townfolk, like those in Waspám, expressed outrage at the Sandinistas' treatment of Fagoth, their elected leader. They were also concerned about their "children," the three thousand young men "on the other side." They seemed truly fearful that Sandinista soldiers with guns would occupy their communities and said that the worst elements had been recruited to the police and army, and that now they carried big guns and intimidated the people. There were no soldiers or police present that night. Although they spoke quite freely to me, a total stranger, and in front of Marcelo and Bobby, who worked for the Sandinista government, they expressed fear that if they spoke of their complaints they would suffer repression. I could hear the preacher's voice spreading misinformation.

We drove back to Wasla, after once again crossing over the rapids in the pitch dark (I could not walk that slippery log—I crawled). The village was prepared to receive us in front of the school. They repeated the same complaints and fears, their anger even more pronounced. Again they graciously shook my hand and thanked me for coming. Some said a few special words of solidarity with all indigenous peoples.

I was exhausted when we arrived back in Waspám at nearly midnight. But Bobby and Marcelo seemed to thrive on this work. I stayed in the same "motel," as they called it, and the next morning found the Latina and her daughter who ran the motel sitting in chairs outside. I sat with them. They told me they were Sandinistas and that they mistrusted the Miskitus, using derogatory descriptions of them in Spanish, not all of which I understood though I got the idea. One word I didn't know but later learned was for monkeys, something to the effect of having to bring the monkeys down from the trees. Complex class and race questions divided the local Sandinistas—that is, Latinos who claimed to be Sandinistas—and Miskitus. I did not know if these contradictions existed within the Sandinista leadership, but I intended to find out.

We awaited the *comandante* of the region. A big mystery, where he was. I was tired after another day and night of community visits, hard traveling with little food or drink, and no baths. Finally, the *comandante* appeared along with the national health minister at an extraordinary event where the Moravians turned over the administration of their hospital in the Moravian mission town of Bilswarkama to the Health Ministry. The ceremony was followed by Miskitu traditional dancing, the dancers attired in the traditional hand-painted tree-bark clothing. As we were readying to depart, a group of white American Moravian missionary women approached me and asked to talk to me alone. A childhood of Southern Baptist preachers and missionaries surged up in me, and I was so repulsed by them I could not bring myself to talk, although I knew very well the Miskitus would not trust me without the Moravian nod.

We ate lunch and left Waspám around 3 p.m., headed back to Puerto Cabezas. We stopped about halfway to visit the Miskitu community of Francia Sirpe, which had a population of about two thousand. The terrain radically changed here from pinewoods to tropical, the principal crop being bananas. All the farmers were meeting in a seminar on maize production, and they were just breaking up. Marcelo arranged for me to speak, and about two hundred, mostly men, gathered in the large open-air meeting room. I spoke, and the response surprised me: they were not hostile but rather quite enthusiastic about the revolution and their own organization, MISURASATA. They were especially proud of the literacy program in the Miskitu and Sumu languages that had been completed. It was such a contrast to the Río Coco Miskitu communities that I wanted to understand why. Marcelo explained that Francia Sirpe was a "new community," one that had been formed in 1960, after the border was changed, and was made up of Miskitus who were forced across the river by Somoza's troops. This model village had been built in cooperation with Capuchin-Franciscan monks, so these Miskitus were Catholic and their missionaries were Franciscans from Wisconsin. That explained the noticeably better conditions of the buildings, including a generator for electricity. They were fortunate, too, in not being located on the border where the US-sponsored counterrevolutionary war was brewing; the Sandinistas trusted them and they appeared to trust the Sandinistas.

On the drive back to Puerto Cabezas, we reviewed our contacts over the last three days. Bobby and Marcelo seemed quite pleased. Yet all that I had heard disturbed me. I realized I was going to be like Lam Phuung, a Vietnamese anthropologist friend in Geneva, who said that when she talked to the minority nationalities in Vietnam, she rallied to their side; then when she talked to Vietnamese government officials she saw their side and all the problems that war-torn Vietnam faced. Of course, that was the situation for the Miskitus who worked for the government, being a part of the process while trying to influence its direction. But working with the Sandinistas did give the appearance of compromise to indigenous groups in other countries, and that was Steadman Fagoth's line to the Miskitus, that those who allied with the Sandinistas were sellouts. I had never before seen a revolutionary process at work so closely, and the most troublesome aspects of the process at that. I decided that I must be very careful in writing and speaking about what I saw and heard about what was going on. It is so difficult to describe movements without either engaging in mindless support or telling the truth bluntly and then having to watch as your words are taken out of context to condemn the process and become an argument for US intervention.

I decided that I wanted to return to Miskitia. I wanted to try to get the International Indian Treaty Council and other North American Native organizations and individuals to rally support for the Miskitus within the revolutionary process, and to try to help the Sandinista leadership understand indigenous aspirations.

Getting to the Miskitia was easier than getting out. I waited and waited. The Ministry of Transportation had grounded the domestic airplanes because of the poor state of their equipment and the lack of spare parts. I spent a day, then two days, then a third, all day at the airstrip on the edge of Puerto Cabezas, a short walk, and then back to the boarding house at sundown, since the planes could not fly at night because there was no radar. There were no telephones either and only two short-wave radios, one controlled by the Sandinistas, the other controlled by the Moravians, each reporting very different information from the outside world. Newspapers, when they arrived, were weeks old. It reminded me of my isolated rural childhood in Oklahoma, where the only information that was regularly available was from the Baptist preacher, who made up whatever he wanted us to think.

Finally, I was able to meet with Dr. Francisco Campbell, who had declined to talk to me earlier, although he provided my guides and arranged my travel. Dr. Campbell was not very informative or inquisitive. He seemed to think he knew exactly what should be done. He believed that the Miskitus were self-defeating. He said that there were many Miskitu villages located precisely where there would always be flooding in the rainy season. One such village, he explained, was two hours off the main highway, then a three-mile walk. It straddled a river that flooded every rainy season (most of the year). The people raised barely enough to eat plus a little yucca to sell. Campbell said that he went there to talk with them and told them that it was impossible to help them unless they would move. They accepted his view of the situation, but refused his suggestion to relocate. It seemed that relocation was on the development expert's mind. That was typical. Governments and development experts always viewed the indigenous population in their countries as mislocated and/or overpopulated, so the solution was to get them to somehow move somewhere else. It never occurred to them that they were establishing priorities rather than finding solutions that the indigenous communities demanded. I had no idea what was at stake there, but in my experience, more often than not, there was another motive—some valuable mineral or oil or other natural resource or water for a hydroelectric dam that could be exploited only if the communities were relocated. I hoped the Sandinistas would not follow that path. I had for years been calling such policies "genocidal." But I could not deny the ferocity of the torrential rain. Rivulets turned to swollen rapids that brought down everything in their wake. That last night in Puerto Cabezas, I thought that the force of the rain would bring the roof down.

During my final wait at the airport, Carlos Alemán Ocampo, also waiting for a plane, introduced himself as a writer who had been recording Miskitu stories for the Ministry of Culture. He was Latino, in his thirties, and from the western region, but he had Miskitu children through his former marriage to Dr. Mirna Cunningham. He described his own dilemma, as a Sandinista since his high school days and the father of Miskitu children, himself fluent in the language, as frustrating but hopeful. Back in Managua, I would learn that he was considered a distinguished poet and writer, and one of the founders of the Nicaraguan writers union. And, thanks to Carlos, I was able to hitch a ride with him on a Sandinista military transport.

5

House Arrest

Managua. June 8, 1981. I was on time, six o'clock, and the sun was almost gone. From the outside, the house looked transplanted—it could have been one of those old brick mansions along Classen Boulevard in Oklahoma City, where the oil-rich lived before they built new, bigger mansions farther north. But the house I was about to enter was out of place in the tropics.

The housekeeper opened the door, and I said I had an appointment with Brooklyn Rivera. She motioned me in, shut the door, and led me down the entry hall to the living room where she left me standing. The interior of the house was as incongruous as the outside. Unlike most wealthy homes in Managua, it was not built around an open interior patio that allowed natural ventilation through all the surrounding rooms. Long, narrow windows were hung with dusty, wine-colored velvet drapes. A small air conditioner in one of the windows barely reduced the humidity, but required that the windows and doors be closed even to achieve that. The ceilings were high and hung with once-elegant light fixtures that were cracked and coated with grease and dust. The bulbs were probably twenty-five watts. The floral-designed wall-to-wall carpeting was threadbare and looked as if it held a number of diseases. Giant cockroaches strutted across it, pausing to mine the fertile field.

The housekeeper returned and nodded toward the left, beckoning me to follow her. We entered a large dining room, and she vanished. Even the twelve-place carved mahogany dining table was swallowed in the cavernous space. At the other end of the dining room was a cluster of formerly fancy brocaded couches that had been abandoned when rich Managuans fled during Somoza's bombing raids in 1978 and 1979. They left with only portable belongings, leaving valuable paintings, furniture, and mirrors. I walked to a sitting area around a massive coffee table that was cluttered with weeks of local newspapers. The wallpaper design matched the floral carpeting. But the walls were bare.

This was the MISURASATA headquarters in Managua, a house abandoned by a wealthy American during the revolution and granted by the Sandinistas to MISURASATA. I was there to meet with Brooklyn Rivera, now the organization's main leader since Steadman Fagoth had fled to Honduras. Everywhere I had traveled in the Miskitia, I was told I should meet him, and that the fate of MISURASATA, the fate of the Miskitu people, was in his hands. I had been back in Managua since June 2 and it had taken six days to get an appointment with Rivera—it was harder to make an appointment with him than with the highest Sandinista ministers. I supposed that he was much in demand.

A tall young man, maybe six-six and blond, entered the dining room from the kitchen. He did not even throw a glance my way. He set the table with a plate, fork, and napkin, returned to the kitchen, and came back with bowls of food; three trips, one place setting. He carefully covered the place setting and the food with cheesecloth, which was quickly swarming with giant cockroaches the likes of which I had not seen since New Orleans, black and oily, clicking whenever they moved. The blond man flailed his arms and ruffled the cloth. A strange servant indeed, I thought.

I decided that the man was probably an American. "Where are you from?" I asked in English, meaning where in the United States. My voice was thin and raspy. Either he did not hear me or was ignoring me. I began thinking I was invisible. I cleared my throat and asked again, louder, though even at top volume my voice was low, asthmatic. At that moment, Brooklyn Rivera entered, coming down the stairway into the living room, not from outside, so he had been in the house all the time and was over an hour late for our meeting. He did not acknowledge me either. Rather, he took a seat at the head of the dining table in front of the single place setting, and then turned and locked his eyes on me, lips curled downwards.

"He's German," Rivera said.

Brooklyn Rivera was a serious-looking young man in his twenties with thick black curly hair, cut short. He was tall and thin, almost delicate. He wore a pale green guayabera shirt and brown polyester slacks—out-of-style bell-bottoms, the pants legs too short for his long frame. Below, worn brown ankle-boots and white socks. He looked like a country boy dressed up for the big city. As a former country girl, I felt a pang of sympathy for him.

Waiting for Rivera to talk to me was becoming a game, my evening project. I felt that I had already learned more about him than I would learn in an actual interview.

The German reappeared and fussed over the food bowls, removed the cheesecloth, and shooed away flies and cockroaches. He silently prepared a plate for Rivera, then covered the bowls again, hesitating a moment at attention, as if awaiting orders. Rivera said, "Un refresco, por favor," and he tapped the day-glo blue metal glass. The German scurried to the kitchen and returned with a bottle of Pepsi, poured most of it into the glass, recapped it, and awaited further orders. Rivera dismissed him with a flick of his hand and began to eat.

After five minutes of eating, Rivera said, in English, without turning to face me, "What is it you wish to discuss with me?"

I looked around the room, and I was the only person. I said, "Are you planning to leave Nicaragua?"

He continued eating and said no more. The German brought two cups of coffee. I salivated and crossed my fingers. I was thirsty for attention as much as for liquid. Alas, the German sat down at the table, and the two of them began chatting in Spanish. After half an hour, Rivera rose from his chair and disappeared into the dark belly of the house. The German began washing dishes in the kitchen—I could hear the ting and clang of china and metal pots, water sloshing. Meanwhile, I had become a potted plant.

The German crossed the dining room and disappeared in the same direction Rivera had. He returned after a few minutes and stood directly in front of me: "Mr. Rivera will receive you now. Please follow me."

I checked my watch: eight o'clock, exactly two hours late. Maybe there had been a misunderstanding about the hour, I rationalized. Rivera was sitting in a small room at a paper-cluttered desk. An old black Remington typewriter held a sheet of blank paper. An effective air conditioner rattled in the window. The German stood at attention, scowling, arms crossed. I glanced from Rivera to him to Rivera: "May we talk alone?"

"Robin is my adviser. He stays."

And I thought he was the cook. Robin Schneider was an anthropologist who, along with his companion, Kristine Ohland, had come to Nicaragua to appraise the indigenous uprising and ended up close to Brooklyn Rivera.

Finally, Rivera spoke: "I would never join the Somocista Contras, but that is not the only alternative if I leave Nicaragua."

"You may not think so now, but the United States government controls the Nicaraguan opposition, and you would surely fall into their net whether you want to or not," I said.

"How is that?" Rivera said.

"If you don't join what they've set up, they are likely to eliminate you. That's how they do things," I said.

"And how do you know this?" Robin said.

"I know a lot about my government. You have to know your enemy," I said.

"The Sandinistas, not the Americans, are my enemy—they are communists and will never allow the Miskitu to be free," Rivera said.

"I disagree. I don't think the Sandinistas are inflexible. But the fact is that the Americans will just use you and use your people, then drop you. They've done it many times in many places," I said. I could hear the pleading in my voice.

The following morning, I woke to the news that Brooklyn Rivera had arrived in Tegucigalpa on the Honduran airline flight from Managua that morning. I realized that he must have had his tickets already the night before.

The first thing I did when I returned to the trade union hospitality house in Managua from the Atlantic Coast was to take a shower. The water was tepid, but it was wonderful. The following day I was provided with a desk at the Atlantic Coast Ministry, which was housed in a mansion deserted by its owners after the revolution, located in Las Colinas, a remote, upscale subdivision. Every day, a ministry pickup truck collected us workers and at the end of the day returned us home, a service provided by all the ministries and other workplaces. A hot lunch was served at noon. It was interesting to experience a slice of workplace practices, such as I had observed when our delegation had visited shop floors and talked with workers.

I spent a month at the ministry, writing a report that my coworker, Julian Holmes, translated into Spanish and Miskitu. Julian was Bobby Holmes's older brother, but quite different: Bobby had been a Sandinista guerrilla fighter, but Julian was quieter and more skeptical, a devout Moravian, and, along with Armando Rojas, the only other Miskitu lawyer. I spent a great deal of time with him and we became friends. Other friends were Minerva Wilson and Hazel Lau, Miskitu leaders who also worked in the ministry. Hazel had been one of the founding officers of MISURASATA and a close friend of Brooklyn Rivera.

My report on my trip was quite frank. I made four major points: First, I recognized that the Sandinistas had inherited a situation with many problems that they had not created, including extreme underdevelopment—far worse than the rest of Nicaragua—labor exploitation, and Anglo-American imperialism. A part of the situation they would have to confront was the internal colonialism that produced western Spanish-speaking Nicaraguans' sense of superiority to Creoles and Indians, and, on the Atlantic Coast, the Creole sense of superiority over the Miskitus (and the Sumus and Ramas, smaller indigenous communities). I suggested that the Sandinistas study various other unresolved situations between Native and non-Native peoples, such as the Soviet Union, Ethiopia, Iraq, Iran, Syria, Mexico, Chile, Guatemala, Guyana, and the Sudan, mostly to get a better sense of what not to do. In the meantime, they should abolish the term and the idea of *integración*, meaning the assimilation and integration of the indigenous peoples as Spanish-speaking Nicaraguans.

Second, I observed that the Sandinistas were approaching the situation with courage and will, but that they lacked enough politically developed indigenous organizers whom they could trust and from whom they could accept bad news. The Sandinistas needed to find such organizers and allow them to initiate a democratic process of nation building within the larger nation-building project.

Third, I suggested that they invite in many of the indigenous groupings that were born of the 1977 international conference of Indians of the Americas to help analyze the problems and to act as interlocutors with the Miskitus, who already had an international consciousness from their own early involvement in international human rights work. In addition, I thought that the Sandinistas, through the Foreign Ministry, should give high priority to promoting the UN human rights forums on the rights of indigenous peoples and to include Atlantic Coast people in their delegations. Nicaragua could thus become a model for indigenous self-determination amid a world of negative examples. In any case, they could expose the way the United States was using the wedge of indigenous dissatisfaction to invade or foment partition of Nicaragua, just as the US had done in Southeast Asia and Iran/Iraq—of course dropping support for the indigenous minorities and the Kurds once it had achieved its objectives and pulled out.

Finally, I reported that I saw serious problems with the way the Sandinista government was currently administering the Miskitia. First and foremost, the Sandinistas needed to develop a declaration on land rights that would follow traditional indigenous land tenure patterns, patterns that were different from the small-plot farming of the western Nicaraguan *campesinos*. The Sandinistas should also acknowledge the significance of the land as ancestral territory, not simply as private or communal property. A second problem concerned the overabundance of police and soldiers in the area. The Sandinistas should put these forces to work in the community, building and fixing things, teaching, bringing in military health care workers, and generally making friends with the local population.

Roberto Vargas took me to the Ministry of Foreign Affairs (MINEX), for which he worked, and organized a lunch meeting for me with the ministry's international lawyers. I brought Julian Holmes with me, and we presented my report, recommending that Miskitu and Sumu Indians be hired in the ministry and included in delegations to United Nations meetings. Julian and I were encouraged by their positive response to our proposals.

The minister for the Atlantic Coast, William Ramírez, was quite accessible and wanted to learn anything possible about indigenous peoples' aspirations that would help him understand the Miskitu discontent beyond the obvious fact of US intervention. Ramírez introduced me to Orlando Nuñez, the director of CIERA, the research arm of the Ministry of Agriculture (INRA). INRA, headed by Jaime Wheelock, one of the nine members of the Sandinista Directorate, was the third most powerful ministry following Tomás Borge's Ministry of Interior (state security) and Humberto Ortega's Defense Ministry. Because the overwhelming majority of the Nicaraguan population was made up of farmers and ranchers, most without land titles, INRA was actually a key institution because of its role in policy making and management of land redistribution. The distribution of land titles to the *campesinos* who worked the land was wildly popular and very successful in western Nicaragua. However, it was the main source of the initial conflict with the Miskitu and Sumu Indians in the northeastern region. For that reason, collaboration between INNICA, the Ministry for the Atlantic Coast, and INRA, the Ministry for Agriculture, was a top priority of both.

Because slash-and-burn agriculturalists work fields far from the communities where they live, their land tenure is a very different system from Western-style land titles. Also, the Miskitus and Sumus resented what they saw as the arrogance of the Sandinistas in "giving" them their own land. If all the population had felt this way, perhaps the INRA would have put off implementing its land-title program on the Atlantic Coast. However, at least half the population in the historical Miskitu-Sumu territory was made up of first- and second-generation Spanish-speaking farmers who the Somoza dictators had encouraged and assisted in "colonizing" the northeastern region for commercial agriculture and stock raising. Many of these relative newcomers to the area were poor and landless, squatting on Miskitu and Sumu traditional lands, and were eager to accept land titles to the land they worked.

Having studied indigenous land tenure in northern New Mexico, I quickly understood the Miskitu-Sumu point of view that seemed impenetrable (and irrational) to the Sandinistas. For one thing, indigenous land tenure, which was communal, not individual, did not lend itself to the collectivization of farmers that was the policy goal of the Sandinistas, based on the model of the Mexican Revolution's introduction of the *ejido* and other socialist models. As a child of a landless farming family, and having studied how the United States had forcibly allotted Native American lands, I regarded socialist collectivization of agriculturalists much as I regarded capitalist expropriation of agriculturalists. I believed that I had Marx on my side, citing his analysis of the stages of capitalism, the first being the expropriation of agriculturalists in order to create a dependent population and surplus labor force; in the case of socialist collectivization, the change in the agricultural system had the effect of controlling resistant rural populations, not of liberating them. The Mexican *ejido* was a better model, but not for the Miskitia.

Orlando Nuñez immediately struck me as a brilliant young researcher and theorist whose mind was quick and open, his arguments challenging, and his knowledge extensive. He was one of hundreds, perhaps thousands, of remarkable young Sandinista thinkers who were not political actors. Later, as US military intervention and Sandinista militarization intensified, little space would remain for open debates within the Revolution. At this point, however, Orlando had accumulated an excellent specialized library and had commissioned studies that were very useful to me. I spent a lot of time in the small library that was a short walk down the street from INNICA, reading and taking notes.

Orlando brought me together with Galio Gurdián, a Nicaraguan anthropologist who had returned after the 1979 revolution following a decade studying at the University of Chicago and working in El Salvador and Guatemala. Orlando suggested ("commanded" would perhaps be more accurate) that Galio and I start a research group, and I agreed that I would return after the end of my academic year in June 1982 to work indefinitely. The first year, 1982–83, would be facilitated by the fact that I was due a paid sabbatical leave from California State University, Hayward, where I still held an academic post and to which I would return to teach in the fall. We would see after that. My work would be unpaid, but I tried to tell myself that this setup would work. I wanted to believe it would work because it was a dream come true to be able to be truly useful and productive using both my research skills and my political commitment.

However, from the moment I met Galio I could tell that he did not like me, and I thought perhaps he did not like working with a woman as equals, or maybe he did not like gringos/as. After I discovered later that his key assistants were US citizens, a woman and two men, I had to conclude that it was my views that he did not like—especially my view of the Miskitus and Sumus as political actors, real people, not the subjects of paternalism, which too often is the stance of Western anthropologists. One clue came to light in that first meeting with him. I was relating the story of my trip to the Río Coco villages and remarked that I had a lot of confidence in the young Miskitus, giving as examples my guides Marcelo and Bobby. Galio reacted as if he had been slapped. The utter hatred in his eyes and expression alarmed me. He said, "I can't stand Bobby Holmes, I can't stand Indians like that." I asked, "Like what?" but the instant had passed and he changed the subject. Bobby was one of a handful of Miskitus who was actually a Sandinista combatant.

Unfortunately, and ominously, I was not able to discuss my final report and recommendations with William Ramírez himself. I had met with him nearly every day at work when he was not traveling, but just as I was finishing the report, news came that William had been in a boat accident on the rugged Escondido River near Bluefields. At the time there were no flights to Bluefields, and the road east from Managua stopped halfway to the coast—the rest of the way was by boat. William had suffered a serious head injury and was in a coma. William eventually recovered from his injuries, but the critical moment to discuss my report with him was lost.

During this period, I remained at the trade union house. The two sisters who were the live-in housekeeper/cooks took care of me like mother hens. Gordita—as she was called because of her plus size—and Anna were war widows in their late twenties, their husbands killed during Somoza's bombing of civilian neighborhoods. The new state tried to provide housing and subsistence to widows and children, often through the creation of jobs such as this one at the union house.

The sisters were determined to keep me in Nicaragua and thought they could do that by matching me up with a Nicaraguan man. Every evening at dinner, some young and good-looking Sandinista would turn up at the table. They were all about half my age—it was difficult to find a Sandinista over thirty. But I enjoyed talking to the young men about their guerrilla lives and their hopes and dreams. They were all from the poorest of the poor barrios of Managua. They had joined the FSLN when they were teenagers and had learned to read using Sandinista reading materials on imperialism and revolution, mostly Marxist texts, but especially Che Guevara. They were still functionally illiterate when it came to writing, but all expressed the desire for more education.

One young *guerrillero*, Oscar, kept returning to talk. He was a born story-teller, and only twenty at the time of the revolution. He was now a member of the Interior Ministry's police, which Chombo commanded. Oscar was fascinated with the United States and the rest of the world, never having been outside Nicaragua except across the Costa Rican border while fighting, and never even in the eastern half of the country; nor had he ever met a Miskitu or Sumu Indian. He loved to look at my credit cards and keys and have me explain how they worked. He was surprised that I carried a bag full of such items, while he carried nothing at all except for his Nicaraguan identification card.

One evening, Oscar took me to his family home—where he still lived—to meet his parents and siblings. They lived in a one-room shack with a rusty tin roof in a shantytown, where women cooked on scrap metal outside. The room was divided by tattered cloth to create a semblance of privacy. There was no electricity or running water; instead, I saw open sewers with swarming mosquitoes and giant black cockroaches. Knowing that what I was observing were the living conditions that prevailed all over Nicaragua, I realized what a lot of work the Sandinistas had ahead of them. The family and the whole barrio were militantly pro-Sandinista, and Oscar was a big hero to them. But how long would that loyalty last if conditions did not improve? I began embracing the logic of the Sandinista argument that there were many needs throughout the country, and that the eradication of dire poverty and provision of housing and health care had to be the priority in the short term. However, I was soon jolted back into that insidious reality of racism in the Americas.

I invited Julian Holmes to dinner at the hospitality house, and Gordita and Anna were so excited that I had found someone of interest, a lawyer working for the government no less. When Julian actually appeared, however, I had an ugly experience of Nicaraguan racism against Blacks and Indians. The sisters would not serve him or sit at the same table. They simply left the room until he was gone. Later they warned me about the "thieving," "savage" people from the Atlantic Coast. The next day I apologized to Julian for the remarks and rude behavior of the housekeepers, but he assured me it was no problem, that it happened all the time and was one of the reasons the *costeños* wanted autonomy and a way of life recognized and respected by the Sandinistas.

My trip to the Atlantic Coast, and then my weeks of researching, had created a problem: my month-long Nicaraguan visa had expired. Under the existing rules, once a visa expired, the holder had to leave the country to apply for a new one, then return. I agreed to ride the bus to Costa Rica for that purpose so I would be able to return to work on my report in the Atlantic Coast Ministry and take part in discussions. However, there was a catch: I could not leave the country on an expired visa. It seemed that the problem had not arisen during the two years the FSLN had been in power, and they did not know how to solve it. I was required to move to the Intercontinental Hotel—at my own expense—under a sort of house arrest, until these issues could be settled. Except for the cost, charged to my credit card, my life continued with no problem. The government owned the hotel, so I reported my movements to security. (I never did receive a renewed visa, nor did I leave to get one, but when I needed to attend the United Nations meetings in Geneva, I had no problem leaving the country.)

I reluctantly moved to the Intercontinental. I was so touched when I left the trade union hospitality house. Gordita called me that first night and nearly daily to check on my well-being, although my affection for her and her sister was soured by their blatant racism, the problem I always had when visiting my relatives in Oklahoma.

The hotel, which had maintained its name under government ownership, had formerly been owned by Somoza, as had nearly everything else in Nicaragua worth owning. US officials railed against the Sandinistas for nationalizing property, but they had never criticized the dictator Somoza for personally owning much of the country: the principle of the sanctity of private property was a little stretched there. The hotel was built as a replica of a Mayan temple and was still quite majestic if a bit frayed. It had withstood the 1972 earthquake that had destroyed the old center of the city, including all the public buildings. Only two modern buildings—the Intercontinental and the Bank of America building—were left standing. They, along with one other modern building farther away, now the Ministry of the Interior, were the only buildings in all of Nicaragua that had elevators.

Toward the end of my stay in Nicaragua, I felt confused and torn. I had seen the Sandinista-controlled state at work up close and personal, and I did not like all of what I saw. My visit to the volatile northeast region, the Miskitu Indian communities, haunted me. It seemed to me that the Sandinistas had to prove themselves trustworthy, rather than the reverse. They expected the Miskitus to prove their revolutionary loyalty without asking themselves why the Miskitus should automatically trust any governance from Managua. The Miskitus, it was true, had been brainwashed by US missionaries (just as I myself had been while growing up in Oklahoma), but that did not make them pro-imperialist enemies.

But what I found endearing about the Sandinistas was what I thought would see them through to an understanding of the Miskitu point of view. The Sandinistas were not rigid and totalitarian, as the US government and press portrayed them. They were trying to build a new society from the ruins left by the rapacious Somoza clique. And President Carter had tricked them into agreeing to assume Somoza's foreign debt in order to get international credits in the future. Now the United States was cutting off their access to credit, but Nicaragua still had to pay its foreign debt. The United States accused the Sandinistas of expropriating private businesses and running them out of the country, whereas in truth they were begging businesses to remain while the US was offering rewards for companies to leave. For US companies, such as Castle and Cook, the banana company that shut its Nicaragua operations, the loss of income from Nicaragua was not significant. But for Nicaragua, a poor country with a population of only two million, the loss of such commercial infrastructure was devastating.

On the other hand, I could feel even in my brief six weeks in Nicaragua a slide toward rigidity. As Reagan's war threats increased and the northern border began to bristle with armed camps on the other side, the Sandinistas began the transition from a guerrilla force to a state apparatus, no longer fighting as long as it might take for ultimate victory, but to protect the impoverished, shattered state they now controlled. One of the first signs of rigidity was the decision to prohibit women from combat service in the army. Sandinista women, who had comprised around 40 percent of the guerrillas and commanders in the struggle for power, were now incensed at this decision by the FSLN Directorate, which was made up of nine men. Similarly, in order not to antagonize the Catholic Church, which was anti-Sandinista, they decided against legalizing birth control and abortion.

However, women were still allowed in the police force and made up a good portion of it. Comandante Tomás Borge, head of the police, one of the original founders of the FSLN and the Sandinistas' elder statesman at the age of fifty, treated women and men equally. I had been impressed on several occasions by the behavior of the police, and coming from me that is an extraordinary statement, as I have a visceral distrust of them. One story making the rounds when I first arrived was that a policewoman, armed and in uniform, was standing on a packed morning bus headed to her job at the Ministry of Interior when a man pinched her bottom. She drew her sidearm, turned, and shot the assailant dead. The policewoman was placed on leave until trial, at which she was found not guilty based on self-defense and returned to her job. Women loved to tell that story and would add that since that incident the men in Managua had left their hands off female strangers in public.

Once while I was staying at the CST hospitality house, Gordita, Anna, and some other relatives who had come for dinner got into a terrible drunken argument, yelling and throwing things. A neighbor must have called the police, because they soon showed up at the door. I let them in, very nervous because this was my first encounter with the Sandinista police. There were two, one man and one woman, both impossibly young. With quiet, calm voices and body movements, they coaxed everyone to sit down in the living room and began to do a conflict resolution session! They stayed for two hours until everyone shook hands (and by then was sober), and left without charging anyone or even taking names.

A similar experience happened to me when I was stopped while driving a rented car. Although I had gained a sense of trust in the police, I thought even they would not look kindly on the fact that I was under house arrest and not at the hotel; rather, without permission, I had rented a car and driven to Granada for the day and was returning. When I saw the patrol car lights flashing, I was certain they had been searching for me. But then I saw that one of the officers had gotten out of the patrol car and was signaling to me to turn around while he held the oncoming traffic at bay. I realized I was going the wrong way on a one-way street. The police, instead of punishing me and investigating me for other possible infractions, as would happen in the United States, simply solved the problem, which is what police should do.

Soon the Sandinista police in Managua would be more suspicious of everyone once the Contra war was in full operation, as they already were in Puerto Cabezas, where Latino racism against the Indians was an added negative.

Despite all these problems, I left Nicaragua in June 1981 full of hope and determination: hope that the power of the Sandinista revolution could withstand US attempts to destroy it, and determination to do everything possible to prevent its destruction. I would concentrate on the Miskitia, doing the work I was most prepared for in terms of understanding the history, complexity, and consciousness of the peoples of that region. I felt that the study I had done in the mid-1970s of the history of land tenure in New Mexico provided a template for me to analyze the issues of peoples toiling under several layers of colonial regimes as well as their contentious relationships with the state.

During the time I worked at INNICA, the trials of former Somoza officials and guardsmen were being broadcast live on radio and television. The backdrop of our workdays had been the live radio broadcasts (also on television but we didn't have one there) of the criminal trials of former Somoza guardsmen, people despised for their atrocities. I was surprised that the dozen or so Miskitus, Sumus, and Creoles who worked in the ministry were very absorbed in the trials. People listened intently, silent, serious. It was actually an early truth-and-reconciliation process. Before trials began, the revolutionary government had abolished the death penalty, and lenient sentences were a reward for truth telling. The counseling I had thought was needed seemed to be taking place on a mass level. I could feel the change in people. But more war and death were looming, being hatched in the halls of Congress, the White House, and the CIA. Soon the country of three elevators and a half-dozen bridges, with a total population half the size of the San Francisco Bay Area, would be prey to the largest military machine in human history, one that boasted that it could (with its spy planes) detect every toilet that flushed in Nicaragua, a claim that didn't impress anyone who knew how few flush toilets there were in Nicaragua. But we got the point.

6

Culture Shock

On my return from Nicaragua I stopped off in Mexico and rode the bus to Cuernavaca, arriving on June 18, 1981, my mother's birthday. Were she alive she would have been seventy-three years old. Coincidences. Waiting for me was a letter from Petuuche, my former brother-in-law in New Mexico, telling me that Phil Reno, my beloved mentor and friend, had killed himself. Phil was seventy-three years old when he committed suicide on May 7, 1981. I tried to think—May 7: what was I doing when he reached that point of despair? I would have been with the trade union delegation. The last night in the Intercontinental Hotel, I had written him a letter and mailed it from Nicaragua, telling him about the beautiful Sandinista revolution and how they could use his expertise. He could not have received it. Maybe if he had, he would have wanted to live, to visit and advise the Sandinistas on economic development as he had done in Guyana and the Navajo Nation.

Petuuche wrote that Phil had left a suicide note saying that he was unable to "start over again" after Reagan's election. Within a year after his death, his Navajo disciples had won control of the Navajo Nation, with Peterson Zah as chairman. They told me later that after the returns came in they began celebrating, and then everyone became quiet. Someone said, "What are we going to do now? We need Phil more than ever."

It had been the rainy season in Nicaragua, and I had been quite melancholy at times. I wondered if I had had some sense of Phil's death. There was actually little to be encouraged about, with the Contra war looming and Miskitu anger at the Sandinistas increasing. The rain, the strangeness of the situation—I thought how oddly my life had gone, how I lived a mechanical life. It was not that my life was monotonous or uniform—to the contrary, it was very full and diverse—but none of the elements of my life had reality except for the vision of revolution. Every minute, whether I was eating or watching television, in meetings or while teaching, my mind was on revolution. It had been that way for fifteen years. Revolution had become my identity.

Sometimes, living like that, it hit me—the responsibility, the collective responsibility that every US citizen should feel for the exploitation, the political repression, the mechanisms required to maintain our wealth, embodied in our daily lives in things so simple as eating a banana or drinking a cup of coffee. For me, that sense of responsibility only toughened my resolve and made me work harder. I wondered if Phil felt that way and decided that he was no longer able to carry on.

I ended up staying a week in Cuernavaca, delaying my return to the United States, mourning Phil, and unsure about my resolve. But I gave talks about the Sandinista revolution to students from the US at three different language schools in Cuernavaca, and on Sunday we organized an all-day protest against US intervention in Central America at the Cuernavaca cathedral. I even assisted in serving mass. When the bishop, Don Sergio Méndez Arce, invited me to do so, I whispered in his ear that I was an atheist, and he said, "No importa." A Salvadoran guerrilla commander of the FMLN spoke, repeating what I'd heard others like him say: "We Salvadorans have been oppressed since the coming of the Spaniards." Yet he went on to claim that all the Indians of El Salvador had been wiped out in the army's massacres in 1933. I was not the only one confused about identity.

While in Cuernavaca, I read that Jaime Pasquier, the Nicaraguan ambassador to the UN in Geneva whom I'd spent many hours talking with in March, had denounced the Sandinistas as communists and "sought exile" in Miami. I wondered what kind of deal he got from the United States. (Johnny Mfanafuthi Makatini, the longtime African National Congress representative to UN headquarters in New York, had told me the fall before at the General Assembly that the ANC had a policy of not leaving anyone—except the absolutely most trusted comrades like himself—in a diplomatic position for more than six months, because beyond that the likelihood was that they would be bought, usually by the CIA.) Soon after Pasquier's defection, the Nicaraguan ambassador to the United States, Arturo Cruz, also denounced the Sandinistas and asked for political asylum in the United States.

I could already tell that the path ahead of me would not be easy. In Cuernavaca, I met a US Capuchin monk who had worked with the Miskitus in Puerto Cabezas for two decades. I hoped to learn more about their lives from him, but he paternalistically depoliticized the conflicts in the Miskitu communities by attributing them to "family rivalries" and "personalities," as if Indians were incapable of politics. Then he said something about God's voice telling the ordained to lead the sheep into the cone of fire because that was the path of humanity. He was no help at all.

In my Cuernavaca lectures, I explained that missionaries were a key part of the problem in the Miskitia. Back in the 1920s, the Miskitus had participated in Sandino's successful attempt to form a guerrilla army in their territory and drive out US fruit companies and the US Marines protecting them. The Moravian missionaries who had lived with (and tried to control) the Miskitus for over half a century were overjoyed by Sandino's death. They acted quickly to bring their Miskitu worshippers into the circle of US influence. The United States as well encouraged more missionaries—other Protestants in addition to the Moravians, as well as US Catholic orders—to pour into the region, bringing US consumer goods with them. By 1961, the United States was so confident of Miskitu support that it used the Miskitia as the launching point for the failed Bay of Pigs invasion of Cuba by US-supported Cuban exiles. After that failed mission, the United States sent in the Peace Corps, and a local radio station, Radio Ver, run by the "Partners of Wisconsin," was set up to teach the natives about the evils of "communism" and the horrors of Cuba and, of course, the "values" of that wonderland, the United States. The counterinsurgency against the Sandinistas began in the Miskitia even before they came to power. Everything was in place already.

But the Moravians and other US-friendly interests among the Miskitus miscalculated the irresistibility of the Sandinista liberation process. Young Miskitus in particular embraced the spirit of the revolution. It was hard for the revolution to reach them, however, in the most literal sense. No roads led from Managua to the Atlantic Coast. Travel was only by prop plane and dugout, both in their own ways arduous and uncertain journeys. There were no phones, TV, or broadcast radio in the Miskitia, and the missionaries controlled the only source of long-distance communication, the ham radios. They used those ham radios to receive and transmit anti-Sandinista propaganda, the most popular lie being that Cubans were going to colonize Miskitu lands and kill their children—this at a time when the Sandinistas invited volunteer Cuban medical personnel to fan out into all parts of Nicaragua to provide immunization shots and develop health clinics.

When the Sandinistas first came to power, the Miskitu and Sumu Indians approached them with enthusiasm. In their assemblies, they formulated demands for these young rulers, and won some of what they had asked for: education in their native languages; roads, vehicles, electricity where none had existed before; and health care for people who took for granted the death of half their infants to curable diseases such as diarrhea. The Sandinistas worked hard to provide the peoples of the Miskitia with medicine for malaria and pneumonia, and immunization against the polio that continued to kill people in the Miskitia long after it had been eradicated in most of the world. Most important, *Sandinismo* brought dignity, self-respect, and self-reliance, and thus threatened to end the dependency that had enabled the US missionaries to wield nearly total power.

However, Sandinistas were in no position to do a lot in a short time, saddled as they were with Somoza's $1.5 billion foreign debt and the devastation from war and the 1972 earthquake. They had to tend to their own base first and could not spare many resources for infrastructure development in the Miskitia. Only a year and a few months after their victory, the Reagan administration declared its intention to throw out the Sandinistas and set about doing so. The fifth column of US-based church people within the Miskitia was not difficult to recruit.

The missionaries exploited every ordinary human error made by the inexperienced young government officials, easily overcome by dialogue in all other parts of Nicaragua, as examples of intentional, even biblical, evil on the part of the Sandinistas. With this message they hammered away at the people from the pulpit and over the radio. They warned the people that they should abandon their villages and crops and flee over the border to Honduras to refugee camps, claiming that the Sandinistas would bomb and massacre them. In fact, as early as August 1980, US-supported forces among the Miskitus began to send out statements to the world at large asserting that such atrocities were taking place, as I had witnessed at that time.

By the time I left Cuernavaca, I had gathered my lectures into the beginning of the paper I would present at a conference I'd helped organize to take place the following month in Geneva. I wrote in my notebook: "How can I talk about all this? How can I describe the vulnerability of the revolution, the difficulty for the indigenous people of knowing whom to believe, the missionaries among them or the excitable, often ignorant, revolutionaries so far away? How can I accurately convey the complexity of the situation in a way that does not cast doubt on the purpose of the revolution or on my own credibility as a member of the Left?"

In the month before I had to leave San Francisco for Geneva, I spoke at Sandinista solidarity events and demonstrations, something I had not done since 1970 in the antiwar movement and for women's liberation. I found it difficult to talk about the revolution because the supporters were so wedded to their idea of Nicaragua as a kind of utopia and didn't want to deal with the reality of the place. The danger for the solidarity movement was not lack of unity, but the lack of tolerance for different views within the movement. I wondered how many would continue to support the revolution if they became aware of its flaws. As I spoke to young people at these events, I almost felt I was speaking to my younger self. I had worried so much, all those years, about being acceptable and accepted by the "Left." Nicaragua had changed me. I had learned new things, hard to accept, hard to take, uncomfortable—my first real experience within a revolutionary process. The three-month trip to Cuba I had taken in 1970 was a prepared experience at a different stage of the revolution. I now understood the reluctance, the silence in those who had been there and had actually been a part of revolution, even the total frustration of those who left, who gave up.

I had been fortunate in my life to be a witness to beauty. I had seen two comets—one at sunset in the western sky, and another at sunrise in the eastern sky. I had viewed the Northern Lights in North Dakota and twice seen the midnight sun—in Alaska and in Copenhagen. I had seen the underwater world of coral and experienced the rapids of a just-thawed rushing river high in the Sierra. I had witnessed time stand still—and finally understood the relationship of velocity and distance—when the waves of the Atlantic Ocean once appeared to me frozen, from 50,000 feet. I had seen the boiling fire in a volcano and the curve of the desert earth. Valley of the Moon, Popocatepetl, Maya pyramid, Alaskan glacier, Indian Ocean, Bolshoi Ballet, Fidel, people awakening like bears from winter sleep. But I had never seen a revolution in process. From where I saw it—the northeastern zone—it was not a pretty sight.

I went back to Mexico for a five-day seminar, organized by Pablo Gonzales Casanova, a notable activist intellectual, and professor at the National University, whom I had met at the Basel conference in 1978. The event was titled "The United States Today," and my topic was the situation of Native peoples in the United States. Only a dozen leftist scholars/activists from the US were invited to participate, all more notable than me, including Immanuel Wallerstein, Manning Marable, Stanley Aronowitz, and Ricardo Campos. We each had a whole morning or afternoon to present our papers and for discussion afterward. Every bit of it was recorded, which made a few participants uneasy since the Mexicans present did not participate but only listened to our presentations, the tape recorder very large and present, on purpose it seemed. The rationale was that a book was to be published, but the book was actually a compilation of our papers and included those of participants who could not be there. I think the Mexican scholars were turning the tables on us gringos, giving us the treatment they received at our conferences, as specimens to be studied. We were treated very well, put up in a nice hotel nearby, shuttled to and from the seminar site, all our comforts provided.

On the return trip, I felt that the seminar was a waste of my time and energy, whereas only months before I would have considered such a gathering, and my inclusion in it, a high mark of my life. But I was preoccupied with the work that the seminar interrupted. Within a few days, I arrived in Geneva for six weeks of meetings at the UN that would be crucial, I thought, for the Sandinista conflict with the indigenous communities.

By the time I landed at Geneva at the end of July 1981 for the month-long Sub-Commission meeting, I felt like a veteran human rights lobbyist. But little did I know what lay in store for me. Up until that time I had observed and studied the process. In this meeting I would be called on to act decisively and aggressively and to put into practice what I had learned abstractly.

Theo van Boven was the director of the United Nations Division of Human Rights (now called the High Commissioner for Human Rights), which was based at the UN offices in Geneva. Van Boven was Dutch and a renowned specialist in international human rights law. As with most of his compatriots, he was fluent in English as well as other languages. Human rights activists adored van Boven, and not surprisingly he was the first to go under the Reagan administration's sword as they gutted international human rights. Van Boven took two initiatives in the early days of the Reagan administration that would seal his fate as well as greatly affect my own. One was to make it possible to create a working group on the rights of indigenous peoples; the second was to organize a UN seminar on racism in December 1981, to be held in Managua.

In a memorable act of generosity and true commitment, van Boven informed me that if anything were to be developed for indigenous peoples within the UN system, it would have to emerge from this meeting in August 1981 of the Sub-Commission on Prevention of Discrimination and Protection of Minorities (informally called the Sub-Commission on Racism). As a subsidiary body of the UN Commission on Human Rights, the members of the Sub-Commission, although nominated by governments, functioned as "independent experts" who could not be recalled during their three-year terms. Van Boven himself had been a member of the Sub-Commission before his appointment as director of the UN Human Rights Center in Geneva, and after his resignation returned to the Sub-Commission.

We had planned since the 1977 conference to get a foothold in the Sub-Commission, since it was a smaller and easier body to lobby than any other. It was the UN human rights body most open to nongovernmental participation and even the initiation of proposals, despite the complaints of both the United States and the Soviet Union. Most importantly, the Sub-Commission in 1972 had initiated a study on indigenous peoples, thanks to Augusto Willemsen-Díaz, the Guatemalan assigned by the UN Human Rights Center to the Sub-Commission. However, we had planned to wait until 1982, the fifth anniversary of the 1977 conference, to mount our campaign. We had even planned a nongovernmental conference on indigenous land rights for September 1981 that we intended to use as a building block for the 1982 lobbying effort. But it seemed prudent to follow van Boven's advice, since he was not a man to make rash decisions.

Van Boven's suggestion put me in a quandary, as I was the only nongovernmental representative interested in the indigenous issue present, and technically I was representing AAPSO, the Afro-Asian Peoples Solidarity Organization, not an indigenous organization. I called the New York office of the International Indian Treaty Council and asked them to send someone. Bill Means, the director, gave me permission to write a proposal on behalf of the IITC to circulate among the NGOs to sign on to, and said he would send Wally Feather over from Northern Ireland, where he was dodging British rubber bullets on a fact-finding tour. Wally, a young Lakota related to the Means family, arrived on the weekend of the first meetings, rather traumatized and carrying in his leg a wound from a rubber bullet, belying its benign name.

Wally and I wrote a statement calling on the Sub-Commission to establish a working group on the rights of indigenous peoples based on the model of a half-dozen other working groups. However, we proposed that the mandate of this group, unlike the others, be broad rather than narrowly legalistic. Also, unlike other working groups, it was to be open to indigenous organizations' full participation, whether or not they had official UN status. Finally, this working group was to have no time limit.

We made copies of the statement in the form of a petition for other human rights NGOs to sign. By the end of the first week of the session we had the signatures of the two dozen or so NGOs present and made copies of the petition to distribute to members of the Sub-Commission. Of course, van Boven and his assistants quietly talked it up with the Sub-Commission members, and the Norwegian expert, Ajsborn Eide, wholeheartedly supported it and began drafting a resolution. Because I had represented the Afro-Asian Peoples Solidarity Organization during the previous four years, I was able to lobby the African and Asian members. The Sub-Commission did not require consensus to take a decision but preferred it, so if a proposal were strongly opposed by any member, it would generally be tabled indefinitely.

Just as we had gotten through these painstaking negotiations and filed the nongovernmental proposal as an official document, a representative for the Indian Law Resource Center (ILRC) arrived from Washington, D.C., demanding that the proposal be withdrawn because they had not been included. I pointed out that no one had barred them from arriving at the Sub-Commission meeting on time and suggested that they submit a letter supporting the proposal that would also be an official document. The lawyer was quite angry and certain that I had deliberately excluded them. They clearly still identified me with the Treaty Council—a problem, since the two organizations had worked together on the 1977 conference but had been divided by power plays and political differences ever since. Tim Coulter, an Oklahoma Potowatomie attorney, was the founder and director of the ILRC and considered the Treaty Council too radical. I had had little contact with Coulter since the 1977 conference, and I didn't know that Armstrong Wiggins, the Nicaraguan Miskitu leader who had left Nicaragua just before I arrived there in May, had been adopted by the ILRC and that they had embraced the anti-Sandinista agenda promoted by the Reagan administration. Later I realized that they might have thought my involvement in initiating the working group was related to the Sandinistas somehow, even though it was not. This was a preview of the vicious ILRC attacks on me during the next eight years.

Despite the ILRC's complaints, the Sub-Commission passed the resolution in favor of the indigenous working group by consensus, although two or three of the members managed to be conveniently out of the room when the vote was called—including the US member, whose term had begun before Reagan took office. It felt like an historic moment—for the first time in history, a formal international law body had committed to creating international law machinery for dealing with Native Americans and other indigenous communities.

After the end of the Sub-Commission, I worked with others—the same groups that had organized the 1977 conference—in Geneva compiling the documents and arranging logistics for our nongovernmental conference, "Indigenous Peoples and the Land." It was intended to be geographically global, but the nearly three hundred Indians from all parts of the Western Hemisphere made up the majority of the delegates. The four topical commissions at the conference were concerned with international treaties and land tenure, indigenous philosophy and land, the effect of transnational corporations on the resources and land of indigenous peoples, and the impact of the nuclear arms buildup and the militarization of indigenous territories and lives.

I was obsessed with one matter—the Sandinistas—and the indigenous communities in Nicaragua. While I had been there in May and June, I had met with the Foreign Ministry and persuaded them to send a strong governmental representation from the eastern region. The three-member delegation included Marcelo Zuñiga, one of the Miskitus who had been my guide. Murphy Almendarez, the young leader of the Sumu Indian organization, SUKAWALA, was also there. The Sumus numbered only a few thousand people living in small remote villages in the mountainous rainforest of northeastern Nicaragua. For centuries, the Sumus, also called Mayagna, had been dominated and nearly absorbed by the much more populous Miskitus, and they struggled to maintain their own identity. Most Sumus spoke Miskitu in addition to their Sumu mother tongue, but no Miskitus spoke Sumu. On the other hand, the Sumus had not absorbed English and US culture and language to the extent that the coastal Miskitus had—if they spoke any European language it was Spanish, which made the Sandinistas trust them more. Heading the delegation from the Atlantic Coast was Comandante Lumberto Campbell, the older brother of Francisco Campbell, who headed the eastern region ministry in Puerto Cabezas. Lumberto was the only person from the eastern zone who held the rank of *comandante* in the FSLN. He had Afro-Caribbean roots like most of the population of Bluefields, where he grew up.

We also expected exiled Miskitu leaders to arrive for the conference, most likely Armstrong Wiggins, who had represented the earlier native organization, ALPROMISU, at the 1977 conference. Brooklyn Rivera, the elected head of MISURASATA I had interviewed so briefly and unfruitfully, was based in Costa Rica, condemning the Sandinistas, and was rumored to be en route to Geneva. However, to everyone's surprise neither of those leaders showed up, but rather Hazel Lau, who had not gone into exile and was an official of MISURASATA. When I met Hazel at INNICA, I had regarded her as a principled defender of the Miskitu people and of the Sandinista revolution, refusing to "choose," an alternative she considered false. Hazel had been a student in the university math class taught by Lumberto Campbell before he joined the armed Sandinista guerrillas. Now she had come to Geneva to denounce the Sandinistas, perhaps to announce joining her compatriot and best friend, Brooklyn Rivera, in exile.

In the opening plenary session of the conference, Hazel wasted no time in taking the microphone and disrupting the ceremonies to denounce the Sandinistas. Staring directly into Comandante Campbell's eyes, she trembled, not with fear, but with an outrage and anger that clearly had its roots in a sense of being betrayed by the Revolution. Since her intervention was out of order and unrelated to the planned program, the conference president and secretary, Romesh Chandra and Edith Ballantyne—who had chaired our 1977 conference as well—deftly suggested a special session on Nicaragua during which the two parties could air their views to all. Both agreed. At the lunch break, Hazel agreed to meet privately with Lumberto, Marcelo, and Murphy, and they all emerged afterward smiling. The special session then turned out to be a demonstration of amazing reconciliation in which Hazel admitted to having been manipulated and fed lies by Brooklyn Rivera.

I had realized at the Commission on Human Rights that the diplomatic world was productive and necessary but also exhausting; and that led me to wonder, again, who I had become. Was I now a diplomat instead of a revolutionary? After years spent as an ultraleftist and Maoist, inappropriately supporting armed struggle within the United States, I had left revolutionary theory and practice behind when I began working in earnest on indigenous issues. I had been seduced by the diplomatic world by the 1977 Geneva conference, by the World Peace Council, by my work with the Afro-Asia Peoples Solidarity Organization. And my turn to diplomacy was doubly reinforced during my time establishing an academic research center at the University of New Mexico.

I struggled with myself over the values of these very different kinds of work. My radical 1970s self believed that all this diplomacy was ultimately a kind of treason, since I was essentially organizing tribal planners to work within the capitalist system, or indigenous leaders to work inside the United Nations. On the other hand, I knew that experts with degrees and publications are needed for legitimatizing liberation movements. I had functioned in that capacity, supporting the Guatemalan oppositions at the UN General Assembly, Native American rights in the United States and at the UN, and now the Sandinistas. I wondered whether I even had the right to be a super-revolutionary when I had the credentials to be a cover of legitimacy for real revolutionaries fighting life-and-death struggles.

This was not the first time I had had to face these choices: that had been in 1967 at UCLA in the months following Audrey Rosenthal's death in South Africa. Audrey was my dearest friend and a sister graduate student in history. She had gone to London with her South African exile boyfriend to finish their dissertations and ended up doing clandestine work inside South Africa, where she died in an airplane crash. I spent the following summer with the African National Congress in London, and felt obligated after this experience to become a full-time revolutionary. I quit graduate school and threw myself into radical organizing for the next three years, when once again I found myself in the position of being a professional, this time a well-compensated public speaker on revolution and women's liberation. This crisis of conscience, the dichotomy between on-the-ground revolutionary and paid professional speaker, led me to go to Cuba in 1970, and to return to form an underground sabotage organization similar to the Weather Underground. Choosing the revolutionary path then had led to criminal court, probation, and alcoholism.

Following the Geneva conference, I accepted an invitation from the Cuban Ministry of Culture to present a paper at its conference on minorities in the United States. That week in Havana helped me clarify my path. I determined to abandon UN work after the upcoming UN seminar on racism in Managua in December. I would spend my sabbatical year in Nicaragua, and then perhaps stay there. It did not work out that way.

7

Red Christmas

That is what the CIA called it, Operation Red Christmas, and by that they meant bloody. They meant the red of fire and of the blood caused by gunfire, not the red of fireworks in celebration of Navidad. Red Christmas was the opening salvo of the US-organized and -financed Contra war to oust the Sandinistas. Not many people knew about it at the time, and little of the reportage and history then or since identify Red Christmas as the beginning of the Contra war. I know only because I was there. It was reported at the time that the US government spent $2.5 billion a year on media for domestic consumption. Against all propaganda to the contrary, my own word was a whisper, the testimony of an eyewitness. From then on, I would try to magnify that whisper.

What was publicized then and is now remembered about Red Christmas is the Sandinista army's evacuation ("removed," "forcibly relocated," "herded into concentration camps," as press accounts read at the time) of all the inhabitants of the Miskitu villages on the Río Coco border with Honduras to five settlements eighty miles south of the border. That evacuation did in fact take place in January 1982 as a response to the start of the Contra military initiative.

In November 1981, the Reagan administration had signed a "finding" authorizing the CIA to spend $19.5 million on the Contra project. The Red Christmas attacks of December 21, 1981, made use of several thousand CIA-trained guerrillas—mostly Miskitu Indians, followers of Steadman Fagoth, who attacked Sandinista forces along the Río Coco. They were trained by former Somoza guardsmen and officers on loan from the Argentine military dictatorship that had been established in 1976 under General Jorge Rafael Videla, masters of murdering civilians, torture, and disappearances until their collapse in 1983.

The aim of the Red Christmas attack was to create a militarized northeastern front to draw the Sandinista military there while the real war would take place on the northwestern Honduran border and the short southern border with Costa Rica. In western Honduras, former Somoza guardsmen were already operating as the FDN (Nicaraguan Democratic Front). Down in Costa Rica, a former Sandinista commander, Edén Pastora, had formed a paramilitary unit, ARDE, funded by the CIA, and was allied with Brooklyn Rivera's MISURASATA. While the Sandinistas were busy putting down a CIA-created Miskitu rebellion, they would be unable to defend Managua from attacks from the north and south. The CIA's other objective was to place civilians, Miskitus, in the crossfire so that the US could accuse the Sandinistas of massacring the Indians.

The Sandinistas were not fooled by this strategy, however. And they had no intention of allowing the Miskitus to be cannon fodder. Yet they had to stop the attacks on their northeastern front. They therefore chose to evacuate the Miskitu border population and create a free-fire zone in the northeast. In part, this choice was forced on them because the Miskitu border zone was the most densely populated of the three areas. But it also was based on Sandinista mistrust of the Miskitus—the Sandinistas did not believe the Miskitus would resist attacks by their own brothers, whereas they knew that the scattered northern mountain villages on the Pacific side and those on the southern frontier were strongly pro-Sandinista and could be relied on to defend themselves. Since then, Sandinista leaders have acknowledged that it was a mistake to have moved the Miskitus, but the Sandinistas were placed in a no-win situation by the US strategy.

Many Sandinista supporters in the United States and elsewhere faulted the Sandinistas for responding militarily without consideration of the alternatives. And in truth, the decision backfired almost immediately. Instead of moving to the camps the Sandinistas had created for them, nearly half the

Miskitu population crossed the river into Honduras. After listening to Moravian and Contra propaganda, they were afraid that the Sandinistas really did plan to incarcerate them in Cuban concentration camps while Cuban settlers would be brought in to colonize their beloved land. They responded to promises made by the missionaries and the Contras that they would be taken care of, even given land holdings, if they joined the Contra side. In Honduras, a refugee camp had been prepared for them—thanks to the US "proconsul" in Honduras, John Negroponte, and his wife, Diane. During his tenure as US ambassador to Honduras from 1981 to 1985, Negroponte oversaw the growth of military aid to Honduras from $4 million to $77.4 million a year, all for the Contra war.

So it happened that a United Nations seminar on racism was scheduled to take place in the midst of Operation Red Christmas. Was the timing a coincidence or was the purpose to disrupt the UN seminar? The $19.5 million in CIA funding for Red Christmas was announced with the bombing of a Nicaraguan airliner at the Mexico City airport, just as I was waiting to board the plane to attend the UN meeting. That day, December 13, 1981, seared my memory with the reality of terrorism and my country's role in state-sponsored terrorism.

Once I arrived at the airport, I lingered as long as possible in its immense continuous main lobby. A microcosm of Mexico City, it was lined with pharmacies, boutiques, banks, cafes, bookstores, art galleries, and taco stands. I had to do some last-minute shopping for items I didn't have time to buy in the rush to turn in my grades, things hard to find anymore in Nicaragua because of the US economic blockade—aspirin, Pepto-Bismol, Bic lighters, batteries, and toothpaste. This airport had been built since my travels in and out of the old one in 1968 amid protests against Mexican government repression during the build-up to the Olympics that were scheduled to be held in Mexico City—protests that culminated in the government's massacre of hundreds of Mexican students. That airport was then a crowded, miserable place, with CIA agents checking the movements of all US citizens to prevent us from traveling to Cuba (which was what I had been trying to do in 1968). One thing hadn't changed: thong-sandaled Indian women padded to and fro across the elegant marble floors, just as they had on the old concrete ones—mopping them.

I checked my watch: 11 a.m., nearly time to go through immigration and on to the gate to catch the Nicaraguan plane. The flight was scheduled for 2 p.m., and even though the flight was notorious for always being late, the ticket agent had told me to arrive at the gate two hours before the scheduled departure time and to stay there. I had arrived from San Francisco at dawn on the Mexicana *tecolote*, the red-eye flight. I had chosen that chaotic flight, filled with Mexican farmworkers wearing jeans and cowboy boots and hats, hugging new boomboxes and portable TVs, in order to secure a seat on the Nicaraguan flight. There had been no way to make a reservation from the United States. The Mexicana ticket agent in San Francisco had told me, "The State Department has a travel advisory on the country. Travel agencies and airlines are not allowed to make reservations for travel to Nicaragua. Just fly to Mexico and get to the airport at the crack of dawn and take your chances."

I took that advice, and at the Aeronica counter I had netted one of the two seats left. I tried to resist checking my carry-on leather duffel bag, but the ticket agent had insisted: "Security," he had said. The word echoed in my head; usually they said that size was the issue.

At immigration on my way to the international area, the Mexican official snatched my US passport and removed the Mexican tourist card. He asked my destination in English, and when I said, "Nicaragua," he looked up at me and smiled. Of course, I knew that Mexicans appreciated us gringos who defied our government. That made me feel good. I bought five cartons of Marlboros in the duty-free shop, as gifts, not for myself, since I had quit, again.

I was two hours early to the Aeronica gate, but I was not the first. It seemed that the other passengers were already there in the austere, modern waiting room—mostly dark, wiry teenagers dressed almost identically in crisp designer jeans, tee-shirts in bright colors, and spotless white athletic shoes. I asked one young woman on the fringe of the group where they were from. They were Nicaraguan students at Mexico's National University on Mexican scholarships, going home for Christmas vacation. But most Nicaraguans who left their country were not returning. They were pouring into San Francisco, complaining that they couldn't make a living in Nicaragua, and there were rumors of war. Suddenly, precious US visas and green cards had, for some people, become easy to obtain.

I looked around and saw only one other possible gringo—a bespectacled young man with closely cropped blond hair. I walked over to him, extended my hand, and asked him if he were going to the UN seminar in Managua. He introduced himself as Clifford Krauss, a Latin American correspondent for Cox News Service in Atlanta. He wasn't aware of the seminar, he said, but was instead on a quest to interview a Salvadoran combatant who he heard was in Managua. He told me he was nervous about the flight because of the CIA program to organize anti-Sandinista forces in Honduras. We discussed the fact that Congress had just granted the CIA nearly $20 million for covert operations, and that the CIA was paying Argentine military officers to train former Somoza national guardsmen. He also said that he didn't trust taking Aeronica but didn't have a choice because the other Central American airlines had stopped flying to Managua under pressure from Washington. He worried that most of the Aeronica pilots and crews had defected, and that there would be no one to fly the plane. He had been waiting two days, because the Nicaraguan plane—Aeronica owned only one jetliner—had not arrived the day before.

Clifford and I drifted apart, and I sat down to read. The book was by the founder of the FSLN, Carlos Fonseca, who had been killed in an ambush by Somoza guardsmen in 1976. I was reading about the eastern half of the country:

> The Mosquitia of Nicaragua, bypassed by Spanish colonization, becomes for a time in the 17th century a refuge for African slaves who daringly escape the captivity imposed on them in the European-owned plantations of the Antilles islands.
>
> Following the consolidation of the colonization of indigenous lands, the Nicaraguan territory is virtually shared by the Spanish and British empires. The Pacific coast and center of Nicaragua remains under Spanish domination. The eastern region, no longer a refuge for fugitive slaves, falls under the domination of the British, who establish what they call "the Kingdom of Mosquitia," which of course is provided with a kinglet.

Suddenly everyone scurried toward the plate glass window. The Aeronica plane had arrived from San Salvador, where it had stopped to pick up passengers, and was even on time. The line formed at once. The students crowded in as close to the gate as possible, and inevitably they had to be coaxed back to allow space for the arriving passengers. The Nicaraguan airline agent scolded the students: "Set a revolutionary example!" The young people inched back in unison, just enough to let the arrivals squeeze through.

Then the agent announced that the departure would be delayed until the replacement crew arrived—they were stuck in the Mexico City afternoon rush hour. I visualized the spectre of the monstrous traffic jams at *la comida*, the early afternoon meal when everyone drives home for two hours, then returns to work, and I reconciled myself to a two-hour wait. I knew that if the plane did not leave by 4 p.m., forget it, because there was no night radar equipment at the Managua airport and night falls all year around 6 p.m. in Central America. I also thought about Clifford's concern about the crews defecting.

An hour passed quickly. The *Nica* students were all curled up sleeping, propped against each other near the gate. The silence of the waiting room was punctuated with flight announcements. I walked toward the airline agent to ask if the crew had arrived. Suddenly, a glaring light blinded me, then blackness. My ears rang and echoed. I was flat on my back on the floor and shards of glass rained down.

An earthquake was my first thought. I lifted my head and took in the sight of people piled on top of each other, writhing, screaming. It was hard to tell that the plate glass window was gone, because every inch of glass had blown out. But the blaze sizzled, and tongues of fire lapped through the gaping mouth that had been the window. I realized that the plane could explode. A man shouted, "Bomba, vámonos."

Somehow, I got to my feet and moved, for I found myself in the corridor leaning against a cool marble wall. Then, a rush of people running knocked me down. I sat cross-legged, head in hands. Someone grabbed me under the arms and dragged me. I looked up into the blood-soaked face of one of the Nicaragua teenagers. She said, "You know that bomb was supposed to go off in the air and kill us all. You see, your government doesn't even care if it kills its own citizens."

As if I didn't know.

I saw Clifford nearby, taking notes, his face smudged with soot. He walked toward me. "Well, there went Aeronica Internacional. Embarrassing to be gringos, huh?" He offered me a Lucky Strike, and I took it, without a thought of having quit.

The Sandinistas later claimed that their superior security measures had delayed the flight and prevented an air disaster, but I think they were just being inefficient as usual. Probably, and luckily for us, the efficient state that sponsored the bombing simply forgot to factor in Sandinista tardiness.

The Mexican investigators would later determine that the bomber had boarded in San Salvador and left the bomb under a seat before he disembarked in Mexico City. The time that passed between the plane landing and the explosion was ample for him to escape into the metropolis. A Mexican baggage handler was killed in the blast, and a Nicaraguan flight attendant who was on board was maimed but survived.

Soon, it became clear to anyone paying attention that the bombing of the Nicaraguan airline announced the launching of the Reagan administration's war against the Sandinistas. Elected in the fall of 1980, the Reagan administration wasted no time in implementing its anti-Sandinista campaign. First, in early 1981, they cut all food aid to the Nicaraguan people who lived in the rubble of Somoza's bombing of Nicaraguan cities. Next, by November 1981, the Reagan administration had cleared nearly $20 million for the CIA to begin the dirty war. They began organizing a mercenary counterrevolutionary army out of the Somoza national guardsmen and wealthy businessmen who had followed Somoza into exile. But the first of many installments of funds for the dirty war was used in the attempted murder of me and of the others on the bombed airplane.

Mexican authorities sealed the airport and held us passengers in a room, taking us out one by one for interrogation and allowing us to claim our baggage. When my turn came, I found my leather duffel burned, torn, and soaked in water, ruining my two weeks' supply of clothing. The three interrogators sat me down and showed me an orange disc, which they said was found in my suitcase, suggesting that it was part of the bomb and may have been in my suitcase. I was terrified, but after an hour of sweating the interrogation, they let me go, even giving me the orange disc, which later I handed over to the Sandinista police, who surmised that it was a piece of the baggage compartment.

Clifford Krauss, the reporter, was questioned after me, and I waited for him—we had been talking. We were taken to the airport hotel and given rooms where we could wait for the Mexican flights promised to us the following day. But both of us were in a hurry to get to Managua, me for the UN seminar and he for his rendezvous. We stood in lines at other Central American airlines trying to find a way to Managua. The only other airline still flying there was the Panamanian COPA, but only from San Salvador, we were told at the TACA Salvador counter. TACA could get us to San Salvador, and we could spend the night and fly out on COPA at 6 a.m. the next morning, arriving in Managua early Monday morning. We took it.

Arriving at the San Salvador airport at sunset, we were not allowed to go into the city to a hotel because of a dusk-to-dawn curfew. So began a long night of fear. We were the only foreigners, but there were dozens of Salvadoran peasants, traders, and businessmen from the highway outside who took refuge there, unable to make their final destinations before curfew. Everyone appeared apprehensive, and with good reason. Gunfire soon erupted outside and the lights went out. We listened to Radio Havana on my shortwave radio and heard that the FMLN guerrillas had announced an offensive and were attacking military bases all over the country; of course, the civilian airport was also a military airbase. With white knuckles, gritted teeth, and gallows humor, my traveling companion and I made it through the night. I nodded off in the uncomfortable plastic chair, and Clifford woke me, reporting the news he'd heard on Voice of America: Polish authorities had declared martial law after sixteen months of Solidarity agitation. I couldn't help but think that the Reagan administration was intervening there as well.

I arrived in Managua a hero, with lots of fanfare and a celebration for my survival. Everyone assumed that I had been the only US citizen holding tickets to board the doomed plane. (My compatriot Clifford Krauss had disappeared into the black hole of Sandinista security from which he emerged a few days later, unharmed but quite shaken, he told me later. He had not bothered to acquire a visa for Nicaragua and then, in customs, blabbed that he was there to interview a Salvadoran guerrilla. He was deported without his interviews.)

The first day of the week-long UN seminar was in session when I finally arrived—I went directly to the meeting in the clothes I had been wearing for two days. Again, I was received almost like a war hero and had to tell my story repeatedly. Sandinista press and television interviewed me. Minerva, my co-worker at INNICA, brought me some of her clothes to wear while there.

Things settled down by the second day, and I immersed myself in the seminar. Since it was a regional seminar (Central America and the Caribbean), and I was invited as an outside observer, I listened and asked questions. Five leaders from the International Indian Treaty Council and three from the leadership of the Canadian-based World Council of Indigenous Peoples were also there as observers, along with a number of anthropologists who specialized in Latin America.

The discussions and papers presented were impressive. The New Jewel Movement led by Maurice Bishop had taken power nearly two years before in the tiny island of Grenada, and their delegation to the seminar played a positive role. The delegation was led by Grenada's foreign minister, Unison Whiteman, who, along with Maurice Bishop and other Grenada officials, would die in a coup in October 1983, followed by a US military "rescue mission" that extinguished all vestiges of the New Jewel Movement. I could see why—working during those days with Unison Whiteman—the Reagan administration might fear a minuscule island of a few thousand inhabitants, the main export of which was nutmeg, the main income from tourism. Grenada was the only English-speaking revolutionary state, and its location was so very accessible to aspiring English-speaking indigenous and African American revolutionaries from North America and the Caribbean. Unison, as he insisted on being called, had an authentically sweet personality and bubbled with energy and enthusiasm, but he was also a serious thinker. His understanding of British colonialism clarified a great deal about the consciousness of the inhabitants of the British-colonized western Caribbean, including the Miskitia. Revolutionary Grenada held the promise of bridging the gap of artificial, colonial-induced hostility between the subjects of Anglo imperialism and Spanish-speaking Americans.

The most urgent issue of racism in the region was what was already being described as the "genocidal" policy by the Guatemalan military government against the highland Mayan Indians, mainly the Quiche speakers (Quiche is the language of the majority of Mayans, although there are twenty-two other dialects of Mayan). Two Mayan exiles were present at the conference and provided evidence of a brutal counterinsurgency meant to destroy the Guatemalan leftist guerrilla movements by what we would now call ethnic cleansing; through terror, torture, and murder, they aimed to force hundreds of thousands of Mayan civilians across the border into the Mexican state of Chiapas, leaving the guerrillas with no population base in their home territory. Bad as things were there in December 1981, they would worsen three months later when a military coup brought General Rios-Montt, a born-again evangelical Protestant, to power for eighteen months of more determined ethnic cleansing, including the burning of homes and crops and the slaughter of whole villages. In talks with the Mayans, Miskitus, and Sumus at the Managua conference, Chockie Cottier (a Sioux from South Dakota and an AIM member) and I decided to start a bilingual newsletter that would publicize the situations of Central American Indians in the context of international human rights. We would call the quarterly paper *Indigenous World/Mundo Indígena*, publishing the first issue in March 1982.

Galio Gurdián attended the seminar and was friendly to me, introducing me to two young US anthropologists. Charles Hale was finishing his doctoral dissertation at Stanford on the Miskitus, and Edward T. (Ted) Gordon was a specialist in fisheries who was active in a nationalist African American organization and interested in the Creole community in and around Bluefields. I met with them at the former Atlantic Coast Ministry building—it had moved into the center of the city—in Las Colinas, which now belonged to Galio's new Atlantic Coast development research center (CIDCA). Charles and Ted were excited about the research and had helped Galio write the paper that Comandante Ramírez presented at the seminar. I hadn't liked the paper much, because it seemd to be the same old rhetoric about integrating the Atlantic Coast into the rest of Nicaragua, but I liked Charles and Ted.

As a part of the UN seminar agenda, the Sandinistas had arranged for all the participants to fly out to Puerto Cabezas and from there to drive to one of the nearby coastal Miskitu villages, Krukira. There we were hosted by the Miskitu pastor of the village and honored with traditional dances and songs.

We were not fully aware of the gravity of the situation—we had no idea, for example, that only forty miles north of us Steadman Fagoth's group, having received CIA military training for the past eight months, was preparing to attack the Miskitu villages on the Nicaraguan side of the Río Coco border with Honduras. On our return to Managua, Theo van Boven held a press conference, summing up the seminar's rather radical recommendations in favor of indigenous peoples' rights. He also condemned "a certain state" for its aggression against Nicaragua, which he viewed as disruptive to the advancement of the indigenous peoples of the eastern region. Soon after, van Boven was forced out of his position as a UN official, as he had predicted.

Along with four of the seminar participants from the Treaty Council—Vernon Bellecourt, Bill Means, Bill Wapepah, and Raul Salinas—I was invited to spend Christmas with Lumberto Campbell, the Sandinista commander I had met at the UN conference in Geneva. Instead of going the easy way by flying, we traveled by land and water, a long and rigorous trip, halfway in jeeps until the road ended, then by motorboat to Bluefields in the southeast. Our boat trip took us down a river enclosed by classic jungle foliage filled with monkeys and all sizes and colors of tropical birds, the noisiest bit of nature I'd ever experienced.

For the next several days, we traveled in a motorboat to Miskitu, Rama, Garífuna, and Creole fishing villages, meeting and talking with community leaders and young activists. It was not my imagination that made it seem that we were experiencing Disneyland's "Pirates of the Caribbean." These coves and foliage-covered waterways had been the lair of those pirates, with the encouragement of the British empire that claimed control of the "Mosquito Coast." Only boatmen who knew every nook and turn of those waterways would be able to find their way in or out of the maze we traveled through.

In Bluefields, we spent many hours with the mayor, Ray Hooker, who was also the local historian. Ray's sister, Miriam, was married to Francisco Campbell, Lumberto's brother. The evening before we left, Lumberto and I talked alone, discussing the following year when, free of my teaching duties in June and on sabbatical, I planned to spend a year in Nicaragua, working on a study and recommendations regarding international law and indigenous peoples' rights.

I returned to San Francisco the day after the New Year and began a new term at Cal State Hayward. It was difficult to focus. Although the Treaty Council appeared to be clear about not supporting any program initiated and promoted by the US government, not so Russell Means, the organization's founder, principal spokesman, and fundraiser through his lucrative lectures, and the brother of Bill Means, the IITC's director. Russell Means had become a loose cannon and craved publicity. Soon after our return, the Treaty Council met in San Francisco, with Russell in attendance. He wanted to focus all resources on his project at Yellow Thunder Camp in the Black Hills, near where Custer's Last Stand and the massacre at Wounded Knee had taken place. Russell believed that the "illegal" encampment he was leading was the best strategy to get the ball rolling for the repossession of the Black Hills. There was much discussion of how we could best bring the issue before the United Nations at the upcoming Human Rights Commission and the first session of the UN Working Group on Indigenous Peoples that would convene in July 1982.

But the main topic of discussion at the meeting was the crisis in Nicaragua. By this time, the Miskitus in the Río Coco villages had been relocated by the Sandinistas, or had crossed the river with the Contras. Roberto Vargas was invited to the meeting to speak during the delegation's report. Russell was quiet and noncommittal, but I became extremely suspicious of his motives when the issue of apartheid in South Africa was raised and he pushed for a resolution in support of Rev. Leon Sullivan, who was close to the Reagan administration.

I had been involved with the anti-apartheid movement since my first year of graduate school at UCLA in the mid-1960s and had always supported the African National Congress's policies. In the mid-1970s the student and youth-based black consciousness movement in South Africa had pumped new life into the stalemated liberation struggle, despite South Africa's murder of leaders like Stephen Biko. Neighboring countries Angola and Mozambique gained their liberation from Portugal in 1975, with the end of white rule in Zimbabwe following in 1979. The apartheid regime was surrounded and its days were numbered. The worldwide anti-apartheid movement expanded, growing to include a US student movement that continued through the 1980s. On college campuses across the country students had built shantytowns to demonstrate how Black South Africans lived under apartheid.

The Ford administration had responded by approving CIA covert actions to overthrow the new governments in Angola and Mozambique, a policy continued by Jimmy Carter. Then, in 1981, the Reagan administration, as promised in its campaign, took that path full speed, delaying South African freedom for another decade. But the political context had changed, and by 1981 not even the Reagan people could openly endorse apartheid—instead, they came as close as possible by enunciating a policy of "constructive engagement" with the apartheid regime. That is, instead of the economic and arms boycott that the African National Congress and UN resolutions demanded, the United States chose to urge capital investment in South Africa based on a set of "principles" for doing business, such as integrated restrooms and minority hiring. These were called "the Sullivan principles," named after their author, Rev. Leon Sullivan, who had started peddling them in 1977.

Sullivan was an African American whose proposal had been roundly condemned by all the mainstream Black organizations in the US, and certainly by the African National Congress. Yet, for some reason I could not fathom, Russell Means had concocted an alliance with Leon Sullivan, and now was demanding that the Sandinista government not only endorse the 1868 Sioux Treaty that guaranteed the Black Hills as belonging to the Sioux, but also endorse the "Sullivan principles." I smelled money behind this alliance, and gross opportunism. Fortunately, in the face of some heavy internal argument from Treaty Council people who knew they would not be able to show their faces inside the UN, the IITC backed away from this proposal. Later in the 1980s, Rev. Sullivan himself backtracked and began demanding divestment in the South African apartheid regime.

To my surprise, a few days after the meeting, Russell called and asked me to serve as an expert witness at his trespassing trial in federal court in South Dakota, in which he was defending himself based on the Sioux Treaty. I did so, and he was pleased with my testimony in which I presented the historical background to the treaty. I convinced myself that he would not become an instrument of the Reagan administration.

During January and February 1982, media coverage of the Miskitu situation in Nicaragua began with a January 3 Associated Press release claiming that the Honduran government had announced that Sandinista soldiers had massacred two hundred Miskitus inside Honduras. The following day, the

Honduran government denied making the statement and denied its accuracy as well. The correction was not well publicized, and the notion of a "massacre" was widely believed in the United States and Europe. For instance, in San Francisco anti-Sandinista Nicaraguans held a well-attended and -publicized mass to commemorate the "200 slain Miskitus."

On February 4, 1982, the US ambassador to the United Nations, Jeanne Kirkpatrick, stated on PBS's *MacNeil-Lehrer News Hour* show that "the Mestizo [she meant to say Miskitu] Indians are being so badly repressed that concentration camps have been built on the coast of Nicaragua in the effort to try to imprison them, to eliminate their opposition." On February 19, Secretary of State Alexander Haig claimed that "atrocious and genocidal actions are being taken by Nicaragua against the Indians on their east coast." On February 25, the assistant secretary of state for human rights and humanitarian affairs, Elliott Abrams, told the Senate Subcommittee on Western Hemisphere Affairs that the "Miskitus are now subject to massive assaults by the Sandinistas." On March 1, Ambassador Kirkpatrick reiterated her charge in the United Nations, saying that the Nicaraguan government's "assault" on the Miskitus "is more massive than other human rights violations that I'm aware of in Central America." In Geneva, at the UN Commission on Human Rights annual meeting that month, US representative Richard Schifter condemned the Sandinistas for "atrocities" against the Miskitus. And, in an extraordinary action, even President Reagan himself referred to the alleged "human rights violations" by Sandinistas against the Miskitus in an address to the Organization of American States that spring.

The deputy director of the CIA, Bobby Ray Inman, one of the weirdest of that cast of spook characters, was featured at a press conference exhibiting grainy photographs that resembled Rorschach inkblot tests. In a seeming parody of a TV meteorologist, he pointed his white stick at various parts of the photograph and recounted a narrative that had nothing to do with the picture, which he then described as unassailable evidence. The story he told was of a massive Cuban occupation of the northeast region of Nicaragua. He claimed that the landing strip at Puerto Cabezas was being prepared for fighter jets to land and that a Cuban military base was being built; the most telling detail of all, he said, was the appearance of a baseball diamond, which proved the Cubans were there to stay. This caused amusement in Nicaragua, where baseball had been the national sport ever since the US Marines had first occupied the country in the 1890s.

I never figured out if Inman was completely insane or quite crafty. In any case, he resigned in March 1982, and his boss, William Casey, was even loonier. At times, it seemed absurd to try to counteract this nuttiness with rationality. But it was not only the spooks; General Alexander Haig, Reagan's secretary of state, held a press conference in the Dupont Circle Hilton Hotel in Washington in which he pointed to another photograph (blown up almost two stories tall) and described what he termed as widespread massacres. The photograph showed human bodies enveloped in flames. Haig claimed that these were Miskitu Indians being burned alive by Sandinista soldiers. Newspapers featured the photograph with headlines screaming of massacres and atrocities against the Nicaraguan Indians. During the following days, tiny correction boxes appeared in newspapers—why it wasn't a big story itself I couldn't figure out—reporting that the photograph was the property of the conservative French daily *Le Figaro*, and was taken in 1978, before the Sandinistas took power. The photo actually showed the Red Cross burning corpses of the victims of Somoza's bombing of civilians in Managua in 1978. The irony was that such massacres were actually happening in nearby Guatemala as Haig spoke, massacres about which the administration said nothing. To my knowledge, no reporter ever questioned Haig about his allegations and misrepresentation of the photograph, nor did he ever admit his deception. The administration was that brazen. Even when corrections were printed, the lies created a kind of populist genocidal logic, in which "exaggerations" were then acknowledged, but people assumed that there must be some core of truth to the charges nevertheless.

In addition to allegations by top officials of the Reagan administration and by the president himself, self-exiled Nicaraguan Miskitu leader Steadman Fagoth was in the United States the week of February 22, sponsored by the right-wing "nongovernmental" organizations, the American Security Council in Washington, D.C., and Freedom House in New York. His presence was heavily promoted by the US State Department, particularly Jeanne Kirkpatrick, whose office arranged many of Fagoth's interviews with members of Congress and the media. He had been the representative of the Indian organization MISURASATA to the Nicaraguan Council of State before his arrest in February 1981 on suspicion of conspiring with the CIA to overthrow the government. On being released from prison, he crossed into Honduras to head up a Miskitu Contra force. Fagoth—I never met him—telephoned me from Washington, having been given my card by someone we knew in common. He claimed to be calling from Ambassador Kirkpatrick's office and told me he was having a ball being the center of attention, riding in limousines, and meeting important government officials of the most powerful country on earth. He tried to recruit me to join the gang and share in the fun—heady stuff it must have been for him.

During this period, I became an obsessive news junkie. Not much for television before, now I never missed the morning, evening, or late-night TV news programs, local and national, often listening at the same time to National Public Radio and Pacifica, turning dials back and forth. Ted Koppel's *Nightline* on ABC and the *MacNeil-Lehrer News Hour* on public broadcasting were particularly important because many of their programs concerned Nicaragua. I spent a lot of money ordering transcripts. I also went to San Francisco's Mission District daily to buy several day-late Mexican newspapers where I could find more reliable and in-depth news of Central America, with excellent editorials and columns condemning US intervention policy. The foreign papers were not cheap. I would hole up in the Mission's only café back then, La Bohème, on 24th Street at Mission, and read every word. Other Sandinista supporters gathered there, and we would share the news.

The US campaign against the Sandinistas during the first three months of 1982 came directly out of government offices, funded by taxpayers. In that short time, the campaign succeeded in changing the terms of the debate and had journalists and international human rights investigators scurrying down to Nicaragua demanding that the Sandinistas prove that the allegations were false. That is when credibility became the crucial issue. And I was one of the few people around with lots of credibility, having actually been there; having spent nearly a year researching, writing, and witnessing events in the country; being a university professor and author or editor of four scholarly books and dozens of articles; and having five years of experience in international human rights work. All that meant that I was definitely someone a whole range of people wanted to discredit.

In the rough times, I tried to hang on to a moment in Bluefields captured in my notebook on Christmas Day 1981: *How can one describe a Christmas in Bluefields, Nicaragua? Dancing and music all night—reggae, Caribbean, not "sacred,"—"Christmas caroling" from 5 a.m. to noon—actually a band with dancers going through the streets, people joining in the parade. I joined. Comandante Lumberto Campbell was in his element, one of the people, one with the people, not a hero to the people, just loved. Practically everyone you talk to, asking what they do, they say they are Lumberto's assistants.*

Nicaragua and the Atlantic Coast region in the mid-1980s. The shaded areas indicate regions where the Contras were active. (Based on a Nicaraguan Interior Ministry map)

8

A Cruel Spring

In the midst of the campaign against the Sandinistas, the Latin American Studies Association (LASA) convened in Washington in March 1982. I was not a member of the organization nor had I ever attended one of their annual meetings. Several colleagues in Latin American history urged me to attend the conference, however, in order to talk to participants about the actual situation of the Miskitus in northeastern Nicaragua. Also, Roberto wanted me to be there, since one of the leading Sandinista *comandantes*, Jaime Wheelock, the head of the Agriculture Ministry, was to speak at the conference, and Lumberto Campbell would be part of the Nicaraguan delegation to attend.

When I arrived, I learned that the program committee had found a slot for me on a panel, one that was sure to draw a large audience. I was to replace the well-known left-leaning Latin Americanist James Petras, who could not be there. Since I already had written the first draft of an article that would be published by *Nicaraguan Perspectives*, I was well prepared to make a presentation. There were more than a thousand people in the audience for that panel, and my paper, "The Miskitus in Revolutionary Nicaragua," was well received. That was the only thing during the days there that went well.

Russell Means and his brother Bill Means of the International Indian Treaty Council also came to Washington in order to meet with the Sandinistas. Lumberto Campbell set up a meeting for us with Comandante Wheelock, one of the nine FSLN members who made up the ruling executive of revolutionary

Nicaragua until elections could be organized. In heading INRA, the agricultural ministry—an extremely important ministry throughout Latin America where *campesinos*, in many places primarily indigenous communities, made up majority populations, and land reform was the top agenda item—Wheelock was a key figure in determining Sandinista policies toward the indigenous peoples of Nicaragua.

Russell Means had brought a copy of my book, *The Great Sioux Nation*, the oral history of the Sioux Treaty developed out of the 1974 federal court hearing, to present to Wheelock as a gift. I was pleased and flattered by the gesture. But I was taken aback when Russell demanded of the *comandante* that he call a press conference, introduce him, and announce that the Nicaraguan government supported the 1868 Sioux Treaty and the independence of the Sioux Nation from the United States. The not very veiled threat was that if the Sandinistas failed to do this, Russell and the Treaty Council would denounce them for mistreatment of the Miskitus. Russell also tacked on a demand that the FSLN support the Sullivan Principles regarding South Africa. A silence fell in the room. Bill Means himself appeared unprepared for his brother's demands, and Lumberto looked as if he might laugh but didn't. I jotted in my notebook: "So embarrassing, that IITC asked Nicaragua to recognize the Sioux Treaty and Dr. Leon Sullivan."

Comandante Wheelock did not refuse Russell's demands, but rather promised that he would study my book and the Sioux Treaty and speak to the other members of the executive to see if Nicaragua could issue a statement of support for the treaty and for Sioux self-determination.

Another incident—this one a misunderstanding—at the LASA meeting infuriated Russell. Jaime Wheelock spoke to a large crowd, maybe everyone in attendance at the LASA conference. Latin Americanists are fluent in Spanish, so there was no translation into English. Russell asked me to translate in his ear, and I was doing so. Wheelock was addressing the issue of Red Christmas and the evacuation of the Miskitu border villages. He used the Spanish word *primitivo* to describe the impoverishment of the Miskitu communities at the time of the revolution. The English word *primitive* was by 1982 considered by Native Americans to be a slur when used to describe them. I translated *primitivo* as "impoverished," but Russell heard the word come from Wheelock's mouth and reacted. He was furious and walked out. I followed him and tried to explain the difference in meanings, but his mind seemed to close completely. However, I suspected that this was insignificant in the midst of all the anti-Sandinista propaganda that had been bombarding him. He had definitely been targeted for recruitment as a big fish, as were a number of other well-known individuals.

Within a month after the LASA conference, Russell had hitched his wagon to the small group of Sandinista-haters around the Indian Law Resource Center that housed the Nicaraguan Miskitu exile, Armstrong Wiggins, and the *Akwasasne Notes* newspaper based in Mohawk Country in upstate New York. The editor was José Barreiro, a Cuban American. Since Russell was not about to attack his own brother, I made a good substitute. And so it began.

Outwardly, Russell still seemed friendly when I met him at a Native American Harvard University student conference in late April. Already, however, he was denouncing me behind my back. In an interview published for *Akwasasne Notes* just a few weeks later, Russell claimed that I pretended to represent the IITC and that I had said that the IITC Christmas delegation had recommended the evacuation of the Miskitus—both lies. Russell did not wait for an answer from the Sandinistas, and instead denounced them "because," he said in the *Akwasasne* interview, "I feel they are Marxists; and I feel that Marxists are the most racist people on earth." When I read the interview, I realized that Russell had already gone for the money and whoever or whatever might hoist him back into the limelight of 1973.

I understood, but could not forgive, the temptations of celebrity hunger. I had had my own "fifteen minutes of fame" in 1968–70 in the women's liberation movement. Such attention can replace a fragile sense of self, so that only more attention can fill the void that remains, and more attention is never enough. Russell was a goner. The next year he was running as a vice-presidential candidate in the presidential campaign of Larry Flynt (of *Hustler* magazine fame), flying around in Flynt's Learjet. After that media scene faded, he became a poster boy for Causa International, a subsidiary of the fascist right-wing Unification Church, Reverend Moon's kingdom on earth and one of the biggest players backing the Contra war against the Sandinistas.

In Russell Means's shadow lurked Ward Churchill, who had replaced Jimmie Durham as Russell's ideologue and speechwriter. Churchill was ambitious and hungry for a central role in something, maybe trying to make up for time squandered growing up in a dead-end Illinois town and spending a year in Vietnam, wanting to break out or break into the limelight. Aggressive in his ambition, Churchill was searching for someone to validate his desire to be an Indian leader, or serve as a vehicle for his climb to the top. Probably he came to introduce himself to me in the fall of 1978 with that in mind. I was in my first semester as director of Native American Studies at the University of New Mexico in Albuquerque, the largest such program in the US. One day, a tall man—whom I took to be a white man—appeared with a group of young Native Americans in tow. I was in the reception area at the center explaining some work to the secretary, and there were several Native students hanging out. Churchill startled me with his booming voice: "Roxanne Dunbar, you were in Weatherman; so was I." Weatherman was a group of antiwar leaders who went underground in 1970, and most were then still fugitives. I had no association with them, and I said to myself, "This man is either a fool or a fed." I informed him that he was wrong, but he only smirked, knowingly. I returned to my office, hoping never to see him again. No such luck. I called Vine Deloria, Jr., who was a professor at the University of Arizona at the time, to find out about the guy. I learned that he was a counselor to Native students at the University of Colorado. Vine said he had never met anyone as ambitious as Churchill, but Vine was always generous in helping anyone who asked. Churchill was editing a book that would be published in 1983, *Native Americans and Marxism*, to which Vine had agreed to contribute. Churchill contacted me by phone to ask me to do so, but I refused. Within two years, he would be Russell Means's right-hand man and one of the most virulent of the anti-Sandinistas.

The primary newspaper of the Native American community was *Ak-wasasne Notes*, published by the Mohawk Nation. Edited by a non-Native, José Barreiro, it had been out in front attacking the Sandinistas, long before even the Prinzapolka clash between Sandinista soldiers and Miskitu opposition leaders in February 1981. When their obsession with the Sandinistas became apparent, I attributed it to the widespread mistrust of governments among indigenous activists. As CIA activity aimed at the Sandinistas increased, along with suspicious disturbances in the eastern zone of Nicaragua, a well-placed syndicated column by Georgie Ann Geyer—a journalist said to have close contacts inside the CIA—appeared in thousands of newspapers nationwide, predicting a CIA-organized Miskitu uprising against the Sandinistas. I began to wonder about *Akwasasne Notes* and Barreiro's motives. Then someone gave me a typewritten seven-page, single-spaced document, "AN OPEN LETTER OF RECENT DEVELOPMENTS IN THE AMERICAN INDIAN MOVEMENT/INTERNA-TIONAL INDIAN TREATY COUNCIL," by Jimmie Durham and Paul Smith. It was dated December 1980.

Despite my many problems with Jimmie, I was convinced by the contents of the "open letter." In it, he wrote that he had resigned as director of the Treaty Council in the summer of 1979 due to the immediate circumstances involving "two individuals we feel did much to reduce AIM to its present state. Both individuals are now in leadership of the movement." Most of the document contains a critical history of the American Indian Movement, showing how its own internal contradictions had led to the vacuum that allowed "two individuals" to take over. One of the two Jimmie accused was José Barreiro of *Akwasasne Notes*. Jimmie's second target was Dan Bomberry, then director of Native American Studies at California State University's Sonoma campus. We had seen Bomberry play a disruptive role in the organizing for the 1977 Geneva conference, and soon afterwards in the nonprofit funding world in which he became the darling of rich white donors, eventually setting up the Seventh Generation Fund. The links between Bomberry and Barreiro were in the open, since Bomberry channeled funds to *Akwasasne Notes*. As early as the spring of 1981, Barreiro was publishing the anti-Sandinista articles that would soon dominate the newspaper. In Jimmie's view, Barreiro and Bomberry were promoting an apolitical or even antipolitical view of Native Americans—that is, of their being outside of politics in another realm, the realm of "the natural world." This was, Jimmie asserted, very appealing to the "land-based" movement of white hippies and communalists, as well as to political liberals who did not want to dabble in radical politics. Jimmie claimed that Barreiro and Bomberry had helped make a reality of AIM's becoming "a small core of dislocated individuals, spiritually correct and politically irrelevant to the Indian people on reservations."

Barreiro's newspaper and Bomberry's money became the basis of an unbridgeable divide regarding the Sandinistas and Miskitus among progressive activists, not only in the United States, but also in Canada and Western Europe. Those who opposed the US campaign against the Sandinistas were completely alienated by what seemed to be an indigenous consensus against the Sandinistas, and the "pro-indigenous" solidarity groups viewed the supporters of the Sandinistas as "genocidal" and "statist." Since I had my feet and heart in both movements, I would spend a great deal of time in the United States, Canada, and Europe trying to help supporters of the Sandinistas understand indigenous issues and the pro-indigenous comprehend the Sandinista situation and see through the US manipulation of the Miskitu issue.

These were all complications that I had not expected to confront. I thought I knew everything there was to know about US imperialism, particularly in Latin America, and about US counterinsurgency, worldwide and at home. I had even experienced some of the domestic variety during my period of militant activism in the 1960s. But I had never viewed US imperialism so up close and personal, as if through a magnifying glass in which a speck is transformed into a complex and menacing creature.

The appearance of Paul Theroux's best-selling *The Mosquito Coast* in the spring of 1982 seemed almost magical to me. "Turn your back and walk away fast—that was his motto. Invent any excuse for going. Just clear out. It had made him what he was—it was his genius. Don't look back." This was Theroux's fourteen-year-old narrator summing up the character of his father, a figure who throughout the book stands as the personification of the United States of America. The story is set on the Caribbean coast of Central America, the Mosquito Coast of Nicaragua and Honduras. Some reviewers at the time claimed that it could have been anywhere remote, any jungle, and that the book was a sort of Robinson Crusoe adventure with a tragic ending. But it was not. It was set in Central America on the Atlantic Coast, the original foothold of US imperialism overseas.

In 1848, adventurers and merchants from Eastern seaboard cities, infected with gold fever, arrived in force on the eastern shore of Nicaragua. They were headed for California, just acquired by military conquest from Mexico. In 1853, the US Marines and flocks of missionaries—at first Protestant German Moravians, then Moravians from the US, then other evangelical sects—followed. Theroux does not refer to this part of the area's history, and in fact ignores particular historical or political events. However, he observes closely, carefully, through the voice of a child, the nature of this land in which one man's life and death are set in the 1970s; US Protestant missionaries are everywhere.

Mutilated and disoriented Native people and Blacks dot the landscape, struggling to survive the final assaults of an apparently benign, but actually vicious empire. They are weary and worn thin. Victims. Theroux's boy narrator figures out that the cause of this disarray is his father. Although he does not carry out the killing of the father that he plots with his younger brother, he does have the pleasure of watching "father" die a slow and hideous death (eaten alive by vultures). Without pity, remorse, guilt, or shame, the boy watches.

I thought perhaps the novel would cause its readers to pose questions about the administration's and media's allegations about this isolated zone with its malaria-infested jungle dotted with US-based religious missions whose demagogic missionaries have their own small airplanes, television monitors, and videos powered by generators, and who enjoy absolute power over the native people. A more graphic picture of the role of missionaries in creating deep colonialism had rarely been drawn in literature, equaling the power of Peter Matthiessen's remarkable novel *At Play in the Fields of the Lord*.

Besides the appearance of that novel, there was another positive development amid all that bad news during that terrible spring of 1982. The dreambusters of the Reagan administration suffered a momentary setback in their timetable for the overthrow of the Sandinistas, due, once again, to their own miscalculations. The CIA had established a terror-training program for anti-Sandinista Nicaraguans based in Honduras and staffed by Argentine military men. A military dictatorship had controlled Argentina since 1976, supported by the United States. During its seven-year tenure, the Argentine military had been responsible for the disappearance of at least 9,000, and most likely closer to 30,000, Argentines and foreigners.

Apparently having felt they had received the green light from the Reagan administration in exchange for their services, the Argentine generals seized the Falkland Islands, which lay 300 miles off the coast of Argentina. The British had taken control of those islands in 1833, and this seizure had remained a source of disagreement with Latin Americans, who thought that the islands—which they called Las Malvinas—rightfully belonged to Argentina.

Despite the Latin American left's hatred of the Argentine regime, they applauded the seizure of the islands. The Argentine military was in trouble at home with a shattered economy and internationally isolated because of its well-documented human rights violations. Margaret Thatcher's conservative government in Britain, with the reluctant endorsement by the United States, sent warships and fighter jets to clear out the Argentines. The Reagan administration's reluctance was based on nearly two centuries of US insistence on the Monroe Doctrine, which proclaimed that no European power could intervene in the affairs of governments of the Western Hemisphere, and was later revived as a Cold war thesis for preventing the Soviet Union from aiding Cuba. The war lasted seventy-two days, with 655 Argentine and 236 British deaths, and with 900 more Argentines killed in the sinking of the *Belgrano* by a British submarine. The following year, Argentine democratic forces were able to rally and oust an Argentine military that no longer enjoyed US support. And loss of its Argentine ally meant that the United States had to end its pretense of not being involved in training the Contras in Honduras.

The Argentine surrender came during the UN Special Session on Disarmament in mid-June 1982, which was marked by a peace march from downtown Manhattan to Central Park. I walked with the small Central American contingent in that demonstration of over one million people. The mainstream US peace movement was happy because they thought the nuclear weapons crisis was close to being resolved. How could they ignore Israel's invasion of Lebanon, leaving 10,000 lying dead? Or the nonnuclear US military role in Guatemala, El Salvador, Nicaragua, and Angola? But the peace people did not trouble themselves with such small numbers, particularly if the numbers were brown Palestinians or Central Americans or Angolans. It was the millions of European and Anglo-Americans who might perish in nuclear war that concerned them. Something about that demonstration bothered me—so far from the politics of the Vietnam War movement, where nonintervention was the demand. But that day I was still smarting from what had happened the week before.

Just after the first issue of *Indigenous World/Mundo Indígena*—devoted to the indigenous peoples in Sandinista Nicaragua—had been mailed, the news of tragedy—even more tragedy—arrived from Nicaragua. That spring, *feet*, not inches, of rain fell day after day on western Nicaragua, flooding lands and destroying crops, burying people and farm animals alive under tons of mud run wild, creating gorges, flattening hills. Some were murmuring conspiracy theories, of the CIA seeding clouds to bring disaster, while environmentalists were already beginning to warn of global warming due to human overuse of fossil fuels and toxic gases. The bundle of newspapers I sent to Nicaragua, I would soon learn, had arrived in the midst of the crisis. This accidental convergence was fateful, or maybe just a convenient excuse.

I had finished the academic year and was in New York for a six-week seminar when the call came. I was free of duties until September 1983, having received a sabbatical leave at half-pay, an easy enough amount to live on in Nicaragua for a year. I planned to move to Nicaragua in August, after having completed the seminar in New York and attending the first meeting of the UN indigenous working group in Geneva. In Nicaragua, I hoped to produce the next two issues of *Indigenous World* as a project with the Miskitu and Sumu communities.

Now I was told I would not be allowed to work with the new institute (CIDCA) that dealt with the eastern region: "You know, people in western Nicaragua, mestizos, suffer too—why no concern about them, rather only the Miskitus?" Galio Gurdián said when he called. He was in the San Francisco Bay Area and had gotten my temporary telephone number from Roberto. The seminar was being held at a Hunter College site on First Avenue, next to Bellevue Hospital, and we participants were being put up in dormitory rooms that had been vacated for the summer. I remember standing there at the wall phone, tethered by a short cord to a small space, unable to sit down—which I needed to do, feeling dizzy, faint, suddenly horribly overheated. I asked if Comandante Campbell or Comandante Ramírez had made this decision. Gurdián said that it was none of my business. It never occurred to me that he had acted completely on his own—I would not know that until I visited Nicaragua six months later.

I was stricken, not only because my carefully drawn plans had been disrupted—I would have to revise my sabbatical application—but because my contributions had been rejected and with such hostility. I did not know Gurdián well, but as time went on I was never able to win from him even cordiality. I think the reasons for his dislike were political, and I must admit that the mistrust went both ways, since I did (and do) mistrust the anthropological worldview. Anthropology, like Christian missionizing, was born of the soft side of European/US colonialism and imperialism. When they were not assisting governments in figuring out how to co-opt the natives, they were "protecting" the natives from corruption—the right and left wings of anthropology and Christianity. Gurdián and other anthropologists had convinced the Sandinistas that only they had the special knowledge of the ways of the indigenous to be able to advise them on indigenous issues. The Miskitu-Sandinista question was now controlled by anthropologists and Christian missionaries. A Marxist-feminist historian attempting to assist in the self-determination of indigenous peoples was definitely a threat to those agendas. That I had no interest vested in fact threatened Gurdián, who did have a design: he sought to calm the Miskitus under the guise of protecting them from the state, from the Revolution.

Thus it was that instead of spending my sabbatical in Nicaragua, I began working with Rigoberta Menchú in the summer of 1982.

9

Getting to Know Rigoberta

Rigoberta Menchú Tum, a Quiche-speaking rural Mayan woman, was twenty-three years old when I met her in the summer of 1982. She was a refugee from Guatemala's genocidal military regime, her parents and brother murdered by the military in 1980. Her two younger sisters had joined the guerrillas, but Rigoberta was secreted out of the country and had legal refugee status in Nicaragua, although she spent most of her time in Mexico working with the tens of thousands of Mayan refugees who poured over the border into southern Mexico.

By the time I met her in New York, Rigoberta was well known in Europe, having traveled to many countries informing groups about the critical situation in Guatemala. She had already met with government officials in Sweden and France, and she had completed a book in Paris with Latin American anthropologist Elisabeth Burgos-Debray. The book, *I, Rigoberta Menchú*, which would appear in English in late 1983, transformed Rigoberta into a major figure: a decade later, she received the Nobel Peace Prize on the five hundredth anniversay of Columbus's first voyage to the Western Hemisphere, the onset of Western imperialism and colonialism.

Rigoberta and the Guatemalan support groups—dominated by anthropologists and liberal Christians—that brought her to New York were organizing solidarity work in the United States. I met and spoke with Rigoberta several times in June, but not until we were paired to speak later that month did I realize how important she could be for the United Nations work on indigenous issues. The event was an annual inner-city youth retreat in the White Mountains of New Hampshire organized by civil rights leader Mel King. King was a Massachusetts state legislator and adjunct professor in the Department of Urban Studies and Planning at the Massachusetts Institute of Technology. The Boston Central American solidarity group had arranged for Rigoberta to spend a day in workshops with the young people, and they invited me as well.

Rigoberta and I flew to Boston, where a young man from the solidarity group met us and drove us to the retreat. There were about a hundred African American and Latino boys and girls in their early teens. It was pouring rain and quite cold the day and night we were there, and the participants were aching to get outside to romp and play. Fortunately, we were able to divert their attention, particularly Rigoberta in her Guatemalan *traje* (the traditional handwoven dress), shawl, and turban folded on top of her head. She was so tiny and young looking that the kids claimed her as one of their own.

Rigoberta and I retired early under mountains of blankets on our bunk beds in the small, unheated room to which we had been assigned. Although I was nearly twice her age, I felt like a student learning from Rigoberta, particularly about the importance of collectivity and community as opposed to individualism. I told her about the UN work I was doing and the upcoming first meeting of the Working Group on Indigenous Peoples in Geneva. It was not difficult to convince her that she should be there, but she said that she had to get permission from her organization, the CUC (Unidad Campesina, or Committee for Peasant Unity), which was associated with one of the four Guatemalan political/guerrilla organizations, the EGP, or Guerrilla Army of the Poor. She already knew about me from the two Quiche Mayans from CUC who had been at the UN Seminar in Managua.

I left for Geneva two weeks later without knowing for sure that Rigoberta would join me. My main concern at the time was not with Guatemala but with Nicaragua: it seemed to me essential that the first meeting of the working group have a clear focus and not be vulnerable to hijacking by the Miskitu insurgents and their US friends. As it turned out, focus on an authentic situation of genocide against indigenous peoples was the best way to undercut manipulation of the working group.

Rigoberta showed up five days before the meeting was to begin, by herself and without money or a place to stay. I thought I had explained that her organization needed to cover expenses and arrange lodging, stressing that I would be happy to train her in the UN work but was no travel agent and did not have money. I explained this again and took her with me to my friend Lee Weingarten's two-room apartment, where I was staying. Good people who lived in Geneva were constantly pressured to house NGO visitors and were often left with large phone bills. Lee had helped those of us doing indigenous work since the 1977 conference and after five years was tiring of constant visitors, so Rigoberta's stay was to be for one night only.

Rigoberta had a telephone number given to her by Julia Esquivel, an exiled Guatemalan poet, for a cloistered and silent order of Spanish nuns outside Geneva. Julia had spent time there, and many of the Spanish nuns had served in Guatemala among the Mayans. Practically all the foreign church people, as well as UN officials, had been driven out of Guatemala in the late 1970s and early 1980s, so they were well aware of the threat of violence against anyone attempting to protect or defend the Mayans.

We called and made plans with the sister on duty—only one sister each day was allowed to talk—and took the train there, about two hours from Geneva. We ended up staying two days because communication was limited to one person on duty, who could not discuss the problem with her sisters. Handwritten notes had to be passed. Rigoberta and I waited. We were given a small room in the centuries-old convent, and prepared our own food in the cavernous stone kitchen. We attended mass morning, noon, and evening in the new, modernist sanctuary with a glass dome, a truly uplifting space where a peaceful silence prevailed. In our room, we could smoke and talk to our hearts' content, and that is what we did.

Rigoberta took the time to explain to me in detail the politics and vision of the Guatemalan liberation movement. I already knew from Marcelo and Mary Zuñiga in Nicaragua about the splits in the movement. They had lived in Guatemala for two years in the 1970s, and Mary was still primarily involved with the Mayan struggle there. She had described to me the evolution of the four organizations that had recently come—shakily—together to form the URNG, or United National Revolutionary Group. The FAR, or Revolutionary Armed Force, composed mainly of Latino Guatemalans, had been the main organization in the 1960s trying to topple the military regime that was supported by the United States. An all-out counterinsurgency, including the use of napalm, had decimated the rebels, but the organization survived, now much smaller than before, organizing industrial workers. The Guatemalan Communist Party, mainly Latino Guatemalans, also organized mainly industrial workers. Both these small organizations had everything to gain by a united front. However, the other two organizations were large, about equal in numbers, and organized the rural poor. ORPA, the Revolutionary Organization of the People in Arms, was the only Christian-oriented of the four organizations (it based its views on liberation theology), and had gained the largest Mayan participation. The EGP had preceded ORPA in initiating armed struggle in the early 1970s, but had more recently begun to focus on the Mayan population supporting CUC, which was a majority Mayan organization.

Rigoberta's father, Vicente Menchú, was one of the grassroots Mayan founders of CUC, and had led the way in affiliating with the EGP. However, Vicente and other CUC activists were massacred inside the Spanish embassy in Guatemala City in early 1980, where they were meeting with the Spanish ambassador, who himself barely escaped death. Then Rigoberta's mother was abducted, raped, tortured, and killed, and her brother was killed by the military.

Rigoberta was supportive of the URNG, the new umbrella resistance organization, but also believed that CUC deserved a central role. The Guatemalan groups were not affiliated with or receiving aid from any country of the socialist bloc. Rigoberta carried with her a stack of CUC materials, and I read all of them, talking to her about the "national" question, that is, the right of self-determination of various nationalities in a country. The view of the EGP, Rigoberta told me, was to topple the military government and initiate a revolutionary socialist order with majority rule. Since the Mayans were the majority, they would presumably dominate the country's politics. However, I had read EGP materials that portrayed the Mayan populations as divided into Mayan language groups, twenty-three in all, each as a separate nationality, and thus argued that there was no such thing as a Mayan majority. This position sounded too much like apartheid South Africa in its tribalization of the majority of Africans into separate national groups, so that no one group outnumbered the white minority. Rigoberta and I debated, argued, and found common ground and some differences. The dialogue would continue for a year, until the EGP split, triggering splits in CUC and solidarity groups as well.

Finally, we got help at the convent. The sister on duty called us to the visitors' parlor and explained the plan. Rigoberta and I would stay with an old, prestigious family of Geneva, the Micheli, the matriarch of which was Spanish. Their daughter, Anita, had died a year before while working with the poor in Nicaragua, and we would be allowed to live in Anita's cottage in the Micheli compound, where nothing had been touched since Anita had left for Nicaragua. The sister drove us to the train station.

The Micheli compound outside Geneva was on the other side of the Rhône on a hillside overlooking the lake, set in a wooded parklike district thick with mansions and compounds. Arriving in a taxi, we were stopped at the gate by a uniformed man who turned out to be from Puerto Rico. Rigoberta explained our purpose to him, and he allowed our taxi to drive into what could have been a small village—two large houses, the cottage where we would stay, and some other structures amid a series of lawns and gardens. The young Spanish-speaking man at the gate wore a familiar uniform, but I could not immediately place it.

In the Micheli home, we were greeted by Monsieur and Madame Micheli and *la señora*, the Spanish matriarch, who was quite impressive in all-black organdy, an aristocratic lady out of a Goya painting. They had a wonderful supper prepared for us, chocolate fondue with fruit and cake to dip. Afterwards, Madame Micheli walked us to Anita's cottage, which was actually a three-bedroom, two-bath, two-story house designed like a ski lodge, all wood and exposed beams. Left alone, Rigoberta and I explored, and we both felt a little intrusive, not wanting to touch anything. In the upstairs bathroom, Anita's toothpaste was open with the toothbrush beside it, just as she had left it. In the bedroom, her nightgown lay across the bed, as if she had left in a hurry. We chose our bedrooms, mine downstairs, Rigoberta's upstairs.

I awoke to the brightest blue sky. It was 8 a.m. and a beautiful summer day outside, a very quiet Sunday. I stood at the window stretching, basking in our good fortune to be in such a place when my eyes locked onto something that did not belong there—a US flag atop a tall flagpole. I blinked and stared, hoping that it would disappear. It did not. I quickly dressed and walked outside. The flag was directly in front of the largest house in the compound, a three-story mansion. I went to the Michelis' house to find out why it was there. I found everyone up and dressed, ready for breakfast. They greeted me, asked me about Rigoberta, who was still asleep, and gave me a cup of coffee. I asked, as offhandedly as I could manage, why the red, white, and blue stars and stripes, definitely not the French tricolor, was flying on their property.

"Oh," Madame Micheli said in perfect English, "didn't you know that we rent that house to the American ambassador to the United Nations?"

"No, I didn't know that," I said, trying to smile.

"Yes, it has been thirty years now. We have met some wonderful Americans," she said.

I excused myself, telling her that I wanted to fetch Rigoberta.

She was still in bed but awake when I knocked on her door. Calmly as I was able, I told her the predicament. Her round eyes expanded, and I thought I detected a mischievous twinkle, then she must have detected something in my look, for we both burst into laughter, the kind that keeps coming back, making it impossible to talk. Finally, we both sobered enough to assess the situation.

"I'll call Juan in Paris," she said. Juan was the URNG representative in Europe, so Rigoberta called and explained the situation to him, then listened a very short time and hung up. She said he would arrive on the 6 p.m. train and we must meet him at the station.

We met Juan, a good-looking, serious young Guatemalan, not Mayan, who spoke very educated Spanish. Of course, Juan was not his real name and no last name was forthcoming. He had only half an hour because he was going to return to Paris on the TVG he had arrived on. Juan scolded both of us for being so inattentive in searching for appropriate lodging, and he gave Rigoberta a name and telephone number in Geneva and urged us to move out of the Micheli house that very night.

And move we did, simply telling the Michelis the truth, that it was inappropriate for me, a US dissident, and Rigoberta, a dissident wanted by a government the United States supported, to remain there. I returned to Lee's couch, while Rigoberta moved to the tiny apartment of a young couple, Pedro, who was Spanish, and Sally, who was English. They worked with the small Guatemalan solidarity group in Geneva. They were the kindest two people imaginable, absolutely at Rigoberta's service. They even took leave from their jobs for a week in order to drive Rigoberta to the meetings.

I arrived at their apartment the next morning, the first day of the Working Group meeting. Rigoberta was on her hands and knees scrubbing the kitchen floor. Sally shook her head in exasperation, saying that Rigoberta had insisted on cleaning up from dinner the night before and had already washed the dishes. Rigoberta had worked as a maid from a young age and maintained that humility. I nearly cried at the realization. My mind returned to the mid-sixties when I had been married to a fellow UCLA graduate student who came from a well-off Mexican family, and of summers spent with them in Mexico City, observing the four maids, very young Indian women, vulnerable to sexual abuse by the four brothers and father, with no future beyond degrading work for rich people.

Rigoberta, her persona, and her urgent message about what had happened to her family and the genocide that was happening to the rural Mayan population riveted the five members of the Working Group and the representatives of observer governments and nongovernmental organizations who joined the meeting, including Amnesty International, the World Peace Council, AAPSO, and a few church-affiliated NGOs. (Each year afterwards, the numbers of indigenous representatives increased and eventually numbered in the hundreds, the largest working group in UN history.) Amnesty International, although not aware that Rigoberta or any Guatemalan Mayan representative would be there, complemented Rigoberta's testimony with a detailed nineteen-page report of their investigation of Guatemala's human rights abuses, listing horrendous massacres of Mayan civilians, a refugee situation with tens of thousands of Mayans fleeing across the Mexican border, and interviews from a dozen eyewitnesses or victims.

We had no problem initiating a strong resolution condemning the Guatemalan government from the Working Group that would be taken up at the four-week Sub-Commission that followed. Rigoberta decided to stay for the Sub-Commission in order to help shepherd the resolution through. I was surprised when Adrien-Claude Zoller, the representative of Pax Christi, an activist Catholic organization, took me to task for having brought Rigoberta to the Working Group under indigenous auspices rather than general gross human rights violations, arguing that the indigenous issue was new (though five years did not seem new to me) and had no future in the UN. I begged to differ, arguing that the Guatemalan situation was clearly an indigenous issue, since the Mayan population was being attacked en masse. I told Rigoberta about the conversation, and she agreed, insisting that she would continue to present her case as an indigenous issue, a stance from which she never retreated. Rigoberta's insistence on including Guatemala's Mayan people in the indigenous project gave credibility to the Working Group on Indigenous Peoples in its first meeting and increased visibility to indigenous peoples' struggles in Latin America.

We were lobbying directly against the government of Guatemala, which brought that country's delegation into the fray; they of course accused Rigoberta of being a terrorist and a communist. No Sub-Commission member was from Guatemala, but the member from Morocco, Madame Warzazi, took up the Guatemalan government's cause. I assumed that the US member would be a problem, but he had brought as his alternate a Lakota Indian from Pine Ridge, Charles Trimble, whose niece had been a student of mine. He recognized my name when I introduced myself because he knew my book *The Great Sioux Nation*. I introduced Charles to Rigoberta and we had a long talk, gaining his commitment not to oppose the resolution.

I launched a reception for Rigoberta, inviting all eighteen members of the Sub-Commission, and all the governments and NGOs attending, timing it to coincide with the indigenous item on the agenda. The Antislavery Society of Great Britain (now Anti-Slavery International) agreed to allow us to use its Geneva office for the reception. Surprisingly, all the Sub-Commission members attended, along with most of the NGOs and even a few government representatives. Rigoberta gave an eloquent appeal for support of the resolution against Guatemala. After all the guests had gone, several friends stayed for the cleanup, again with Rigoberta washing the dishes and scrubbing the floors.

Rigoberta and I were invited to most of the government receptions that were staged during UN meetings, including ones to which few NGOs were invited. In the end, we won passage of the resolution. Even the Sub-Commission members opposed to it managed to be absent when the vote was taken, and it passed by consensus. After the passage of this resolution, Rigoberta agreed to go with me to the upcoming United Nations General Assembly that would open in New York in September.

O n the eve of the opening of the General Assembly, representatives—all men and non-indigenous—from the Guatemalan opposition organizations arrived, making clear that they did not want Rigoberta to dominate the UN lobbying. The ORPA representative had a completely different lobbying strategy from the one Rigoberta and I had formed, and the indigenous issue was not a part of it. As ORPA saw it, only the Western European missions should be approached, not the nonaligned countries. I believed that it was particularly important to lobby the African representatives, since it was the African region's turn to chair the upcoming UN Commission on Human Rights that would meet for six weeks beginning in February. The group had chosen Uganda ambassador Olara Otunu as chair, and I had set up meetings with him and with other African ambassadors. The ORPA representative was not interested in the indigenous resolution we had shepherded through the Sub-Commission and had brought one of his own, which spoke of "campesinos" rather than Mayans. Thanks to the efforts of Frank LaRue, a Guatemalan labor lawyer who had been forced into exile by death threats and physical attacks, we reached a compromise and merged the two resolutions as well as arranged a meeting with the African group. Frank was a great unifying force, noncompetitive and open to new ideas, such as allying with the international indigenous movement. Having a US-born Anglo father and a Guatemalan mother, Frank was bilingual and bicultural and an effective lobbyist.

Rigoberta was invited to attend an American Indian Movement rally in the Black Hills, protesting Mount Rushmore and Columbus in October. She accepted the invitation and went, much against the wishes of the Guatemala solidarity committee, who, like the Pax Christi representative, was dubious about linking the Guatemalan political/military situation to the indigenous issue. They appeared to blame me for Rigoberta's decision to go to the Black Hills, but it was her choice. She found the experience bracing and exciting, as she had never before set foot on sacred Native North American land.

Besides lobbying at the General Assembly, I was trying to publish the third issue of *Indigenous World*, which featured Rigoberta and the Guatemalan Mayan struggle against genocide. Chockie Cottier at the San Francisco American Indian Center was putting it together with other volunteers. The most difficult aspect was translating from English to Spanish. I could translate the Spanish to English, but finding someone to do the other was always hard; however, we were determined to publish a bilingual paper. The other problem was money. We had none. I had paid for typesetting and printing the first two issues out of my own salary, but now I was on half-pay during my sabbatical and could not cover the costs. Frank LaRue came to my rescue. He had been invited as a keynote speaker at the annual gathering of progressive grant makers to be held in Maryland and could bring a guest, and Frank and I flew to spend a day at the conference.

This turned out to be a magical opportunity, because there I met Maya Miller, a liberal philanthropist from Carson City, Nevada, who happened to be interested in the Central American indigenous situation. Her daughter, Kit, had lived for a time in Guatemala and had raised money for a Maya women's weaving project. But Maya Miller had also been asking to meet anyone who knew anything about the Miskitu situation in Nicaragua. She mistrusted Dan Bomberry, now a member of the Grantmakers group, who founded the Seventh Generation Fund for indigenous projects. He had early on condemned the Sandinistas for human rights abuses against the Miskitus, and now he insisted on symmetry between the Guatemalan and Nicaraguan indigenous situations, that is, blaming the Guatemalan genocidal generals and the Sandinistas equally. Phil Hutchings, director of Vanguard Foundation in San Francisco and an old friend of mine, was also at the conference. He was surprised but glad to see me there and took me to meet Maya Miller.

Maya and I hit it off. She had substantial knowledge about Native American issues, particularly those in Nevada to which she had contributed: resistance to nuclear testing and grazing restrictions, as well as support for honoring the 1863 Shosone treaty with the US government, the Treaty of Ruby Valley. Maya amazed me because she had already figured out that reports of the Sandinistas abusing the Indians of Nicaragua were exaggerated, and she refused to go along with the idea of symmetry. But she wanted the unvarnished truth of the situation in the Miskitia, and that is what I gave her: there were serious problems, I said. I also told Maya about the *Indigenous World* newspaper and outlined our plans to form a UN-affiliated organization, and she pledged her financial support. Maya's money came from an inheritance from her parents, who had owned the Mission Inn in Riverside, California. She devoted the money to social causes, particularly those that affected women or were organized by women. I was a perfect candidate for her small grants, which allowed me to carry on my UN lobbying as well as investigations of the situations in Central America, and especially the Miskitu issue in Nicaragua. I returned to New York with the burden of finding funds for the newspaper lifted.

U N headquarters in New York is a far more difficult venue for NGO lobbying than Geneva (and has become virtually impossible since the 2001 World Trade Center attack). The New York Police Department handles security and, at least as long as I have known it, is much more under US government control than UN security at the Geneva offices. The NYPD was not so much strict as arbitrary, one day allowing entrance to the Delegates' Lounge, a key place for lobbying, and the next day refusing, not even allowing one to signal the diplomat waiting for an appointment. In those years, the NYPD reflected the US government's disdain for NGOs, particularly those involving women's issues, and this attitude had only hardened under the Reagan administration. Unlike the UN in Geneva, the New York headquarters' General Assembly Hall was designed to keep NGOs corralled in a high balcony, with no floor access unless a government brought us in—and that was usually not an option for any NGO that wanted to remain nongovernmental. Even the smaller committee meeting rooms segregated NGOs, unlike Geneva, where one had full access to government delegations. But I had no problem once I began working with Bianca Jagger.

Bianca, a Nicaraguan who famously had been married to Mick Jagger of the Rolling Stones in the 1970s, had made quite a splash and a name for herself in the hot nightclubs and with the Andy Warhol crowd, so that she was a celebrity in her own right. She had divorced Mick, won custody of their daughter, and was now living in New York. In 1978, she visited refugees from Nicaragua and brought attention to Somoza's torture and killing of civilians. In 1981, she visited El Salvador on the Honduran border where Salvadoran refugees were trying to flee the civil war, and while there witnessed the massacre at El Mozote, a story powerfully told by Mark Danner in *The Massacre at El Mozote*. From that time, Bianca has been a dedicated human rights activist and promoter of the United Nations.

I was introduced to Bianca by Francisco Campbell, who had been head of the Miskitu region when I visited in 1981, and was now an ambassador to the United States and member of the large Nicaraguan delegation at the UN General Assembly in the fall of 1982. The Nicaraguan government was running for the Latin American revolving seat on the UN Security Council. Although the regions nominate their candidates, the entire General Assembly votes on them at the end of the session. Usually the region presents a single candidate they have decided upon, but when the Latin American states chose Nicaragua, they came under intense pressure and threats from a furious Reagan administration to change the selection. They compromised and nominated two countries, Nicaragua and Costa Rica. Francisco asked me to help Bianca lobby.

What fun it was to lobby with Bianca! She was stunning then (and still is in middle age), and had the glamour and carriage of a celebrity. When she walked into a room, heads turned and talking stopped, at least among the men. With Bianca, I had no problem getting past the NYPD guards into the hallowed space of the Delegates' Lounge, or even onto the main floor of the General Assembly Hall. As far as I could tell, she had no credentials of any kind, but no one ever stopped her. If we approached a diplomat to speak about Nicaragua, the man would fall all over himself to make all the time in the world, seemingly hypnotized by Bianca's presence. Then I would move in with my mantra of voting for Nicaragua and not allowing the US to bully him, and I would provide a packet of literature, which included my article on the Miskitus and the Sandinistas. I do believe Bianca won the vote for Nicaragua, by the narrow margin of one in the General Assembly. Fortunately the vote for seats on the Security Council was by secret ballot, since it was apparent that quite a number of diplomats voted in opposition to their governments' instructions.

When the vote was taken, Bianca and I were sitting together in the guest section on the main floor, right behind the government delegations. The serious gathering turned into a rally for Nicaragua on the announcement of Nicaragua's victory. Delegates crowded around the Nicaraguan delegation. Nicaraguan foreign minister Miguel D'Escoto, the rotund and sweet former

Maryknoll priest, was hoisted into the air. I was having enormous fun watching this unprecedented display. Then Bianca nudged me, saying, "I need to go to the bathroom."

"Sure, go ahead," I said, rather annoyed.

"You must come with me," she said.

I resisted, but she took my arm and off we went. It was the first time I had been irritated with her, and I remember thinking, well, maybe she is a bimbo after all.

In the long, broad hallway that leads from the General Assembly Hall to the corridor appeared dozens of news photographers and television camera crews in a pack, walking backwards, and I noticed that Jeanne Kirkpatrick, Reagan's ambassador to the UN, was in front of us. I saw her straightening her hair and taking on that certain pose to be filmed, slowing down her stride. The pack of news people swept by her and stopped in front of us. Reporters shouted questions to Bianca, and she charmingly jousted with them. I kept my eyes on Kirkpatrick, and in one of those revelatory moments saw her turn around to see what was happening. Her face revealed disappointment and then, recognizing Bianca, cold hatred. She turned and practically ran down the hall. Of course, Bianca had seen Kirkpatrick walking out, noticed the waiting press, and wanted me to witness the comeuppance.

By the time of Nicaragua's victory in the United Nations, I was exhausted and feverish from what I thought was a bad cold. I had an airline ticket to fly to Mexico City the following day for a two-day seminar on the hemispheric indigenous movement and would have to return to New York for the final week of the General Assembly. Despite feeling increasingly ill and weak, I found the seminar an exciting opportunity to convince key activists of the importance of participating in the UN's new working group on indigenous peoples. However, the venue was questionable, and I would not have agreed to participate had Rigoberta not urged me to do so. She wanted me to meet her Mayan compatriot, Pablo Ceto, who would be there.

The seminar was cosponsored by and held at CEESTEM (the Spanish acronym for the Center for Economic and Social Studies of the Third World), a think tank founded by the former president of Mexico, Luis Echeverría Álvarez, on the grounds of his personal estate south of Mexico City. The other co-sponsor and organizer was CADAL (the Spanish acronym for Anthropologi-cal Documentation Center for Latin America), whose founder and director was an Argentine anthropologist living in Mexico, Nemesio Rodríguez. I had met Nemesio the summer before in Mexico, along with other Latin Ameri-can anthropologists and sociologists who had begun to work in collaboration with the growing indigenous movements in Latin America—Rodolfo Staven-hagen, a Mexican sociologist at El Colegio de México (in 2001 appointed UN Special Representative for Indigenous Peoples' issues); Guillermo Bonfil Batalla, Mexican and head of the National Museum of Anthropology and di-rector of Nueva Imagen publishers; Carlos Guzman-Boeckler, a Guatemalan anthropologist; and Stefano Varese, a Peruvian anthropologist then working in Mexico for the National Indian Institute, among many others who would be at the seminar. Just as the more liberal Christian churches had ceased missionizing and began supporting Indian struggles, so too had many Latin American anthropologists who had previously considered Indians to be only informants for their studies. In January 1971, the World Council of Churches had assembled the leading Latin American anthropologists in a meeting on Barbados to hammer out a common policy known as the Barbados Declara-tion, which committed support to the pan-Indian movement.

All this seemed fine, but Pablo Gonzales Casanova, my Mexican colleague from the 1978 nongovernmental conference on racism in Basel, cautioned me about getting involved with CEESTEM, or anything related to former Presi-dent Echeverría, who had been the infamous minister of the interior (and thus head of the national police) during the Díaz-Ordaz presidency and was responsible for the 1968 student massacre in the Plaza de las Tres Culturas at Tlatelolco. Pablo had been chancellor of the National University, UNAM, at the time and was fired that year, although he continued as a UNAM professor. As a reward for his brutal repression of all radical activity in Mexico, Echever-ría was chosen to be the next president. I had been married to a Mexican citizen at the time and had spent a great deal of time in Mexico City and was involved in planning the 1968 protests—I was not present during the mas-sacre, although my husband was—and I detested Echeverría. Nevertheless, following Rigoberta and her Mayan colleagues' lead, I cautiously took ad-vantage of the vast resources offered by CEESTEM until it was perfunctorily closed and all of Echeverría's property seized in 1983 by the new Mexican president, Miguel de la Madrid Hurtado (1982–88). But for eighteen months, CEESTEM was useful to my work.

I was wowed by the center and would never have imagined that such a complex and developed outfit suddenly would disappear from one day to the next. It was similar to a liberal arts college campus and even offered a credentialed master's degree in development studies. Echeverría's own villa and compound were next door to the beautiful campus of meticulously kept gardens, ponds, and fountains, and elegant buildings that housed offices, meeting rooms, a superlative library, a large auditorium, and restaurants. CEESTEM also hosted the national offices of a number of United Nations agencies, each of which had a bookstore. CEESTEM published studies and had its own printing facilities for book publishing; it had produced some of the best work on the New International Economic Order and the New International Information Order, United Nations and UNESCO initiatives of the 1970s that sought to limit Western imposition of laissez-faire economic development programs and First World media on former colonies and other impoverished countries.

The seminar turned out to be even more exciting than I had hoped. In addition to Pablo Ceto, there were a dozen other indigenous observers present—Guatemalan and Mexican Mayans, Mexican Mixtec and Zapotec, and a Quechua from Bolivia. They were all men, and I asked where the women were. They said women were the backbone of their movements.

Pablo and I talked alone. He was now representing URNG, the united front of the four Guatemalan guerrilla organizations, in Mexico. Pablo was an Ixil-speaking Mayan from Nebaj, a land he told me, dreamily, of mountains, waterfalls, and streams. He had become a guerrilla combatant with the Guerrilla Army of the Poor in 1976. Since the Ixil area was where the guerrilla army operated successfully, it was the first bombed by the military, but that was nothing compared to 1981–82, when 26 villages and 145 hamlets, including Nebaj, were destroyed by the Guatemalan military, producing 80 percent of the internal refugees in Guatemala, now under the control of the military in concentration camps. Hundreds were tortured and killed. General Rios-Montt was in charge and called the operation "Draining the Sea." The EGP had not expected nor were they prepared for the massive assault. They were not able to arm and care for the refugees, the lucky ones of whom made their way to Chiapas, Mexico. Although Pablo Ceto did not admit it, the Guerrilla Army of the Poor was defeated and scattered, and its combatants like Pablo forced into exile.

10

Drinking for Courage

I started drinking again on December 10, 1982. I know the date because I wrote it in the journal I was keeping in those days. Those days.

I can even pinpoint the exact moment. It was 4:30 p.m., in the Delegates' Lounge of the United Nations in New York. I had returned from Mexico late the night before and had been up most of the night coughing. I was still feverish, my throat was so sore I was unable to swallow food. I told myself that I had to make it through the week, the last week of the General Assembly, in order to make sure that we would have enough votes for a Guatemalan resolution at the UN Commission on Human Rights that would open in Geneva six weeks later. Then I could fly home to San Francisco and see a doctor, and everything would be all right.

The floor-to-ceiling windows of the Delegates' Lounge were black with the winter darkness outside. I was awaiting an appointment with an assistant to Olara Otunu, the Ugandan who had been elected chairman of the upcoming Commission session. He was late, and I kept my eyes on the entrance and my ears attuned to the paging calls. Finally, an hour later he walked in, smiling as always, effusive with apologies as if I were someone of importance rather than an irritant. He offered to fetch us drinks from the bar. Maybe some hot tea, I said, adding that I had a sore throat and a bad cough.

"The General Assembly will do that to you," he said, adding, "I know what will help." Off he went to the bar and returned with a large steaming cup of dark liquid that looked like tea. I took a sip. It was a hot toddy, pure brandy with a lemon slice floating in it. I drank the whole cup as if seven and a half years of sobriety had been a fantasy, although it took a full year of starts and stops for me to get back into the groove of being an alcoholic.

And thus began fifteen more years of alcohol abuse, except for brief periods of abstention. Later, in recovery, I would learn that many alcoholics quit drinking for a time and return to it, which reinforces their delusion that they can stop anytime they wish, that they are choosing to drink and are therefore in control. In that entire time of drinking, I never returned to a recovery program. And along with the drinking came heavy smoking.

In retrospect, I see my own relapse into alcoholism as parallel to the melting of global political resistance to United States power and oppression, especially in Central America. In this deeply personal way, I was reacting to the Reagan and Bush administrations' creation of scarcity and fear, punctuated by the AIDS pandemic. Turning to drink in 1982 was a repeat of my first bout of alcoholism a decade earlier, when the powerful resistance of the 1960s began to implode. In the early 1970s, I had begun to feel increasingly isolated until I became involved with the American Indian Movement. Now again, in 1982, I felt that increasing sense of isolation: AIM was weakened and splitting, its leaders courting the press, then Hollywood, some even turning to cocaine. That I survived, once again, that I am writing now, two decades later, alcohol-free and reasonably healthy, is inexplicable and marvelous, although I am not without a measure of survivor's guilt for all those who did not make it.

On the other hand, I do not believe I could have done what I did for the next five years had I not been fueled by alcohol to dull the fear and live with the exhaustion. Although the life-threatening risks I took and what I believe I accomplished added up to perhaps nothing in the end—the Sandinistas were defeated—I was a witness. I was a witness, and because of that, I cannot regret anything. I only ask pardon of those family and friends who were helpless in their concern for me.

I took that one drink in the UN Delegates' Lounge as medicinal and did not deal with its implications. I returned to San Francisco and healed quickly on antibiotics, then celebrated the holidays with my daughter, now in college, and with friends. I got out the *Indigenous World*, mailed copies, and finished the manuscript for the book I had been working on since 1980, *Indians of the*

Americas: Human Rights and Self-Determination, sending it off to London for publication by the small, leftist publishing collective Zed Books (the book finally appeared in the spring of 1984).

Writing was a kind of release and relief. I had worked on the subject so long that writing the book was more like reading, the words almost forming themselves. My mind and body became a kind of word processor, disappearing into the work. I loved—still love—the way writing allows me to put pieces together into meaningful wholes, or at least ones that give meaning to me. I cannot function without trying to see the whole.

In a way, perhaps, this quilting together of experience is what is easiest for me. It is a discipline, so unlike the craziness of an activist life. Were it not for my sense of an obligation to be active, I could have lost myself in writing. It was my old dilemma again—community organizing vs. academia or UN work, the revolutionary vs. the writer. In 1982, however, I knew I would not be able to keep myself away from the revolution for long. To write without acting when Reagan was loose in the White House would be too irresponsible. Soon I would be back in the jungles of Central America.

As I wrote the book, I continued to drink, carefully, at several holiday parties. I received a bottle of Kahlua as a gift, which I rationed out over several days of finishing the book. But it was exactly one month after the hot toddy that I began really abusing alcohol again.

I had been invited by AAPSO to join their delegation at the Non-Aligned Movement's (NAM) meeting in Managua in mid-January 1983, and I had told myself that I would go if I finished the book and the newspaper mailing. In the Mexico City airport, awaiting the flight to Managua, I bought another bottle of Kahlua in the duty-free shop, supposedly as a gift for someone in Managua. Practically the entire Nicaraguan airline was filled with delegates from all over the world traveling to the NAM meeting, along with a few Nicaraguan foreign ministry hosts on the flight to greet us. I was acquainted with a number of the African delegates from the liberation movements. Along with the free drinks served on the flight, I opened the Kahlua to share with my seatmates.

I was buzzed for much of the conference. Having been sober for nearly

eight years, I did not have to drink much to be drunk. No one appeared to
notice, though, since nearly everyone else was drinking at receptions and din-
ners. Bill Means, Vernon Bellecourt, and Tony Gonzales were there for the
Treaty Council and American Indian Movement, but they did not comment
about my drinking, probably because I did not drink in their presence. We
alcoholics can be very canny about when and where we drink. The Guatemalan Mayan delegation invited the IITC people and me to meet with them, a
meeting that turned out to be a ceremony honoring me for my work on their
behalf at the UN. They presented me with a beautiful handwoven Mayan
blouse to mark the occasion. After the meeting, the IITC men tried to take it
away from me "for the organization," but I refused, pointing out that I was
no longer a part of their organization, and that I had done the work for which
they had received unearned credit. Most likely, I would not have stood them
down had I been sober.

The meetings themselves were stimulating. There were serious discussions
of the Reagan administration's threats of a "first strike" use of nuclear weapons and its ongoing use of proxies in wars against Nicaragua, Angola, and
Mozambique, as well as its increased support for the South African apartheid
regime and the Israeli occupation of Palestine. Even the insipid Carter-initi-
ated Camp David Accords had ceased to be US policy following Israel's invasion of Lebanon and its attacks on the Palestinian refugee camps there. US
support for recruiting fanatic Islamists from Saudi Arabia, Egypt, and other
countries into the CIA-created Mujahadeen movement in Afghanistan was a
cause of serious concern for the Arab delegates. They were prescient in realizing that a unified, mobile, and armed group of fundamentalist Islamic terrorists would be a threat to Muslim and Western countries alike, much more so
than the mullahs of Iran. As part of the AAPSO delegation, I was well aware
of the danger, since the Egyptian head of the organization had recently been
assassinated by Islamists. Finally, the endless US sanctions and covert actions
against Cuba were taken up and denounced. None of us even guessed that
during the year just beginning the United States would bomb Tripoli, Libya,
and invade Grenada, destroying the New Jewel Movement, although both the
Libyan and Grenadan delegations raised the issues of US sanctions and covert
actions against their countries.

The Treaty Council delegation and I, representing AAPSO, lobbied delegates to support indigenous initiatives in the United Nations. At the top of our agenda was our opposition to a new initiative proposed by the Spanish, Italian, Vatican, and US governments to acknowledge the five-hundredth anniversary of the "encounter" of Europe and the Americas in the form of the landing of Columbus on October 12, 1492, by celebrating that event in the United Nations in 1992. Since 1977, we had been calling for October 12 to be declared a day of mourning for the indigenous peoples of the Western Hemisphere, and for 1992 to be declared the UN year of mourning. I had been in the General Assembly meeting in October when Spain presented the "encounter" proposal. I was shocked by it, then disgusted when the Irish and the Norwegian ambassadors teased the Spanish that their countries had instead been the first to "discover America." After half an hour of general hilarity, one of the African delegates suddenly stood up and walked out of the room, followed by all the other African representatives. A recess was called, and the Western European and North American delegates appeared dazed and confused. I heard one say, "Why on earth would Africans even be interested in the issue?" When the African bloc returned an hour later, its elected spokesperson read a statement that condemned the call to celebrate the onset of "colonialism, the transatlantic slave trade, and genocide" in the halls of the United Nations.

That killed the proposal for the time being, but it did not faze the supporters. The Vatican even wanted to expand the concept of the Columbian "encounter" to include a phrase about the "gift" of bringing Christianity to the heathens. During the decade that followed, Spain, the Vatican, Italy, the United States, and all the Latin American countries they could bribe brought full pressure on the African states to agree, but they never budged. Only Cuba among the Latin American states refused to participate in the project; unfortunately, Nicaragua did. Meanwhile, the international indigenous movement and local indigenous groups of the Western Hemisphere opposed it and insisted on a declaration of a year of mourning. We won in the end. To pacify Spain and the Vatican for their total defeat, 1993 rather than 1992 was named the "UN Year for the World's Indigenous Peoples," followed by a UN Decade (1995–2004) of the same name. Rigoberta Menchú was appointed UN special ambassador for the year and the decade, and she was given the 1992 Nobel Peace Prize, which she accepted in the name of the indigenous peoples of the Americas and the world. The Non-Aligned Movement, and especially the southern African states and liberation movements, were thus critical to the advancement of indigenous peoples within the UN system.

At the Managua conference, Comandantes Lumberto Campbell and William Ramírez, the two commanders of eastern Nicaragua, arranged for the Treaty Council delegation and me to travel overland to Puerto Cabezas, on the edge of the war zone. We would visit the new settlements for the Miskitus and Sumus who had been evacuated from the border region, and also meet Miskitu prisoners who had been captured in fighting and ask questions of the people and the Sandinista authorities. I was the only one of the four of us who had visited the border villages before the residents were relocated, and I looked forward to seeing people I had met eighteen months before. Lumberto and William also took me aside and asked me why I had not come to work in the Miskitia as I had promised. I told them that Galio Gurdián had called and told me not to come.

Clearly, the Treaty Council guys—Bill Means, Vernon Bellecourt, and Tony Gonzales—were not pleased having me along, nor was Galio Gurdián, but the *comandantes* insisted. We traveled in two Toyota four-wheel-drive vehicles—the Jeep types—my male comrades in one jeep with Galio Gurdián, and I the only passenger in the other one with Julio Rocha, a *subcomandante* to Comandante Ramírez. It was a long and intense trip, and Julio was an excellent guide to every detail.

The overland road had been built since my 1981 stay. It was dirt and not passable in many parts during the rainy season, but it was dry at this time of the year. We stopped in Matagalpa, which I had visited in 1981 with the trade union delegation, but from there to the coast was all new territory for me. After Jinotega, we were in mountainous terrain, full of Sandinista soldiers, the road strung out as close as five miles from the Contra-infested border with Honduras. Mine sweepers walked ahead of us, making progress slow, along with obligatory stops at military checkpoints. At each checkpoint, though, we were able to get out of the vehicles and talk to the soldiers. One told me that he would be happy when the US stopped sending mercenaries to kill Nicaraguans because he wanted to go to the university and "learn all the languages of the world—Miskitu, Sumu, Rama, and Creole," the latter meaning English. He was naming only Nicaraguan languages, but that was a completely new world for a child of the Managua poor and illiterate. On my previous visits I had not met many soldiers, mostly commanders and officers, but on that drive I talked with hundreds of the least militaristic soldiers I had ever met. All the officers had been Sandinista guerrillas, many of them poets, writers, artists, and teachers before they became guerrillas. The relationship of officer and soldier was more like teacher to student, very kind, patient, and supportive, none of the barking and terrorizing of recruits characteristic of US military training. It broke my heart to think that many of those sweet and idealistic young people would be killed by "Washington bullets," as the British punk group The Clash put it.

All along the road, handmade signs stuck out of the ground like wooden flowers: "Welcome to Vietnam." The whole experience had a profound effect on Bill Means and Tony Gonzales, who had been combat soldiers in Vietnam. Everything reminded them of Vietnam—maybe in part because of their fear of that kind of war happening again. I saw tears leaking from their eyes more than once.

On January 21, we stopped at the mining town of La Rosita, which had been transformed into a center of revolutionary resistance. Using La Rosita as our base, we visited each of the settlements the Sandinistas had created—Wasimona, Truslaya, Sasha, Sumubila, and Columbus—over several days. I had never before visited a refugee camp, but once I had I realized that Tasba Pri was just that, only far better than most. I was relieved to find that the Sandinista authorities did not regard the situation as permanent, and that the displaced Miskitus fully expected to return to their Río Coco homes once conflict ceased. Like all refugees that I would meet over the next six years, they longed for their ancestral villages and they missed neighbors and relatives who had fled across the river to Honduras when fighting began.

Each of the settlements contained contiguous Río Coco villages; within each settlement, houses were arranged by village and by neighborhoods within villages. At first, the people had lived in tents, but now each family had a small wooden house with a zinc roof. They had individual and communal gardens and had become self-subsistent in basic foods. There were sports teams, crafts workshops, schools, churches, clinics, all bare-bones, of course, but in fact the people were physically better off in many ways than they had been in their river villages. Yet as river people, with many also from areas near the Caribbean, they missed fishing and the freedom of movement it allowed. Less than three years later, they were able to return home and rebuild, taking their dismantled settlement houses and roofs with them.

I found people I had met on my 1981 visit to the Río Coco villages. Word had spread in the settlements that the Sandinistas had killed all their relatives and neighbors who had chosen to go to Honduras. I had no way of knowing for sure, of course, but I was certain that this was not the case. I took names and promised people that I would try to find out, but it took two years for me to gain access to the Honduran camps that were administered by World Relief (an arm of the fundamentalist Christian National Evangelical Association, based in Wheaton, Illinois—Ronald Reagan's hometown) with oversight by US ambassador John Negroponte and his wife.

After the Miskitu settlements we visited the resettled Sumus from the villages of Waspuk and Umbra in the upper Río Coco region. They lived in two settlements near La Rosita—Santo Tomás and Spanolito. The Sumu Indian organization SUKAWALA was more or less in charge of the camp. The people spoke freely and complained about the lack of educational materials in Sumu. Although all the Sumus also spoke Miskitu and Spanish, they preferred their mother tongue, and the initiatives for education in indigenous languages had been displaced by war. The Sumus were firm and vocal about returning home as soon as possible. They urged us to visit a real Sumu village, Fruta de Pan, and we did so.

Located in a mountainous rain forest above the Bambama River, Fruta de Pan had a Shangri-La feel to it. We had to leave our vehicles and cross the river in dugouts, then climb the mountain to reach the village. As in the Miskitu villages, the Moravian church was the center of all community life. There was no sign of Sandinista presence. The villagers had developed a poultry cooperative, but taking goods to market was difficult and dangerous because of the war. It was good to confirm that the Sandinistas were not interfering in villages where there was no military threat.

After finishing our tour of the settlements and villages, we drove to Puerto Cabezas, crossing the broad Río Wawa on the car ferry that moved by pulling a cable overhead. Although Puerto Cabezas was the largest town and capital of the northeastern region, on my last visit it had been quite small, with a population of two thousand. Now Puerto Cabezas had swelled to ten thousand people, including soldiers from the western region and more refugees from the border area, people who had relatives to stay with and did not wish to live in the settlements. There were few places to stay since the soldiers took up nearly all the rooms while barracks were being built.

We were given two tiny rooms, each with twin beds, in the same boarding house where I had stayed in 1981. Bill and Vernon took one room, leaving Tony and me to the other, but he balked. So I was taken to a women's police barracks on the beach and given a cot. The lights were always on, and Interior police constantly came in and went out for guard duty. AK-47s and Browning automatic sidearms, bandoliers, and bullet clips lined the walls and were scattered on the beds and floors. Despite the discomfort, it was interesting to talk with the women, as well as the men housed next door. Except for a few Miskitus, most of them were Spanish-speaking and far from their western Nicaraguan homes, and they said that they felt uncomfortable and unwelcome among the Miskitus. They were well informed about the region and were required to take daily classes in the Miskitu language. Their commander was José Gonzales, head of the Ministry of Interior in the region, who appeared to respect and admire the Miskitus, even the ones fighting against the Sandinistas. He believed that he could win them over if dialogue could be initiated, and he would be proven right within two years.

The Miskitus in the Interior forces were impressive. Jimmy Boppell was assigned to accompany us on our trips to nearby villages. One would not guess that Jimmy was Miskitu, or even Nicaraguan, since he was fair-skinned and had blond hair and blue eyes, a throwback, it seems, to a US Marine getting into the bloodline during the 1920s. Other members of his immediate and extended family were dark, including his cousin Armstrong Wiggins, the Miskitu exile on the staff of the Indian Law Resource Center. Both Jimmy and Wiggins were from the Miskitu village of Karata. I learned more about Wiggins from Jimmy, who was a decade younger than Wiggins but remembered well the period when Wiggins was president of Karata, 1974–76, during which time he had collaborated with the Somoza regime. Wiggins had left Karata to go on scholarship to the University of Wisconsin and returned to work for the US embassy in Managua. Spending most of three days in

Jimmy's company, we became his admirers. He was dedicated to the freedom and self-determination of the Miskitu people and believed that the Sandinista revolution was the means to achieve that goal. But the pro-Contra Miskitu guerrillas marked every Miskitu who worked with the Sandinistas for death. Not all were killed, but two years later Jimmy was, after being brutally tortured, perhaps for days.

I had intended to stay only one week in Nicaragua, but the trip turned into nearly three weeks. I had only a few days in San Francisco before I flew to Geneva for the United Nations Commission on Human Rights, a grueling six-week-long meeting.

During the 1981 Commission, I had become friends with Jelka, a young woman born in Yugoslavia but raised in Cleveland, Ohio, where her father had taught. When her father died, the family returned to Zagreb. Jelka had gone to Geneva to work at the International Labor Organization (ILO) and invited me to stay with her during the Commission. I was pleased to not have to intrude once more on my friend Lee's life. Besides, Jelka had a prize apartment in a landmark eighteenth-century building on the cobbled main street, Grand Rue, of the walled old town, next door to what had been the home of Jean-Jacques Rousseau. It was large enough for the two of us, with its tiny living room, one bedroom, small kitchen, and study filled with Jelka's books and a table that took up all the floor space. The living room was my room. Not until I was settled into the place did I realize that Jelka had hundreds of friends who would drop by at any hour, many of them staying over, some for days. It was a never-ending party, except for the few days when Jelka's mother visited from Zagreb. The study became the workroom for me and my Guatemalan comrades, Rigoberta Menchú and Pablo Ceto. They often stayed over as well. Jelka was always cheerful and generous, driving us to the Palais every day, buying groceries and wine, lots of wine. During those weeks, I returned to drinking one to two bottles of wine a day, always half-drunk, drunk, or hung over.

Yet we worked tirelessly on the Guatemalan resolution. A dozen or so Guatemalan representatives had come from the four organizations, most of them from ORPA, so that nearly as much energy was expended on internal

discussion as on lobbying the delegates. I developed a good working relationship with the president of the Commission, Ambassador Otunu from Uganda. He supported the idea of appointing a special rapporteur on the human
rights situation in Guatemala, but the government of Guatemala, backed by
the United States, was opposed to it. Had it not been for Rigoberta's high-profile personality and effective work at the General Assembly (most of the same
representatives were now in Geneva), we would have failed. As it was, what
we got was a double-edged sword. We compiled lists of names as possible
appointees, which Otunu would present to the Guatemalan government, and
which they of course would veto. Finally, toward the end of the Commission, the US and Britain came up with Viscount Colville of Culross, and the
Guatemalan government agreed. From the minute he took the post through
its expiration in 1986, Lord Colville saw his role as defending the Guatemalan
government to the world community. He was worse than useless. Rigoberta,
Frank LaRue, and I met with him several times, and each time he scarcely
tolerated us. We had invested so much energy in that session, all for such
rotten results.

   I was exhausted from stress and lack of sleep, bloated from drinking, stuck
with a constant hack from chain-smoking. I decided to stay an extra week
and go to Valmont in nearby Montreux to quit smoking and drinking. Valmont is a Swiss health clinic, of which there are many, the one in Davos made
famous by Thomas Mann's novel *The Magic Mountain*. I wanted to go to a
magic mountain. Luckily, they had one room for $90 a day, which included
meals, consultation daily with a doctor, and some massage and mineral water treatments. The clinic consisted of one medieval mansion, with terraces,
large parlors and dining rooms, and a library. Although less than a mile up
from Montreux, it seemed remote. It overlooked the lake, and the manicured
grounds had flower gardens (the first day of spring passed while I was there),
paved walking paths and benches with scenic outlooks, and a small teashop
nearby. I never took my meals in the dining room, rather in my room, first
because I wanted to be alone, but also because wine was served in the dining
room. I was the only English-speaking guest, but the Swiss employees spoke
English. Most of the guests were twice my age. I felt transported to another
century. I slept around the clock for the first two days, except to take my tray
of food, which I did not always eat. On the third day, I began taking walks and

having tea at the teashop, reading in Valmont's small library—the only books in English being old leather-bound novels of Henry James. It was so nice to rest, read, and walk. I could not recall the last time I had experienced such leisure and solitude.

On the last evening at Valmont, I went to an ornate lounge I had not visited, where there was a television set. There on the screen was a picture of Marianella Garcia Villas, a founder of the civilian Salvadoran human rights group. She had documented human rights abuses in El Salvador and presented them at the United Nations, and she was beloved to all of us who were doing human rights work. She had not shown up for the Commission as was expected. Guillermo Ungo, who was representing the Salvadoran opposition at the Commission, had become concerned when he was unable to reach her. He said that she had found evidence that the Salvadoran military was using napalm and white phosphorus—supplied by the Reagan administration—against civilians in rural El Salvador. She was scheduled to present those charges at the Commission—and now her maimed body had been found in El Salvador.

During April 1983, while I was working on publication of the third issue of *Indigenous World*, I had speaking engagements that took me through California as well as to Albuquerque, Denver, Nashville, and Washington, D.C. In Washington I spoke on a panel on women and the law, but I stayed on a week in order to meet with Frank LaRue, Rigoberta, and Rigoberta's boyfriend and comrade, Domingo (Mingo) Hernández Ixcoy, who was also Quiche Mayan, and active in CUC and the EGP. Although we did not discuss it, we all were concerned about the EGP's military actions, which may have enflamed the Guatemalan military's war of annihilation against the Mayan communities. These rumblings would remain internal for another year before precipitating a bitter split in the EGP.

But our immediate concern was the situation of the Mayan refugees in Chiapas. The Mexican government, under the new president, Miguel de la Madrid Hurtado, was militarizing the border with Guatemala, preventing refugees from entering, and rumored to be forcing refugees back across the border to certain death. This was causing uproar among Mexican students and intellectuals, who were supporting the liberation movements in Central America as well as opposing US intervention, particularly against the Sandinistas. Rigoberta and Mingo urged me to meet them in Mexico City to arrange a visit to the refugees in Chiapas, many of whom were living under private protection.

I spent two weeks in mid-June 1983 with Rigoberta, Mingo, Pablo Ceto, and many other Mayan exiles in Mexico City, talking and brainstorming. We attended a Mexican trade union meeting to lobby for a resolution on Guatemalan refugees, and I accompanied them to a meeting with Congressman Stephen Solarz and to the International Press Club, where they made a presentation. I met with Mexican journalist Sergio Aguayo, who had written a series of investigative articles condemning the Mexican government's resistance to welcoming war refugees from Guatemala, accusing it of being racist against Indians.

Finally, Pablo Ceto gave me instructions to meet a priest in Mexico City, who in turn gave me sealed letters of introduction for me to show to a list he provided of nuns and priests in Chiapas. In addition to visiting the clandestine refugee centers, the CUC people also asked me to drive along the border of Chiapas and Guatemala all the way to the Pacific Ocean in order to assess whether the Mexican military had demilitarized the border. I had never been to that part of Mexico.

I flew to Tuxla Gutiérrez, the capitol of Chiapas, and rented a Mexican VW bug. I was to drop the car four days later at the airport in Tapachula, a city near the border close to the Pacific, and fly back to Mexico City from there. I drove almost four hundred miles in that little car, which reminded me of a mountain goat. It had the personality, too, or perhaps I saw a bit of myself in the car. I found out, for example, that its windshield wipers did not function in the middle of a rainstorm while I was driving on a mountainous dirt road. My head out the window, I kept on going. Stubborn, both of us.

My first stop was San Cristóbal de las Casas, the Spanish colonial religious center deep in the heart of Mayan country that Cortez had granted to the Spanish bishop Bartolomé de las Casas as an *encomienda* (meaning a territory along with all the indigenous residents within its bounds), second in size and population only to Cortez's self-granted *encomienda* in central Mexico. In the immediate area around San Cristóbal live the Tzeltal-Tzotzil Mayans. They were unrelated to and lived in a different region of Chiapas from the Guatemalan Mayan refugees.

My instructions from the priest in Mexico City were to present a sealed letter of introduction to a priest in San Cristóbal, whom I was to meet in front of the cathedral at 11 p.m. on the night of my arrival. That priest would then tell me where to go from there.

I arrived in San Cristóbal at 6 p.m. and checked into a motel, ate dinner, and waited until the appointed hour. I was at the cathedral steps at 11 p.m., but no one was there or anywhere to be seen. It was eerie with the wind whipping around me, creating a ghostly whine, so that I began imagining the voices of Mayan survivors driven to Bishop las Casas for protection in the wake of Spanish soldiers burning their villages and crops, raping women, plunging swords into babies, their armored Presa Canario war dogs, trained to relish human flesh, eating the wounded. The survivors, seeking refuge from that long-ago genocide, fell into the arms of the other Spanish colonial institution, the Church, where they were made into obedient servants and laborers for las Casas' *encomienda*, making his Dominican order wealthy.

With these ghosts of colonialism beginning to obsess me, I felt like leaving. Why should I trust priests? But before I could leave, a man in regular clothing (at that time, priests and nuns were forbidden by Mexican law to wear clerical garb in public) appeared out of the dark at midnight and told me to follow him.

We walked to his car parked nearby and began driving on increasingly narrow, curving, and unpaved roads going uphill. I was perplexed because I knew from my Guatemalan exile friends that the refugees were being housed clandestinely in towns far from San Cristóbal. After driving in silence for a while, the priest apologized for being late and explained that he had had to make some arrangements. "I understand that you work for international rights of the indigenous peoples. I want you to meet some friends so that you may understand what is going on in Mexico."

We stopped on a dirt road and walked about a mile along a path to a small clearing, where a dozen or so young men and women sat in a circle around a small fire, each cradling US military M-16s. I listened to them tell me their ideas and goals for their struggle, and they asked me many questions about the international indigenous movement and about Native peoples in the

United States. We talked until the sky began to lighten, then they got up and disappeared into the rain forest.

These revolutionaries would, a decade later, become known to the world as the Zapatistas. During all those years of the 1980s and early 1990s, while one after another political/military liberation movement was quieted or crushed, its revolution declared dead, I thought about those young Mayans and wondered what had happened to them, hoping they were still in the mountains, still organizing, still planning. When I heard the news of the Chiapas uprising on New Year's Day, 1994, I knew it must be them. When I visited the Zapatista-controlled villages in Chiapas in 1998, I would recognize the road we had taken that night fifteen years earlier.

Bleary-eyed from little sleep but full of energy from the meeting, I drove to the next stop on my quest, Comitán, a town closer to the Guatemalan border. There I met a nun in the designated place and handed over her letter. To my surprise, she was from the US, a very serious woman, large-boned, fast-moving and fast-talking. She hustled me into my car while she got in the passenger seat and navigated me to the dozen or so clandestine centers that housed the Guatemalan Mayan refugees. She allowed me to take pictures and even posed the women who were weaving beautiful and colorful traditional *trajes*. Every center was a workshop of one kind or another—weaving, wood carving, furniture making, printing—the products of which would be taken to Oaxaca and other big tourist market centers to sell. The nun wanted to make certain that the refugees did not become dependent and docile, that they be self-sufficient economically. They even raised their own food in one location and operated a clinic in another. It was an impressive operation, completely hidden from the authorities and the public eye. My host gave me directions to several other small centers in nearby Las Margaritas.

Having met with Mayan refugees and confirmed their stories, I came to the second part of my quest—to check out the border for signs of the Mexican or Guatemalan military, a potentially dangerous task. Before embarking on it, I bought two pint bottles of tequila and a carton of cigarettes, breaking my three-month abstention from both.

I drove west on Mexican Highway 211, which runs parallel to the border, and turned south at every crossroads I came to. Some turnoffs dead-ended, and it was not clear if I had crossed the border or not. Most of them led to an isolated border checkpoint, several of which had no one manning them, others with only one or two Mexican border police who were friendly and helpful, not even asking for my papers. They would have allowed me to cross into Guatemala, but I did not want to. Then I ran into a terrible rainstorm and made it out of that crisis, I am certain, only by pure luck and drunkenness. The dirt mountain road was sliding away as I drove it, sometimes narrowing down to the width of the VW. I arrived in the coastal border city of Tapachula at night, drunk, soaked, and exhausted. But I could return with the good news that the two armies had pulled back from the border, thanks to Mexican public pressure.

I checked into the first hotel I found in Tapachula, a glitzy tropical paradise filled with what appeared to be gangsters, guns strewn everywhere. Later I would learn that it was a gun- and drug-trafficking town, and that the hotel was indeed a gangster hangout. I was too tired to go anywhere else, so I took a room, a very large and vulgarly fancy one, with a sliding door to the swimming pool and poolside dining. I was starving and out of tequila, so I ate at the restaurant, eavesdropping on some exotic discussions far removed from the realities of the Mayan refugee camps.

The following morning, I found the airport, checked in the car, and flew to Mexico City to report my findings. A few months later, thanks to widespread campaigns by Mexican citizens, the government authorized the UN refugee agency (UNHCR) to construct refugee camps in Yucatán and welcomed the Guatemalan Mayan refugees.

11

International Law— and International Lawlessness

After the Chiapas trip, and especially after meeting the Zapatistas, I realized that I needed to stop everything and figure out how I might be most effective in the long term. I did not consider reentering an alcohol recovery program, although I did not drink for two months after that harrowing journey along the Guatemalan/Mexican border. I was doing what alcoholics do—denying and justifying my drinking, telling myself I could stop anytime I wanted to, and proving that by doing so for months at a time. But I did realize that I had in the past two years become my own rapid response network, reacting instead of acting, moving without political direction.

Teaching, which I had long considered my passion and my calling, was no longer central to my identity; it had become a means of income to do other things. I desperately wanted to continue writing, to begin a new book, but I now felt that writing was an unaffordable luxury in the face of the imperialist aggression and proto-fascism of the Reagan administration. I returned to the vow I had made when Reagan was elected: to fight the Contras and help prevent the US from invading Nicaragua.

What troubled me was that, over the past year, I had followed no consistent path in implementing my commitment. My work at the UN on international indigenous rights had been important, but had little to do with stopping US intervention in Nicaragua. In fact, though I was technically still connected to AAPSO, I felt as if I had acted at the UN as a free agent, working for whatever group or proposal seemed most important at the moment. Having been blocked by Galio Gurdián from working with CIDCA, the research institute of the Ministry for the Atlantic Coast, in the Miskitia, I had assisted the Guatemalan struggle for a year, but there too I had no clear role. Above all, my link with the American Indian Movement and the International Indian Treaty Council was frayed—that was clear on the trip with their leaders to Puerto Cabezas in January. I needed some kind of organizational connection and clear purpose for my activism. I joined a group in the San Francisco Bay Area—Line of March, a kind of Marxist think tank that also organized activities and actions and published a newsletter and a journal. It was good to be able to anchor my work in the context of others who were doing labor, immigrant, and community organizing, with a fine group of veteran left organizers as well as the many young people in the organization. But I was away from the Bay Area for much of the time, and I realized that my international work needed other connections to become more coherent.

In May and June 1983, in between giving talks in various parts of the country and publishing another issue of *Indigenous World*, I gave considerable thought to this situation and came to a decision. Rather than thinking of activism and diplomacy as two separate spheres, I would try to combine them in a concerted and purposeful way. I would become an expert in international law, particularly human rights law, and lobby more effectively at the UN to aid indigenous groups and revolutionary organizations. As a first step, I decided to apply, along with Chockie Cottier, who was director of the San Francisco American Indian Center, for United Nations consultative status for nongovernmental organizations for an organization we named the Indigenous World Association. The application deadline was June 1983, to be considered two years later by the UN governmental committee that met biannually. While waiting for that application to be approved, I decided to fill in what I knew to be the large gaps in my knowledge of international law, especially humanitarian law (such as the laws of war). I also wanted to learn more about the regional systems—the Organization of American States, the European system, and the Organization of African Unity.

Justice Frank Newman, the former Boalt Hall School of Law professor and my friend, urged me to study at the International Institute of Human Rights in Strasbourg, which had begun granting degrees in 1970. His colleague at

Santa Clara School of Law, Dinah Shelton, organized a group each year from the United States to participate in the annual month-long intensive course. If accepted, a participant could choose to take exams for the prestigious degree, a *diplôme* of international and comparative human rights law, or not. Ordinarily, you were expected to take two consecutive courses over two years to go forward for the degree. I applied and was accepted for the July 1983 course.

The institute was housed on the campus of the University of Strasbourg, and participants in the course stayed in university dormitories. Classes were held in the Faculty of Law. The cost for food and lodging for the month was $100, along with a $100 registration fee, making it amazingly affordable. (The French government largely subsidized the institute.) Strasbourg is the capital of that long-disputed province of Alsace, where the majority of the population speaks German; a Nazi death camp, now a museum, looms on the city's outskirts. I immediately felt that I was in an occupied city even though there were no soldiers. Before arriving, I had not reflected on Strasbourg as a place, but I was haunted by the echoes of two world wars in which this place had been one of the spoils and losses of German aggression.

I often passed by a Goethe statue and sometimes sat on a bench contemplating his work, which had influenced me as a young woman, not only during my university studies, but also as a child in western Oklahoma hearing his poetry recited by neighboring German farmers. I even learned the German words to a few poems: *Wer geht so spät durch nacht und wendt/das est der vater mit seinem kindt*; and, recalling Goethe, the reality dawned on me that Strasbourg was deeply German in language and culture. Few citizens spoke English, and the German speakers, who were largely blue-collar workers, small shopkeepers, and beer hall owners, refused to speak French, while the French speakers, who made up the upper class and ran the government, did not know a word of German. All my fellow students appeared oblivious to this history and reality, but it haunted me for the whole month I was there, and I never felt at ease enjoying the Alsace cuisine and wine for which the province is famous.

But Strasbourg was a good place to study international law, particularly the European system, because located there were the European Parliament, the Council of Europe, and the European Court and Commission for Human Rights, a judicial body of the Council of Europe. These were the building blocks for what would become the European Union. Our training in that part of the course included hands-on observation of those bodies in action.

The US contingent of participants that Dinah Shelton chose was around half a dozen, a tiny number among the more than two hundred participants who came from all over the world, even from Vietnam, Nepal, and the People's Republic of China. Many of the African participants worked in their foreign ministries and were sent by their governments for training in human rights law. A few were from national liberation movements, such as José Ramos Horta, who was in exile from East Timor, the former Portuguese colony that had declared its independence once the Portuguese withdrew in 1975 and was quickly annexed by Indonesia (after President Gerald Ford and Secretary of State Henry Kissinger gave General Suharto the green light to invade). East Timor would receive its independence only in 2002, after a long struggle that cost a quarter of a million Timorese lives. During that two-decade-long resistance, José, based in the Mozambique mission in New York, represented the East Timorese liberation movement at the UN. From 1985, when the Indigenous World Association received UN credentials, to 1989, José registered with our organization. Following independence, he became East Timor's foreign minister, after having picked up the Nobel Peace Prize along the way. But in 1983, when I met him, he and East Timor's struggles were little known.

One of the gifts of the course was learning about human rights issues in a nonlobbying situation. Every evening after dinner I took a walk in the park of the Orangerie, then headed to the dormitory recreation room to listen to the heated discussions that took place there. Political enemies who would not have talked with their adversaries in other situations did so there. I doubt that they changed each other's minds, but for the rest of us it was a rich learning opportunity. One participant was a government representative from Ethiopia; another was an Eritrean. At that time, a bloody civil war was being waged between what now are two separate countries. But in Strasbourg, these two opponents debated, and we listened. A Sherpa man from Nepal, who was studying law in Yugoslavia, informed us about an indigenous insurgency against the royal family. Moroccan and Algerian participants argued about the status of the Western Sahara, the Moroccan defending his government's claim to the former Spanish territory while the Algerian supported the Polisario insurgents fighting for an independent state. Participants from Greece and Turkey debated the issue of Cyprus, whose Greek (Christian) and Turkish (Muslim) communities were deeply divided. I argued about ethnic conflict with a Tamil lawyer from Sri Lanka, who predicted the civil war that would explode the following year. Later I would meet him as a representative of the insurgent Tamil Tigers.

The participant I became closest to (and lifelong friends with) was Julia Messina, who worked for the United Nations High Commissioner for Refugees (UNHCR), based in Geneva. She was married to an official in charge of Latin America at UNHCR, Leonardo Franco, who had been a political exile from Argentina until the generals were ousted in 1982. Through that friendship, I was able the following year to gain admission to visit the Miskitu refugees in the Honduran refugee camps. Julia also generously extended hospitality to me on many occasions in Geneva.

The course itself absorbed me. Having a good basis of experience in the UN system, I found it easy to quickly absorb the lectures and learn the class materials. The first lecturer was familiar to me: Theo van Boven, the former director of human rights at the UN, who had helped create the Working Group on the rights of indigenous peoples.

The deadline for deciding to go for the *diplôme* was the end of the second week. I had not applied with the thought of doing that, but after the first week I felt capable of passing, and the degree gave me a goal to work toward. Only seventeen others declared. For the next two weeks, I studied in the library during every minute I was not in class, eating, or sleeping.

A full day was allocated for the written exam, which required a long, analytical essay in response to one question. Eleven of eighteen of us passed the written exam and were allowed to take the oral examination. The entire faculty sat on the committee and could ask any question for three hours. Those exams were as demanding as my doctoral exams, but I was one of six who received the *diplôme*.

From Strasbourg, I took the train to Geneva to begin six weeks of meetings. My friend Lorraine Ruffing had left me a three-story, two-hundred-year-old farmhouse in Vallery, a tiny French farming community about thirty miles from Geneva, to house- and dog-sit. The commute was difficult, especially since I had to go through customs twice daily, with trucks often backed up for miles at the border. But it was a great luxury to have a place to myself, a car, and a sweet and devoted German shepherd.

The one-week Working Group on Indigenous Peoples (WGIP) overlapped the first week of a two-week conference on racism that marked the end of the UN's first Decade to Combat Racism, Racial Discrimination, and Apartheid. Following those meetings, the four-week Sub-Commission on Human Rights met; its last two weeks, in turn, overlapped a conference on the "Question of Palestine." The Working Group and the Sub-Commission met in the old Palais building, while the two special conferences convened in the newer UNCTAD building, which, although attached, required a very long walk that was slowed to a snail's pace by unprecedented security checkpoints along the way. In preparation for and during the conference on Palestine, the Swiss army was out in full force, and the UN grounds were cordoned with concertina wire while tanks were hoisted to the roofs of the buildings.

These security measures were to protect Palestinian officials, most notably Yasser Arafat, from Israel's assassination attempts. Several PLO diplomats in various countries had been assassinated during the previous year. Rafic Khouri, the main representative of the PLO to the UN in Geneva, was required to stay off buses and taxis; he walked everywhere, usually alone, although I sometimes walked with him. The year before, Israel had invaded Lebanon, where the Palestine Liberation Organization had its political headquarters and thriving businesses in the Palestinian refugee camps. Two months after the conference, Arafat and the PLO would be driven out of Lebanon and relocated in Tunisia (until the Oslo accords of 1993 brought them to the West Bank).

Israel and the Reagan administration boycotted both the racism conference and the Palestine conference, the latter having been organized to entice the United States to participate in the racism conference, which the Carter administration had boycotted in 1978. It did not work. Ostensibly, both the Carter and Reagan administrations cited the inclusion of Zionism as a form of racism in the UN Decade to Combat Racism as the reason for their boycotts. Many of us were convinced that the United States did not want its own institutionalized racism to be discussed, nor did it want to discuss apartheid, not even to tout its own policy of "constructive engagement" with the South

African regime. While the rest of the world called for an economic boycott of South Africa and the UN disallowed South Africa from taking its UN seat, the United States called the African National Congress "communists" and "terrorists," claiming that the apartheid regime was "making progress."

I had AAPSO credentials for all four meetings, but I was an active member of the AAPSO delegation to the conference on Palestine. I was surprised by the large nongovernmental delegation from Israel, which included former army officers and soldiers, many of whom had served long jail terms for opposing Israeli occupation of Palestinian territories acquired in the 1967 war and supported creation of a Palestinian state according to the 1947 UN partition plan. The Palestinian delegation was large and included Edward Said and other notable Palestinians. But I was most impressed by a number of brilliant women on the PLO delegation, none of them wearing head scarves, most of them secular, whether from Muslim or Christian families. My biggest surprise was meeting Alfred M. Lilienthal, whose 1953 book *What Price Israel?* I had read as a first-year college student at Oklahoma University during the Suez Crisis. I carried my old copy of that book—given to me by a Palestinian student—around for years as a reference to the Middle East.

As we gathered on the fourth day of the conference, news came that a Korean Air Lines (KAL) passenger jumbo jet, oddly numbered 007, had been shot down by the Soviet Union in its airspace over the Pacific Ocean. This caused a considerable stir among the participants and government delegates, fearing that the Reagan administration would unleash nuclear war in response. War was in the air in those days, with Reagan's threats and the reality of US proxy wars in Central America, Angola, Mozambique, and Afghanistan. And there we were, surrounded by heavily armed troops and tanks. The despair was palpable that day and the days after. Information about the event trickled in. The Soviets said that they had believed the plane was an unmanned US spy plane when they brought it down. They accused the United States of intentionally diverting the KAL airliner as it passed over Alaska into Soviet air space in order to test their air defenses. I thought that made sense, but it was also well known that Soviet monitoring technology was out of date. The Reagan administration needed to exaggerate Soviet military capability as an excuse to build Reagan's expensive and loony "Star Wars" missile defense system. In the end, the Reagan administration's refusal to allow supercomputer technology to be sold to the "evil empire" only made an accident such as the shooting down of the Korean plane, or even an accidental nuclear strike, far more likely.

I sobered up after this conference, which had been for me a month of heavy drinking, and for the next three months remained sober. I returned to teaching, published another issue of *Indigenous World*, and devoted myself to a new think tank conceived in Managua.

P olicy Alternatives for the Caribbean and Central America (PACCA) was formed in early 1983. Reagan had established by executive order the National Bipartisan Commission on Central America, better known as the Kissinger Commission, after its chairman, Henry Kissinger. Created on July 19, 1983, the fourth anniversary of the Sandinista Revolution, the Kissinger Commission was given six months to report on "the elements of a long-term United States policy that will best respond to the challenges of social, economic and democratic developments in the region, and to internal and external threats to its security and stability." Those opposed to US intervention in Central America believed that the Kissinger Commission had been established to provide credibility to the Reagan administration's Central America policy, which was coming under increasing congressional and public criticism. Indeed, at the end of its tenure the commission would recommend that US military assistance be significantly increased to the Salvadoran government; that the US continue its support for the Contras; and that the United States consider using force against the Sandinistas as a "last resort."

To counter the Kissinger Commission, the members of PACCA decided to write and present a series of position papers at a meeting set for October 20–22 in Washington, D.C., at the liberal Institute for Policy Studies. The main architect of PACCA was Xavier Gorostiaga, a Spanish (Basque) Jesuit who founded and directed the Nicaraguan Institute for Economic Studies (INIES) in Managua. Orlando Nuñez, the director of CIERA with whom I had worked in 1981, was the only Nicaraguan Sandinista involved in PACCA. Roger Burbach, a long-time researcher and writer on Latin America based in Berkeley, was PACCA's US coordinator. The rest of us were US academics, researchers, and writers, each with specific research areas. My task for the

October conference was to assess the situation and policy needs of the indigenous populations in Central America.

When the meeting was finally held, we were distracted from our work by the events leading up to the US military invasion of Grenada on October 25. Most of us knew Grenadan officials and found it difficult to believe that Maurice Bishop, the head of government, along with most of the government ministers, had been killed in a coup the week before led by Bernard Coard, the New Jewel minister who controlled the military. It would take years for the documentation of the US covert actions that provoked those murders to be compiled. On the final day of our meeting, Sunday, October 23, we heard the news that 240 US Marines had been killed in Beirut by an Islamic fundamentalist suicide bomber while they slept in their barracks. I observed that someone or some country would pay for it. Later, one of the participants, a journalist with State Department sources, brought in the information that the United States would invade Grenada on Monday, the next day. He turned out to be wrong—by one day. I proposed that the US citizens among us fly to Grenada—the civilian airport was still open—an activist response that might even prevent the invasion. We did not suspect then that the justification for invasion would be "rescuing American medical students" on the island, although they were in no danger. But no one agreed with me, observing correctly that the United States would pretend to have rescued us, or worse, would kill us and say the Grenadans did it. Yet it was shameful that no US journalists were on the ground at the time of the invasion and that none were allowed to accompany the Marines.

The invasion of Grenada—code name "Operation Urgent Fury"—marked a sharp change in US interventions in the past decades, harkening back instead to the pre–World War II pattern of "gunboat diplomacy," which began soon after the birth of the nation. The Marine anthem, beginning "From the halls of Montezuma to the shores of Tripoli," celebrated the invasion of Mexico in 1846 and the shelling of Tripoli (Libya) in North Africa "to open sea lanes for free trade." After World War II, the United Nations was founded on the principles of decolonization, disarmament, and nonintervention. In response, the US Central Intelligence Agency was established to do covertly what no longer could be done brazenly. Both the Korean and Vietnam wars began with covert operations that became all-out wars, neither won by the

United States. Many hoped that the humiliating loss in Vietnam would bring a change in US belligerence, but covert operations in Iran and Iraq, Afghanistan, southern Africa, and Latin America, and especially against Cuba and in Central America, continued without a pause. Apparently, however, these covert operations did not satisfy the Reagan administration, because Grenada marked a return to open US military aggression, with the Reagan administration "sending a message," as they like to put it.

Four days after the invasion of Grenada, I was in Houston for a three-day colloquium, "Ethnicities and Nations: Processes of Inter-Ethnic Relations in Latin America, Southeast Asia and the Pacific," organized by the Rothko Chapel, a cultural institution of the Schumberger family of Houston oil fame. My presentation was on the Miskitu situation in Nicaragua. I ended by saying that I believed the invasion of Grenada was very likely a stepping stone for invading and occupying the Miskitia of Nicaragua. After my talk, two middle-aged women approached me and invited me to lunch. One was Texas attorney Frances "Sissy" Farenthold, a former Texas state legislator, well known in the liberal wing of the Democratic Party. Sissy introduced the other woman as her cousin, Genevieve Vaughn. I was astonished when Gen said, "I want to publish everything you just said in a full-page ad in the Sunday *New York Times*." I laughed, but she said she was serious. I said I thought it would cost a lot. She asked how much, and although I had no idea, I said at least $5,000. She asked me to check when I returned and get back to her. I was right about the "at least $5,000"— the cost was $30,000, which I was certain would cause Gen to back off. But instead she sent a check. The ad appeared in the November 13, 1983, issue of the *Times*.

The top quarter of the full page was filled with a giant headline:

(Grenada was a dress rehearsal)

EARLY WARNING OF A U.S. PLAN TO INVADE & OCCUPY THE
MISKITU INDIAN REGION OF NICARAGUA

Two graphics broke up the long text—a map of the northeastern border region being attacked by the US-backed Contras, and a Sandinista poster depicting the east coast peoples. A longish text explained who the Miskitu were, described the "Operation Red Christmas" covert action of 1982, and entreated readers to send a cutout letter protesting US support of the Contras and arguing for nonintervention to George Schultz, then US secretary of state.

Just over a month later, on December 19, 1983, the predicted Contra offensive was launched, but as a psychological war rather than a military intervention. I believe the ad could well have been a factor in the Reagan administration's decision to continue to fight the war via proxies instead of sending US troops. Instead of launching a new military initiative, MISURA, a part of the Contras, was able to convince the entire population of the Miskitu town of Francia Sirpe, over twelve hundred people, to flee to the Honduran side of the border. The Francia Sirpe "Christmas exodus" was a propaganda coup for the administration: Nobel laureate Elie Wiesel trumpeted it as analogous to the Jewish exodus from Egypt. A filmmaker, Lee Shapiro, had accompanied the well-staged event and his footage was all over the television news programs. (Shapiro was an official of Causa International, a part of Reverend Moon's Unification Church, which financed and distributed the film.) From the footage, Shapiro created a one-hour documentary, "Nicaragua Was Our Home," which was later broadcast on PBS. He was killed in 1987 while doing the same kind of Moonie-CIA propaganda work in Afghanistan.

In a short time, the State Department had produced a six-page internal draft paper to develop its official interpretation of the mass exodus. The classified document, dated February 1984, was titled "Nicaraguan Repression of Miskito Indians: The Christmas Exodus." I did not see this document until nearly three years later, when I was able to obtain State Department documents through the Freedom of Information Act. Much of the wording in the classified internal paper later appeared as opinion columns and in newspaper articles in the months following the event. The draft paper makes clear that manipulation of refugees was the central strategy of the Reagan administration's attempts to discredit the Sandinistas: "Since the forced internal deportations began and other Sandinista violations of human rights intensified, thousands of Miskito Indians have sought a better way of life. They have 'voted with their feet,' with most of them going to Honduras." Regarding the staged "Christmas exodus," the draft paper tellingly states:

On December 19, 1983, the residents of the resettlement town of Francia Sirpe in northeastern Nicaragua attended Mass in a festive mood, knowing that plans had been made to depart to Honduras on the following day. According to the Indians, the Sandinistas were preparing to transplant the Indian population of Francia Sirpe to the mountainous region north of Managua.

The use of the term *resettlement town* to describe Francia Sirpe was interesting, implying that it was one of the settlements created two years earlier by the Sandinistas. But Francia Sirpe had not been created by the Sandinistas: it was built when Somoza forcibly resettled Miskitus from north of the Río Coco to south of the new border in 1960. Francia Sirpe was in fact distant from the border, and the Sandinistas had no plans to relocate its population. Before handing over the area to Honduras, Somoza had sent his National Guard into the disputed zone to force Miskitus south of the Río Coco—after all, they were cheap labor in the mines. Several settlements were established for those relocated Miskitus, one being Francia Sirpe, which was organized by French Capuchins and later by the Partners of Wisconsin. MISURA had made a false promise to these townspeople that they would be able to reacquire the lands they had lost north of the Río Coco, in what was now Honduras.

I had spent a day at Francia Sirpe in 1981, and the Miskitus had told me the story of that brutal forced relocation. The elders still longed to return to their ancestral land. No wonder they listened eagerly to Contra tales of taking back their homeland in what is now Honduras. No wonder they left Nicaragua so quickly and so joyfully. It seemed to me such a cruel story of deception.

12

Guide

New Year's Day 1984 dawned in Managua, and I had a hangover. I had started drinking again five days earlier in Tegucigalpa, Honduras. I had been invited to join a fact-finding tour of Central America that was dubbed the Women's Alternative to the Kissinger Commission. It was the brainchild of lawyer Sissy Farenthold of Houston and former New York member of Congress Bella Abzug, a longtime fighter for civil rights in general and women's rights in particular. Sissy had invited me to be the historian on the trip, and because I would be the only member of the delegation who had been to the countries we were to visit—Honduras, Nicaragua, and El Salvador. But at the last minute Sissy had to go to trial and didn't make the trip. I didn't know the others, and my role wasn't clear. The other members of the delegation were Faye Wattleton, then president of Planned Parenthood; Gloria Molina, the first Latina elected, in 1982, to the California State Legislature; Jessica Govea, a labor organizer for the United Farm Workers Union; an activist nun, Sister Maureen Fidler; Ramona Ripston of the Los Angeles office of the American Civil Liberties Union; Ann Bright, a colleague of Sissy's; Diane Ladd, the wonderful actress who starred in Martin Scorsese's *Alice Doesn't Live Here Anymore*; and Sonia Johnson, the 1984 Citizens Party's presidential candidate and a hero to me because of her outspoken leadership, including a hunger strike, during the late 1970s struggle for the Equal Rights Amendment (ERA) to the Constitution. Jacqueline Jackson, or, as she preferred to be called, Mrs. Jesse Jackson, was also a member of the delegation chosen by Sissy.

Unfortunately, Jackie Jackson and Bella Abzug made a combustible pair. Bella's dominance was challenged from day one by Jackie's presence: Bella had endorsed Walter Mondale, the anointed Democratic Party primary candidate for the 1984 presidential election, while Jesse Jackson had entered the race in late November 1983 to the annoyance of the Democratic Party establishment. Jesse Jackson was, at the time of our trip, on one of his publicity-grabbing missions, this one to negotiate the release of two African American airmen being held in Syria. That drama played out during our ten-day journey, creating a buzz around Jackie everywhere we went.

Jackie Jackson, who was always exceedingly dignified, polite, and charismatic, seemed to bring out the worst in Bella, a volatile personality who clearly was used to being the center of attention. To rein in Jackie, Bella enlisted Faye Wattleton, or perhaps Faye volunteered. Faye was the only other African American besides Jackie in the group, and she was a tall, elegant, young, intelligent, and independent woman, but she seemed to have virtually no sense of being African American, something that disgusted Jackie. The rest of us were like children in a dysfunctional family, walking on eggshells. I began drinking on the second day of the trip, making me reckless in my responses to the conflict. I was excited about Jesse's Rainbow Coalition and became Jackie's second, as Faye was Bella's, a part of the problem rather than helping to resolve it.

What at first appeared to be a manifestation of women competing with each other, indulging in decidedly unfeminist behavior, was actually an extension of the poisonous racial conflict that forms the template of social relations in the United States. Had I not been observing this scenario through Jackie's eyes, I doubt that I would have detected Bella's racism, not against black skin—Bella was not racist in that way—but against African American politics and identity with peoples of the colonized world.

In Tegucigalpa, we met with Contras, US embassy officials, Honduran government and military officials, a business leader, and representatives of Honduran opposition organizations, many in the large conference room at our hotel. The Contra political leadership of the Nicaraguan Democratic Front (FDN)—Adolfo Calero, Arturo Cruz, Alphonso Rubello, and Edgar Cham-

orro—came to our hotel to meet with us. Bella knew Chamorro, a former Jesuit, and chided him for being in such company. He appeared embarrassed. A
few months later, he broke with the Contras, denouncing CIA management,
including their issuance of a manual of terrorist tactics titled "Psychological Operations in Guerrilla Warfare." That manual infamously instructed the
Contra forces to "neutralize" Sandinista local leaders and to shoot informers,
and went on to coldly state, "The torture situation is a contest between the
subject and his tormentor."

However, the sleaziness of the CIA and FDN leaders paled in comparison
with the thugs occupying the US embassy in Tegucigalpa, headed by Ambassador John Negroponte, who had been groomed as an assistant to Henry
Kissinger during the Vietnam War. Honduran activists called him the "proconsul," that is, the real ruler of militarized Honduras. In our meeting at
the embassy we were submerged by a deluge of propaganda about the Francia Sirpe "exodus." I had informed members of our group about the obvious staging of this event and the lies told to the Miskitu townspeople, so we
were not interested in hearing more about it from the US embassy. Instead,
we questioned the embassy diplomats closely on the Contras and on human
rights abuses by the Honduran government, including the recent disappearance of a US citizen, a priest. They refused to answer our questions and referred us to the Honduran government, pretending to have no say in matters
concerning that state.

We then met with Honduran government and military officials, and
they stalled us. The most interesting meeting we had was with the head of
the Honduran business association, the Alliance for Progress of Honduras
(APROH). This association was actually an alliance of General Álvarez and
other right-wing military men with right-wing businessmen who wanted a
cut of the action in supporting the Contras. The leader, with no sense of
shame or hesitation, proudly told us about the handsome payments (he called
them "investments") Honduran businessmen were receiving from Reverend
Moon's Unification Church.

The Honduran activists we met with were a breath of fresh air. They came
to our hotel to tell us about the effects of the US military presence in Honduras. The previous denigrating nickname for their country, "Banana Republic," was quickly being superseded by "US stationary aircraft carrier." The

six-month US–Honduran war games ("Big Pine") in the Miskitu region of Honduras were winding down, leaving the country with two permanent US military bases. A third base had been planned on the north Caribbean coast of Honduras at Trujillo, but had been thwarted by the locals, the Garífunos. Professor Victor Meza, a Garífuno, was one of our guests and told us about the local uprising that stood up against the US empire.

The Garífunos, also known as Black Caribs, are descendants of the enslaved Africans from the Caribbean island of St. Vincent who successfully escaped into the mountains, merged with the indigenous Caribs, and forged their own society and language in the eighteenth century. In 1797 the British navy rounded up most of them and deported them to the Bay Islands off Honduras, and from there they expanded their settlements along the mainland coast of eastern Central America and built free Afro-Indian communities. In 1984 there were 77,000 Garífunos living in fifty-three Garífuno autonomous towns—six in Belize, two in Guatemala, two in Nicaragua, and forty-three in Honduras. Dr. Meza told us that his people were militantly independent, their oral history based on their successful struggle for freedom, and that they were generally left alone by Honduran authorities. The Honduran government had warned the US military not to set up a base in a Garífuno town, but the Reagan administration sent the Corps of Engineers there anyway to start construction. Thousands of locals responded by blocking their way, and the US had to withdraw.

This inspiring story of resistance was followed by another one. The young woman from a US solidarity group who served as our scheduler and translator in Honduras arranged for us to meet a group of landless farmers, mostly women, who were occupying land from which they had been evicted, land adjacent to a new US base. On the way there, we stopped on the road outside the base, got out, and took pictures, bringing ourselves to the attention of the Marine guards, who told us to leave. We yelled questions to them about what they were doing there. Meeting with the courageous women occupying the land, we experienced what was daily fare for them—intimidation and repression. After introductions in the middle of a field the women were attempting to plant, four US Huey helicopter gunships landed nearby. A Honduran officer approached us and ordered us to leave. We were certain that the orders had come from the US officers at the nearby base.

One of the purposes of our mission was to create publicity back in the United States, and, if possible, locally. The Honduran press was heavily censored, so we did not expect anything from it, but we were surprised that the dozens of US reporters and television crews that were based in Honduras were "unavailable" to meet with our delegation. It seems they were all following the "exodus" story.

We left Honduras for Managua and a reception quite different from the one we had received in Tegucigalpa. The Managua airport was full of local press and television journalists covering our arrival. Jesse Jackson was a hero in Nicaragua, and Jackie was greeted like a queen. I was also treated with warmth and attention, and was even touted as the next US ambassador to Nicaragua if Jesse won the election. The press swarmed around Jackie. I took a *Nuevo Diario* journalist I knew aside and quietly explained that Bella was the head of the delegation and to make sure that her photo was on the front page. It was, but unfortunately with Diane Ladd's name and description underneath. They had never heard of Bella Abzug, so the mixup was accidental, but Bella was furious.

This was not a good beginning, and the problems did not end with that gaffe. In a meeting the following morning, Foreign Minister Miguel D'Escoto and Vice-Minister Nora Astorga assumed that Jackie was our leader and appeared to know nothing about Bella. Bella was boiling mad. I could see that the young woman from the solidarity group who had scheduled our visit did not have close connections with the Sandinista leadership and did not understand Bella's importance. I suspected that she had sold our delegation—there were dozens of US groups visiting at any one time trying to get high-level meetings—based on Jackie's presence.

I decided that something had to be done to assuage Bella's ego. I feared that she might turn on the Sandinistas out of spite and use her high-profile status to denounce them. I had seen it happen more than once—US journalists and human rights activists, unable to get what they wanted or meet whom they wished in Nicaragua, would turn on them, as if the Sandinistas were vulnerable to blackmail for access. Unfortunately, they were.

I called my old friend, Walter "Chombo" Ferretti, who was head of the National Police under Comandante Tomás Borge, and told him the problem. I asked him to try to set up a meeting for our delegation with the *comandante,* and he agreed. Borge was the only living founder of the FSLN and was one of the nine FSLN directors who formed the collective governing executive. He was possibly the most powerful Sandinista leader, the oldest but also the most militant, and the most hated by the Reagan administration. I had only heard Borge speak on several occasions, and I did not know what to expect. As it turned out, I could never have dreamed of what he would do.

We first met with him in our hotel, the Intercontinental, where he had a suite for that purpose. It was a good, but formal, meeting in which we asked questions. He did, as I had asked Chombo to tell him, defer to Bella as the leader, having her sit beside him. I was pleased, and Bella swelled with pride.

The next day was New Year's Eve. Borge's assistant called me, inviting our group to be guests at Borge's New Year's Eve dinner party at the hotel. He then asked me very detailed questions about each member of our group—hair color, age, profession, and style of dress—which I assumed were for security because Borge was the number one target for assassination by the Contras. We gathered that evening in the large meeting room of the hotel at the appointed time. No one else was there. Soon, the *comandante* burst in, followed by a number of assistants bearing gifts for us. Then I realized what the questions had been about—each gift was perfectly selected for each woman. Borge first presented Bella with a handmade, handwoven Nicaraguan sun hat—Bella's hats were her trademark. Then he presented each gift along with a personal tribute for each of us. Jackie received a fine woven Nicaraguan hammock, "to hang in airports where she and Jesse could make love when they crossed paths." For Sonia, he had a book of poems he wrote while on hunger strike in prison, telling her how much he admired her courage, as he too had been through that ordeal. I received a Miskitu traditional bark rug, along with a tribute to my work and love for the Miskitu people. Each of us was amazed by Borge's knowledge of our better selves. Then we walked to the terrace by the pool where a feast awaited us. All evening we were Borge's special guests, and he never strayed far from our company. Every Sandinista leader passed through, meeting and talking with us.

I felt certain that the rest of our trip would go smoothly. We were to leave for San Salvador on January 2 and had New Year's Day free as a rest day. Yet for some reason Bella attacked Jackie that day. I was not present when it happened, and the women in our group who were there could not explain what had brought it on—an explosion in which Bella was out of control and screaming at Jackie, who did not respond. Within an hour, Jackie was on an airplane to Miami and home. Later she would tell me that she had called Tomás Borge, who had given her his private telephone number, and asked him to get her home that day. He had arranged it.

We left for San Salvador the day after that, Bella seemingly unshaken, even triumphant, that she had driven Jackie away. She was quite cheerful during our three days in El Salvador—while the rest of us were quiet and on guard not to become the next target. We stayed at the El Camino Hotel where the US press was based. Reporters and television newspeople had returned from the Honduran "exodus" show. Bella was in her element because she knew most of the journalists, and Julie Preston, who was correspondent for the *Boston Globe* (and later the *New York Times*), was her friend. In my opinion, we had far too many meetings with reporters, none of whom wrote anything about our delegation or the report we drafted and gave them on our last day in San Salvador.

Our first meeting was with the Jesuit deans and professors at the University of Central America in El Salvador—Ignacio Ellacuría, Segundo Montes, Amando López, Joaquín López y López, Juan Ramón Moreno, and Ignacio Martín-Baró. Always under threat, they were murdered in 1989, along with their housekeeper and her daughter, by the Salvadoran military. The US government apparently wanted to make sure that they were not involved in the peace process that had by then begun.

A few months before our visit, the army had murdered the internationally known and admired Marianella García Villas, president of the Salvadoran Human Rights Commission. The human rights office across the street from the cathedral where Archbishop Romero had been assassinated in 1980 was now nearly deserted. We met with a handful of nervous human rights workers before going to the army headquarters in downtown San Salvador to question General Vides-Casanova. To every question he responded with a sentence than contained the word "communists." No wonder the Reagan administration adored him. What amazed me was how the general and his high command could spend hours with eleven women from the United States. It must have been because the United States was running everything in El Salvador, and they didn't have anything better to do.

We had been able to obtain permission from the general to visit an imprisoned FMLN commander in the women's prison, Ilopango, just outside of the
capital. We knew her only as "Maria." Thirty percent of the fifteen thousand
armed FMLN combatants were women, and women comprised 40 percent
of total FMLN membership. We met with Maria in a large room, separate
from the general prison population. Like every FMLN combatant I had met,
she was skinny. She told us how the political prisoners had organized to teach
other prisoners to read, as well as studying history, politics, and revolutionary theory. A young woman who said she was a journalist from the United
States had suggested that we meet with Maria, and she had gone with us to
the meeting. As we were leaving, a member of our delegation saw the journalist pass a piece of paper to Maria, and all hell broke loose when we were
outside. Bella Abzug and Gloria Molina were furious with the young woman,
charging that she had risked the credibility of our delegation by delivering a
message from the FMLN. Several of us thought they were overreacting. I was
glad we could be of some use, since we hadn't accomplished much else.

I was glad to leave San Salvador. Every shop had not just armed guards, but
combat-ready soldiers toting M-16s. Banks and McDonald's shops had squads
of them. There were few people on the streets, and inside the stores were
empty shelves. The effect of US intervention on the people was much the
same in right-wing El Salvador as in left-wing Nicaragua—there was no room
left for normal life. On the other hand, anyone who left Nicaragua for the
United States received immediate political refugee status, while Salvadorans
who fled certain death in their own country were deported if they managed
to get to the United States.

I returned to Managua alone rather than traveling on to Miami with the
Women's Alternative group. I had made plans to meet there with the editor
and publisher of Navajo Nation Today, Mark Trahant and Loren Tapahe, and
accompany them to the Miskitia war zone. Mirna Torres-Rivas, who was in
charge of the foreign press and a good friend, had arranged their press passes:
few journalists were allowed in that zone. She asked me to take along another
US reporter, whom it turned out I knew. Richard Gonzalez worked at KPFA,
the local Pacifica radio station in the San Francisco Bay Area. My main goal

was to take the reporters to visit a Miskitu town on the coast that Brooklyn Rivera's Miskitu exile group claimed had been bombed by the Sandinistas in early January. I wanted to report on the Miskitu situation in Nicaragua at the UN Commission on Human Rights in Geneva in February to counteract the lies that were sure to be circulated by the United States, and I wanted reliable and credible witnesses. I had confidence in Loren and Mark's objectivity. Both were astute and knowledgeable but apolitical, interested only in accuracy, and Mark was trained as a journalist. They were also Native American: Loren was Navajo, a businessman and a practicing Mormon, and Mark was Shoshone-Bannock from the Fort Hall, Idaho, reservation (he later became editorial page editor for the *Seattle Post-Intelligencer*). They would not be so easily fooled by MISURASATA's Brooklyn Rivera, Armstrong Wiggins, and their American Indian supporters, who claimed to be "pro-Indian" rather than pro–United States. This implied that those who questioned them were anti-Indian. Mark and Loren would see through that binary.

The only means for reaching the coastal town of Wounta, the allegedly bombed Miskitu community, was by boat. Comandante William Ramírez allowed us to ride along with soldiers on an old ship that had been converted to a troop carrier. Fifty or so Sandinista soldiers were being taken to Wounta to relieve the troops already there, with whom we would return the following day. The *comandante* assigned Henry Herman, a thirty-six-year-old Miskitu, a former teacher, and now a member of the local Sandinista militia, to accompany us. He was from a mixed family, his father from a family of German immigrants who had intermarried with Miskitus, his mother Miskitu. They owned a small grocery in Puerto Cabezas. Henry was fluent in English as well as Miskitu and Spanish, and was very well read, smart, and charming. His younger brother, Roger Herman, was one of the exiled leaders of Steadman Fagoth's MISURA Contra forces. As we were boarding the ship, Galio Gurdián arrived to join us and insisted on pulling seniority on Henry. This was unfortunate because of his overbearing paternalism and contempt for Miskitu leadership.

We arrived in Wounta and explored the small town and its surrounding area thoroughly, finding no sign or word of Sandinista bombing or destruction. The residents told us that MISURASATA had arrived by boats and occupied the town, gathering them into the Moravian church to warn them that the Sandinistas were going to bomb the town, and tried to persuade them to leave. People were terrified and some hid in the bush nearby, but hours and days passed and no bombs fell. This kind of manipulation and fomenting of unwarranted fear for propaganda purposes diminished Brooklyn Rivera's claims to "pro-Indianism," and it reeked of CIA dirty tricks programs.

Henry took Loren, Mark, and me to meet the elder of the village, a Miskitu woman thought to be more than a hundred years old. She was frail, with long white hair, wearing a long white shift, clear-minded but mystical, speaking only in Miskitu. Henry translated. She said she was not surprised to meet Native people from the North, as she had foreseen our visit and was waiting for us, saying that she was confident that once again the indigenous peoples of the North and the South would come together to rid their world of foreign invaders.

Back in Puerto Cabezas, Comandante Ramírez gave us a jeep and a driver/translator and allowed us to travel around a large area for several days. Judith Butler accompanied us. She had come to Nicaragua to work with Galio Gurdián at CIDCA. Judy was a writer and editor of the journal of the North American Conference on Latin America (NACLA), and was in charge of starting the CIDCA journal *Wani*. We attended festivities in the villages of Kambla and Lamlaya celebrating the annual crowning of the Miskitu king and queen for the year. There I finally met Dr. Mirna Cunningham.

On a sadder note, we went to Sukatpin, a town of 2,000 that I had visited on my first trip, before the Contra attacks. It was now reduced to 300 people, all the young men having been forced to join MISURA, and the only industry and employer, a successful sawmill, had been destroyed by the Contras. We also visited Tasba Pri, the settlements of the evacuated Miskitus. Conditions had improved since I had been there a year earlier, but people longed to return to the river. Hazel Lau was there when we arrived. She told us she was concerned that INRA, the agricultural ministry, had introduced a cash crop, palm, for the extraction of palm oil for the market. She worried that this would divert the communities from raising their own food and remaining self-sufficient. Everywhere, Loren took photographs, Mark conducted interviews, and Richard taped.

They were surprised and impressed with how many Miskitu leaders, especially women, were in the top leadership in the region. Mark and Richard interviewed a dozen Miskitu leaders, including Cesar País, the Puerto Cabezas chief of police; Dr. Mirna Cunningham (six months later she was appointed the region's governor); Miskitu nurse Mildred Levy; Jimmy Boppell, now promoted to army lieutenant; Miskitu lawyer Armando Rojas Smith; as well as people like Hazel Lau, Virgilio Taylor Gil, Oscar Hogsdon, Railly Saunders, Minerva Wilson, Gabriel Bell, Marcelo Zuñiga, and Indira Brigette, a nineteen-year-old militiawoman, one of the Miskitus making up 70 percent of the regional militia. Mirna, Oscar, Virgilio, Railly, and others had established a new organization, MISATAN. These brilliant leaders were dismissed as "sellouts" and were considered traitors to be shot by both Rivera's and Fagoth's Miskitu exile organizations. Because most observers outside Nicaragua, even those who supported the Sandinistas, had romantic views of Native Americans as unsophisticated people of the land, they tended to believe the lie that these Miskitu leaders were government lackeys.

The *Navajo Nation Today* published a three-part feature over the following weeks. I took multiple copies with me to Geneva, along with my own detailed report, which I distributed and presented orally. I had expected the US State Department/CIA to bring Contras, whom they called "freedom fighters," to the UN Commission on Human Rights, but I was stunned by the arrival of a large contingent of Miskitus from the Honduran-based Contra-affiliated organization MISURA.

A Louisiana Coushatta tribal official, Ernest Sickey, whom I had met before, accompanied these Miskitus. He had no idea what he was doing with that crowd. He said that the National Tribal Chairmen's Association (NTCA, an organization funded by the federal government) had appointed him to represent them on the delegation, which had been co-organized by Freedom House in New York, an organization devoted to investigating human rights abuses "behind the iron curtain." Since they regarded the Sandinistas as Soviet allies, they had taken up the cause of the Contras, particularly the Miskitus. R. Bruce McColm, the Freedom House director, was appointed that year by the Reagan administration to represent the United States on the Inter-American Commission on Human Rights, an arm of the Organization of American States. The other sponsor was unfamiliar to me at the time. The American Security Council, based in Virginia, was made up of former generals, admirals, and government officials, all extremely right-wing, along with emerging

neoconservatives like Richard Pipes and Richard Bissell, as well as CIA operative Ray Cline. What surprised and disappointed me most was that the State
Department had persuaded Amy Young, the director of the International Human Rights Law Group, to provide NGO credentials to this Contra delegation, a move that was intended to give the Contras credibility but in fact only
eroded the credibility of US-based human rights groups.

One of the Contra-allied Miskitus turned out to be Roger Herman, the
brother of Henry Herman, the Sandinista-allied guide we had traveled with
during the previous month. Because I knew Henry and their parents, Roger
was willing to speak with me. As we talked in the Delegates' Lounge, his eyes
kept rising to scan the mezzanine. Following his glances, I caught a glimpse
of a man whose face I did not know but whom I would never forget. In 1985,
I would meet him in Honduras, and in 1987 his face would become familiar to
every television viewer during the Iran-Contra hearings—Marine Lt. Colonel
Oliver North of Reagan's National Security Council. At the time, I did not
learn his name. When I asked Roger if we could meet in town over the weekend, he said he would have to ask "Ollie," who, of course, said no.

The US Mission produced another surprise—Moonie filmmaker Lee Shapiro and his film on the Francia Sirpe "exodus" in December. A declassified
State Department telegram from the US Mission in Geneva that I would later
obtain stated: "To illustrate as vividly as possible actual living conditions for
Miskitos, members of the Commission saw a film showing refugee camp
conditions and whole Miskito communities fleeing for their lives with their
few basic household effects on their backs."

Actually, no members of the Commission were present at the film showing, although the ambassadors of El Salvador, Costa Rica, and Honduras attended. Six NGO representatives and one British journalist came to see the
film, but left in disgust halfway through, muttering that it was gross propaganda. I stayed.

The central theme of the film was that the town's bishop, Salvador Schlaefer, a contemporary Moses, had led his flock out of Nicaragua. However, to
my surprise, the bishop stated clearly in the film that he followed the people
and did not lead them, and that at any rate he had little choice since the MIS-
URA had mined the road behind them and had blown up the bridges. Declassified State Department telegrams to Washington from Tegucigalpa reflected

nervousness regarding Schlaefer's public statements, since they contradicted the propaganda version. US officials were particularly upset that one month after the "exodus," Schlaefer returned to his work in Nicaragua without any problem. Curiously, the US media did not notice that.

Lee Shapiro gave a short talk after the film. I spoke at length with him afterwards, and he gave me his business card with the address 401 Fifth Avenue, New York, the well-known location of the headquarters of the Unification Church in the United States and its Causa International. Shapiro told me that he was an independent filmmaker and had contracted with the US Information Agency (USIA) to make the film. Even though USIA-produced materials, according to its own charter, may not be distributed domestically in the US, either directly or through another organization, the film was broadcast nationally on PBS in June 1986. Soon after the Commission premiere, the film was shown on German public television. Amazingly, it turned up in the 1985 Telluride film festival. Then it began to appear at Causa-organized meetings throughout the United States, often with Russell Means speaking.

By the time I met Shapiro, I had learned more about Causa from researcher Fred Clarkson. It was headed by Bo Hi Pak, a former South Korean intelligence career officer who served as military attaché in the South Korean embassy in Washington. Pak was the second-ranking official to Rev. Moon in the Unification Church, the central element of the World Anti-Communist League (WACL), which Clarkson called "the international fascist network." Vietnam commander General John Singlaub, founder of *Soldier of Fortune*, was the president of WACL.

In a 1991 speech, Reverend Sun Myung Moon spoke about the Unification Church's work in saving Nicaragua from communism and paid tribute to the late Lee Shapiro, who had been killed in 1987 while filming the Mujahadeen in Afghanistan. Here is a portion of Moon's speech (he refers to himself as "Father"):

Father made a special film on Nicaragua called *Nicaragua Is My Home*. That film was made by our dear brother Lee Shapiro. His wife is here. Linda, could you please stand up. Lee Shapiro made this film upon Father's order. This film was shown at the White House first. President Reagan wrote a letter of commendation after viewing it. It was shown on PBS, to different localities all around the country, and that completely turned around public opinion. Nicaragua today is free. Communism is gone, they have freely elected a president. As soon as Violetta Chamorro became president, she wrote a letter to thank Father.

Despite the successful propaganda campaign, there was a tangible shift in the politics of the Contra war in the spring of 1984. The Sandinistas were preparing for national elections, which they hoped would give their revolution greater international legitimacy. Congress meanwhile suspended aid to the Contras. This injected some starch into the nationalistic elements of the Honduran military command, and they ousted US ally General Álvarez, who left for a comfortable retirement in Florida.

To keep up the pressure, Robert "Bud" McFarlane, head of Reagan's National Security Council, secured a pledge of $1 million a month from Saudi Arabia in support of the Contras in Honduras. Within a year, the Saudis more than doubled that amount, which was further embellished by pledges from the Sultan of Brunei and others, leading up to the 1986 Iran-Contra scandal when it was revealed that the administration had sold arms to Iran at profit and used the money to aid the Contras. Another source of funding for the Contras was cocaine running using US-chartered resupply aircraft. Those of us on the ground in Central America knew all about it, but Contra drug-running operations were not documented and exposed at the time. Although the CIA continued to operate in the Contra war, the National Security Council took the lead, run by its gung-ho psychopath Oliver North, whom Reagan cast as a young John Wayne. Alexander Haig, who had been Reagan's initial secretary of state, did his bit by commissioning an anti-Sandinista (and anti-Cuban) movie, Red Dawn—Haig sat on the board of MGM—which premiered in the White House around the same time as the Moonie film. To ensure that the Sandinistas would not gain credibility, the Reagan administration pressured most of the opposition parties to pull out of the forthcoming national elections.

The US ambassador to Honduras, John Negroponte, reshuffled the Contras, focusing on the Miskitus because sympathy for them was far easier to elicit than for the Somocista ex-Guardia murderers who made up the Contra command structure. MISURA became KISAN, with Steadman Fagoth out.

Brooklyn Rivera and his group, MISURASATA, were soon allowed to operate out of Honduras. The mass exodus of Miskitu refugees to Honduras became the pattern of operation and the basis for pro-Contra propaganda; as part of this strategy, journalists and human rights observers were allowed better access to the Miskitu refugee camps in Honduras. At the same time, the Sandinistas continued to restrict US mainstream media from traveling in the Miskitu war zone. I thought this was a mistake, but the Sandinistas assumed, rightly as it turned out, that the mainstream US media were easily manipulated by the Reagan administration's Office of Public Diplomacy for Latin America and the Caribbean, which had been established in 1983 with Otto Reich at the helm. It was Reich who had designed the "exodus" drama.

I experienced the shift in Contra propaganda in the summer of 1984. In June, after I gave a lecture on Nicaragua at University of Colorado, Denver, Dr. Vincent Harding, a scholarly liberal theologian and sixties civil rights activist, invited me to accompany a group he and his wife had organized to visit the northeast region of Nicaragua in order to learn "the truth" about the Miskitu situation. He said he had made all the logistical arrangements through the Moravian Church. I told him I thought the delegation would be better informed if they didn't limit themselves to a Moravian agenda. He agreed and asked me to set up meetings for the group and to accompany them. I arrived before the group did and met with Dr. Mirna Cunningham, now governor of the region, who was in Managua. She agreed to organize meetings in Puerto Cabezas. However, when we arrived at the Puerto Cabezas airport, two separate official delegations were there to meet us, Dr. Cunningham and several Miskitu leaders on the one hand, and the Moravian hierarchy on the other, all Creoles except for one Miskitu pastor. The two host groups were eyeing each other suspiciously. Mirna took me aside and said it would be best if we went with the Moravians, and the government delegation faded away after greeting our delegation.

They took us to a large hospitality house where we would stay and also have our meals, gave us a tightly scheduled agenda for three days, and left us to settle in. Dr. Harding's groups decided everything in meetings to reach consensus. Since I was an adviser to the group, I didn't have veto power (which is what consensus comes to), but I expressed my disagreements, then went along with what they decided. They did agree with me to alter the agenda to include meetings with Mirna and other nonreligious Miskitus. Mirna had given me the agenda she had worked up, and the group inserted some of those meetings. When we met with the Moravian hosts, they were not pleased with the changes and stared at me while they said so, but agreed. As they took us around, including to Tasba Pri, I was able to pose questions challenging their assertions that the delegation otherwise would not have been able to do. But one evening when I had gone to dinner at the Herman family's home on my own, I returned to find the delegation missing. We always met at 10 p.m. for a discussion about the day's events. I was asleep when they returned around midnight. The next morning at breakfast they informed me that they had met with "the mothers of the disappeared," and that they now believed that the Sandinistas had committed serious human rights abuses. I said that the Miskitus were being fed lies and that the supposedly disappeared were actually in Honduras. Dr. Harding said, "Mothers don't lie," and I said that I didn't mean that the mothers lied, but in fact mothers *do* lie. But I lost them in that discussion, which made me determined to find a way to get into the refugee camps in Honduras and prove that the missing Miskitus were there, which I would do a few months later.

On the way to Nicaragua to meet Harding's group I had stopped over in Cuernavaca to give some talks in the language schools. Harriet Goff, director of the Cemanahuac school, presented a proposal that I arrange for a *Time* magazine reporter to go to the Miskitu zone of Nicaragua. The reporter, David DeVoss, had just finished a month-long course in Spanish at the school and taken up his post in the Mexico City *Time* bureau. He had expressed to Harriet his desire to visit the Miskitia but had had no luck obtaining permission at the Nicaraguan embassy in Mexico City, and other journalists had warned him that it was impossible. Harriet thought of me. I was dubious, not only because he worked for *Time*, but also because Harriet said he was a native of Dallas and a Republican. However, I trusted Harriet's reading of character, and she had found him to be sincere and honest.

I met with DeVoss in Mexico City, and my impression of him was the same as Harriet's. He was a quiet, serious man, older than any of the other reporters I had met in Central America. It seemed to me an important opportunity for a top US weekly to get the Miskitu-Sandinista story straight and counter the White House propaganda. I spent hours telling him everything I knew about the situation, especially the US manipulation of refugees. He was an old hand at dealing with refugees as propaganda from his post in Southeast Asia during the Vietnamese "boat people" crisis. I gave him my book *Indians of the Americas: Human Rights and Self-Determination*, which had just been released and included a section on the Miskitus and Sandinistas. DeVoss also told me that as a senior correspondent, he had the right to refuse editorial changes that he disagreed with. I was convinced, and told him that I agreed to try to arrange his trip and would call him from Managua with the outcome.

While the Harding delegation met with religious leaders in Managua, I spent hours and days trying to gain permission for DeVoss to enter the Miskitia, finally succeeding by appealing to Comandante Borge. No photographer would be allowed, however, and I was to travel with him.

DeVoss was given a great deal of freedom to travel and talk to anyone. He mainly wanted to interview the Miskitus who had been evacuated from the border in January 1981. I was impressed with his professionalism and his patience with the difficulty of travel, lodging, even finding food. I saw and heard everything he saw and heard and was confident that finally a truthful story would appear in the mainstream press.

13

City of Refuge

W hat happened?" That was the text of the telex I sent to David DeVoss
in Mexico. Simply, "What happened?" It was early September 1984,
and I was still in Geneva after the Working Group on Indigenous Peoples and
the UN Sub-Commission had ended. I had been offered and accepted a five-
month contract as a researcher, and every week I checked at the train station
where the magazine store stocked *Time* magazine. Then, ten weeks after the
trip with David, there it was, on pages 10 and 11. The issue was dated August
20, 1984, but US magazines always arrived a couple of weeks late. I knew the
minute I saw the article that something was wrong. The photographs were all
of Miskitus funded by the CIA.

I bought the magazine and, without opening it, went to a nearby café and
ordered a carafe of white wine. I downed a glass, then read the two-page
story. There were three pictures breaking up the text. One was captioned,
"Miskito fighters pass through an Atlantic coast settlement after an antigov-
ernment foray," showing three men in uniforms with guns on horses, followed by a dozen people on foot. Another showed seven men in camouflage,
one with an enormous M-60, in a canoe on a river, captioned, "In a canoe on
the Coco River, preparing to infiltrate Nicaragua." The third was captioned,
"Women train for war at a camp near the Honduran border," showing a few
women in skirts led by an equal number of uniformed men, all jogging. Two
of the photographs were attributed to Denis Reichle, whom I would soon

find out had assisted Werner Herzog in making a documentary, *Ballad of the Little Soldier*, for German state television.

The headline to the story shouted, "Indians Caught in the Middle: A Jungle War Flourishes over the Right to Land and Autonomy." The first paragraph set the tone:

> Of all the territory caught up in Central America's diverse wars, none is less hospitable than the steaming jungles, malarial swamps, and sluggish rivers that make up Nicaragua's Atlantic coast. There, bands of Miskito Indians, their uniformed shoulders draped with bandoliers, travel on foot, by leaky dugout canoe and on horseback. Using modern, US-made M-16 automatic rifles and M-60 machine guns, they are carrying out a hit-and-run campaign of harassment and sabotage against the government. Their mission: to regain the ancestral lands and autonomy that they feel were taken from them by the Sandinistas who have ruled Nicaragua for the past five years.

This was a completely different story from the one David had sought to report. I looked to the end of the article and found this attribution: "By George Russell. Reported by David DeVoss/Tasba Pri." Except for the second paragraph about Tasba Pri, the rest of the article was a glowing and romanticized tribute to the Miskitu insurgents. The Reagan administration's support and funding of the insurgents was mentioned only to be dismissed as a Sandinista ploy to paint "the native rebels as mere pawns of the CIA."

I returned to my office, half-drunk and shaky, and used the telex there to ask that question: "What happened?" Every kind of self-deprecating thought raced through my mind. How could I be so naïve as to trust a *Time* reporter? I will never again trust my judgment of anyone. I am a stupid peasant, not capable of this work. The Sandinistas will never allow me to go to the Miskitia again. I broke down crying. Fortunately, everyone else had left the office and I was alone. I waited for the telex to spit out an answer to my question.

The response came from David a short time later, saying that he had written to my San Francisco address, but would resend to Geneva. Two days later, the letter came, David apologizing to me and telling me that he had resigned over the article's attribution of the story to him as if he had reported it. He also enclosed a copy of his telex to *Time*'s editors protesting the fabrications and distortions. But he wrote that he did not want to make the issue public and that *Time* had agreed. The following January, when I was next in Managua, I asked Julia Preston of the *Boston Globe* what she thought about David quitting, and she claimed that he had been fired for skimming money in Thailand when he was bureau chief there. I told her that I didn't believe that was true, but she believed it and said that everyone in the press corps knew, and, indeed, every US reporter I asked repeated the same story. I wrote David that *Time* or someone was defaming him, but again he said that he did not want to deal with it, that no reporter wants to become the subject of a story, and that a public controversy would ruin his career. I knew that was true, but had hoped that he would do what John Gerassi had done in the early 1960s under similar circumstances when he was the Latin American correspondent for *Time*—he denounced the magazine and was fired, and although he went on to work for short stints at the *New York Times* and *Newsweek*, he soon became a lifelong anti-imperialist activist, teacher, and writer. To my knowledge, David never revived his career as a war correspondent; he ended up as a travel writer, publishing a coffee-table book on Thailand.

Two years later, I would acquire a confidential State Department memorandum revealing to what ends that office would go to manipulate the media. Dated March 13, 1985, from Otto Reich's assistant, Jonathan Miller, to White House Director of Communications Pat Buchanan, the memo presents "five illustrative examples of the Reich 'White Propaganda' operation." It reports that an attached *Wall Street Journal* editorial detailing the alleged Nicaraguan arms buildup had been written by a consultant in Reich's office, which "officially had no role in its preparation."

Another "illustrative example" was a favorable report on the Contras from correspondent Fred Francis on *NBC News with Tom Brokaw* on March 12, 1985: "This piece was prepared by Francis after he consulted two of our contractors who recently had made a clandestine trip to the freedom fighter camp along the Nicaragua/Honduras border. The purpose of this trip was to serve as a pre-advance for many selected journalists to visit the area and get a true flavor of what the freedom fighters are doing." Third, "Two op-ed pieces, one for *The Washington Post* and one for *The New York Times,* are being prepared for the signatures of opposition leaders Alphonso Rubello, Adolpho Calero and

Arturo Cruz." In the fourth instance, the office was sending Calero around to all the media offices for editorial interviews. Finally, there was an attached cable from a congressman visiting Nicaragua, together with the note: "Don't be surprised if this cable somehow hits the evening news." Reich's assistant ended his memo by writing, "I will not attempt in the future to keep you posted on all activities since we have too many balls in the air at any one time and since the work of our operation is ensured by our office's keeping a low profile."

The *Time* article was only another blow added to the others of that summer. With the US propaganda machine running at full tilt, I had been ready for some controversy at the August UN meeting around my new book, *Indians of the Americas*, but nothing like what happened. The book began with an analytical summary of the European colonization of the Americas, and then moved to the development of US colonialization of North America and the indigenous peoples' struggle for survival and self-determination. I told the story of the formation of the International Indian Treaty Council in 1974 and reviewed current theories of self-determination and oppressed minorities. I concluded with two case studies, one on Native Americans in the United States and the other on the Miskitus in Nicaragua. In analyzing the Miskitu situation, I particularly tried to capture the complexity of a people seeking indigenous self-determination in a revolutionary state that itself required nationalist consolidation and was experiencing intervention and sabotage funded by a powerful state.

I was well aware that the NGOs supporting the Miskitu Contras would hate the book, but I was surprised by the size and force of the campaign waged against me, a campaign that hounded me until the Sandinistas lost power in Nicaragua in 1990. The first salvo came from the International Indian Treaty Council, apparently initiated by Russell Means but signed by Mario Ibarra, the IITC representative in Geneva. The letter was addressed to the UN Secretariat, saying that I did not represent the IITC and should not be allowed IITC credentials; of course, I did not claim to represent the IITC and did not want or need to do so. The real purpose of the letter was to discredit me, because copies were circulated to every member of the Sub-Commission and to all the NGOs. I was infuriated and tried to talk with Mario, but he refused to discuss it or to talk with me at all. The most disturbing attack came from several North American indigenous women, who had been at the Strasbourg Institute the month before. Mario Ibarra, Augusto Willemsen-Díaz, Ester Prieto, and I had organized a special course parallel to the July international human rights law institute that I had attended the year before, this one for indigeous participants only. I had arrived late because of the Democratic National Convention taking place in San Francisco at the same time—I was supporting Jesse Jackson and the Rainbow Coalition. My co-organizers were angry with me because they were all non-indigenous Latin Americans and the indigenous participants were all from Scandinavia, the Pacific, and North America. We had bitter disputes over who was to blame for the course not going well, and my solution was to drink. I deserved criticism, but not the way it was done by these women, which was hostile and dismissive.

Paranoia overcame me, and I felt isolated and miserable. I told Lam Phuong, a friend who worked in the UN Human Rights Center, about what was happening, and she said: "It's the book—they are jealous." And perhaps it was that, at least for some of the North American Indians who accused me of making money off the book. Clearly, they didn't know anything about publishing—academic books don't make much money, and besides, I asked for books to give away rather than cash royalties.

I hoped that the accusations against me would die down, but they followed me wherever I went. After I gave a talk about UN human rights work at the World Council of Indigenous Peoples' General Assembly in Panama in September, a man I knew from the South American Indian Council took the microphone on a point of order and denounced me as a known spy (he did not say for whom) and not an Indian. He had been in Geneva the month before and had heard the rumors. Later, I talked to him, explaining what had happened in Geneva, and he apologized, saying that he had seen me talking to the Miskitus from MISURASATA who were present at the WCIP meeting and thought that I had brought them. But the damage had been done in front of over a thousand indigenous participants from all over the world.

Two events kept me going, kept me believing that my work was important and that attacks on me were inevitable given the kind of work I was doing. The first was a chance encounter. I stopped for several days in San

Francisco after the Panama trip to do some scheduled readings from my new book, and to gather things I would need for the fall and winter in Geneva. I flew from Panama to San Salvador, where I had to change planes. While waiting for my TACA flight to San Francisco I saw a man, also waiting, whom I figured to be a drug lord. He was dressed expensively, smoking a cigar, and surrounded by several young Latinas wearing skin-tight designer jeans and very high-heeled shoes. They were all drinking champagne and laughing. Since I was the first to check in, I was the first to be allowed on the plane. I took a front window seat—TACA and other Central American airlines did not have first-class or reserved seating. Then on came the man and his entourage. Someone followed with a box of food and drink. The man sat down next to me, and the women sat in the three seats across the aisle. After we were in the air, they broke out the sandwiches and champagne, offering some to me. I accepted and got into a conversation with the man. He told me his name was Félix Rodríguez, which was familiar, but not until he told me what he was doing in El Salvador did I realize that this was the Cuban-American CIA operative who was present when Che Guevara was summarily executed in Bolivia. He claimed that he was now retired from the CIA and simply had been invited by the chief of the Salvadoran Air Force to teach paratroopers how to find and fire on FMLN guerrillas from helicopters. He boasted that he had ended up fighting on the ground as well. According to a March 14, 1992, *San Francisco Chronicle* feature on Rodríguez, he purportedly showed off his many relics from his counterinsurgency career to reporter David Adams. One souvenir was a black bra, which he claimed he took from Nidia Díaz, a FMLN commander he captured in 1985. Others included Che's watch, which he claimed to have taken off his arm after he was killed; a bloody Viet Cong flag; a CIA citation signed by George Bush the First; and coded messages from Lt. Colonel Oliver North.

Rodríguez said to me as he disembarked from the airplane in Mexico City, "They all seem so nice, the Salvadorans—that shoeshine man, that woman selling something, that schoolboy—but they kill so easily." The words were exactly what people like him had said about the Vietnamese, or, in other times, about the Filipinos, the "Mau Mau" of Kenya, the Native Americans—all people engaged in defending themselves against invaders and colonial overlords. Rodríguez viewed them all as categorically available for killing. I felt that I needed to take a shower after he left the plane in Mexico City, but this meeting made me realize how important it was to keep going, to stop killers like Rodríguez.

In San Francisco, I was met with a local attack on me in the *East Bay Express* by Bernard Nietschmann, then a senior geography professor at the University of California, Berkeley, and an adviser to Brooklyn Rivera. In late August 1984, Paul Rauber had written a feature in the free weekly paper titled "The Nietschmann File," in which he mentioned me only once, writing that "Pro-Sandinista Indian activist Roxanne Dunbar-Ortiz has this to say about Nietschmann's early works: 'These papers by the scholar, turned Contra, indicate a romantic, indígenista view which could later be easily manipulated by the CIA program of psychological warfare to discredit the Sandinistas, and purportedly to favor the Miskitos." This Rauber took from an article by me and had not interviewed me. The two-page diatribe by Nietschmann in response to Rauber filled two pages of the newspaper, beginning with a personal attack on me:

> The first place I'll turn to is another file labeled 'Roxanne, Don't Turn On the Red Light,' my collection of quotes from Chairwoman Rox (-anne Dunbar-Ortiz). Rauber quotes from her bibliography of literature on the Miskito where she calls me a 'scholar, turned *Contra*,' but he should have read on a little more as a reality check on this Managua Rose.

Nietschmann began writing regular opinion pieces in the Unification Church–funded newspaper, *Washington Times*. He was a precursor of the kind of right-wing pundit that became regular fare following the election of George W. Bush in 2000, a sort of male version of Ann Coulter, an individual filled with hate and scorn for liberals and leftists, perhaps with good reason—many of them believed what he had to say despite his affiliation with Reverend Moon's fascist operations. He was older than the Reagan-inspired budding right-wingers of the time, and perhaps was taken more seriously because of that. He was also a tenured professor and author of one book, *Between Land and Water*, about the Miskitus, which was long out of print but re-issued thanks to his newfound fame.

About the same time, there was a surprise attack on the Sandinistas from an unexpected source. Werner Herzog was the director of two of my favorite films, *Aguirre: Wrath of God* and *Fitzcaraldo*, both about the colonization of the indigenous peoples of the Andes. Commissioned by German state television, the documentary, *Ballade vom Kleinen Soldaten* (Ballad of the Little Soldier), aired on German television on November 5, 1984, the day after the Nicaraguan elections in which Daniel Ortega was elected president. It was also the time when Brooklyn Rivera had been invited by Tomás Borge to visit for peace talks. In a review in *Die Zeit* on November 2, 1984, film editor Siegfried Schober wrote: "Herzog says today, that he and his German-French colleague Denis Reichle had been falsely quoted. The damage was, however, done: Herzog had, the effect could not be otherwise, broken the lance of the Sandinistas." Herzog's film had been interpreted by anyone who saw it as confirming US allegations of Sandinista massacres of Miskitus. He had traveled with Miskitus associated with the Contras, and filmed whatever they told him.

Reichle, whose photographs had been published with the *Time* magazine article, was a German-born French journalist who first traveled with the MISURA in the fall of 1983, during which they had briefly occupied Wounta. He filmed those travels and tried to persuade Herzog to produce the film. Herzog initially rejected it, but then accepted Reichle's challenge to go there himself, which Herzog did in early 1984. Herzog filmed the second part of the film, which took place in Tapamlaya and Rus Rus, two refugee camps in Honduras near the border that were controlled by the MISURA and were outside the supervision of the UN High Commissioner for Refugees. Actually, the film is two contradictory films in one, the first half a pro-Contra narrative, and the second half—Herzog's—denouncing the use of children soldiers and showing them being trained by a former Somoza national guardsman, who says in the film that children's minds are not yet formed and that they can be told to do anything.

I was working in Geneva in late October, when Phil Agee called me from Hamburg, where he lived in political exile. Agee had left the CIA in the late 1960s and wrote a bestselling book, *Inside the Company*, which had not been authorized as required by the CIA. Agee had acquired a copy of the videotape and wanted me to fly to Hamburg to look at it and comment. I spent two days at the Agee home, studying the film, some of which was in English, but most in German, with Agee translating for me. I figured that if Herzog could be manipulated to participate in such a film, almost anyone was vulnerable.

I wrote Herzog my thoughts on the film, and he replied in English in a very long handwritten letter, in which he said that "my camera tells the truth," but refused to face the fact that his camera had only been taken to the refugee camps, and that the first half of the film was pure Contra propaganda.

I was encouraged, however, by the 1984 findings of the Inter-American Commission on Human Rights regarding the Miskitu-Sandinista case, which the commission took up in response to petitions and testimony collected by the Indian Law Resource Center and MISURASATA alleging that the Sandinistas had bombed villages, murdered people, and threatened to eliminate "the indigenous race." The Nicaraguan government accepted the jurisdiction of the commission and replied extensively, the commission reported. Although the commission favored the collective rights of the Miskitu people, and by extension the rights of all indigeous peoples, it did not find the charges against the Sandinistas to be valid.

Another incident then occurred that brought home the fact that the US solidarity with Nicaragua movement did not understand the Miskitu situation or indigenous peoples in general. The St. Augustine, Florida, Committee on Central America called asking me to recommend "an Indian" to be a part of a delegation on their "Cargo and Peace Ship," which was scheduled to sail from St. Augustine directly to Puerto Cabezas. Normally the Sandinistas didn't allow foreign ships to dock there, but they did give the green light for this project. The ship was loaded with clothing, food, medicines, and other items for the Miskitu refugees in Puerto Cabezas and the settlements. They called me only a few days before the scheduled departure, because a Sandinista official insisted that they include Native Americans in the delegation that would accompany the ship. Clearly, it was an undesirable requirement to the project director's way of thinking.

I was able to persuade my former husband's brother, Gilbert Ortiz (Petuuche) from Acoma Indian Pueblo, to go. His report upon returning was disturbing. He said that on the ship, named *Fri*, there were six crew members and six "witnesses" including him, the others white and one African American—Petuuche called them "Americans." When the group visited the Miskitu village of Krukira, Petuuche received special recognition from the people, because he was Indian. He wrote me:

> As the meeting progressed, I was asked to speak and the indigenous people wanted to hear me talk in my language. I spoke to them in Acoma and translated in Spanish. After the meeting the community people wanted to take a group picture with me. They sat me in front of them in a big wooden chair and someone handed me a months old baby to hold. Then they made the Americans take the picture. They didn't include the Americans in the picture. I think the Americans felt I held a special relationship with the indigenous people, and this was unnerving to them. I know the indigenous people treated me differently.

Several other situations of special treatment took place. Then, the ship's leaders called a meeting with the local FSLN to discuss Petuuche. Petuuche said that the Sandinistas were gracious, and made it clear that he could go wherever he wished and talk to anyone. But, he wrote, the solidarity group didn't agree:

> They scolded me and said that if I believed so much in the indigenous cause I should just stay and assist them in their fight and that I could find my own way back home. Yet, I also think one of them said I had the right of free speech as long as I didn't foment a revolution. I thought then this was a strange word to use.

They gave him money for airfare, and he returned alone. With friends like that solidarity group, the Sandinistas did not need enemies.

Some people, maybe most people, keep their distance from someone under attack. Fortunately for me, not Zia Rizvi. Toward the end of the Sub-Commission in August 1984, I had received an invitation to meet with Dr. Rizvi, who was then the secretary-general of the Independent Commission on International Humanitarian Issues (ICIHI). Ever attuned to all happenings at the UN, Zia had heard about my book and the campaign against me and invited me to visit the ICIHI office in Geneva. He got right to the point, asking me why I was so controversial. I explained and he listened, and then he hired me to work as a consultant for ICIHI, which I did for the next five months. I was determined to persuade Zia to take up the issue of indigenous peoples, which he did two years later.

Zia had been groomed as a young man for international diplomacy, but, like many others from wealthy families from the formerly colonized world, sought his education and career in Europe or the US Zia had studied at the Sorbonne, completing a doctorate, and then began his international career with the United Nations High Commission for Refugees (UNHCR). In 1971, he gained near heroic status by designing a solution to the crisis of ten million Bengali refugees that resulted from the Bangladesh war of independence from Pakistan. That brought him to the attention of the high commissioner for refugees, Prince Sadrudhin Aga Khan, who drafted Zia to be his personal assistant.

Prince Sadrudhin, who died in 2003 at the age of seventy, was the son of Sultan Mohammed Shah, Aga Khan III, the spiritual leader of the world's Ismaili Muslims, and uncle to the Aga Khan IV. In 1978, after having served twelve years as high commissioner, Sadrudhin was forced out by the Carter administration because of his unwillingness to take US orders regarding Southeast Asian refugees from the "American war." Zia was marginalized in the UNHCR office in Rome until 1980, when he was called upon to work his magic on the chaotic Southeast Asian refugee crisis in the wake of the Khmer Rouge genocide in Cambodia. Soon after Reagan was elected, Zia took leave from UNHCR as the administration began its work of reshaping and sabotaging international organizations.

During the 1981 UN General Assembly meeting in New York, the body called for a "New International Humanitarian Order," and the following year mandated the formation of an independent commission to be composed of leading figures in the humanitarian field along with former or standing government and international officials. In 1983, the Independent Commission on International Humanitarian Issues was established, co-chaired by Prince Sadrudhin and Prince Hassan bin Talal of Jordan, brother of King Hussein. Zia, who had been working closely with the two princes in shepherding through the project, was hired as secretary-general of ICIHI.

I had a private office in the ICIHI suite of offices near the Palais, the UN headquarters, and lived in a studio with a kitchen in the hotel across the street. I worked daily on various reports and statements. Nearly every weekend that fall, I was invited to speak on the Miskitu situation and took every opportunity to do so: at the Sorbonne in Paris, to Kurdish and Turkish workers in Oberhausen, Germany, in Rome, in Amsterdam, and many places in Switzerland.

As the other consultants and I worked researching and writing on the issues to be taken up by the commission—street children, refugees, famine, desertification, deforestation, warfare, disappeared people, youth, mass expulsions, displaced persons, statelessness, disaster management, urban migrations, man-made disasters—Zia would come up with ideas and ask all of us to write something up, giving us a short deadline. It was exciting and stimulating intellectual work, if a bit frustrating working for such a high-powered and brilliant boss. And it was always awkward being the only US citizen and not a French-speaker, although all the other researchers spoke English.

The majority of the high-profile ICIHI members was non-Western and included only one other royal—Saudi Prince Talal bin Abdul Aziz al-Saud. Other members included Shridath Ramphal of Guyana, then head of the Commonwealth Commission; Salim Salim, the Tanzanian foreign minister and later head of the Organization of African Unity; and Desmond Tutu of South Africa. Two judges of the International Court of Justice were members—Manfred Lachs from Poland and Mohammed Bedjaoui of Algeria. The founder of independent Senegal, Léopold Sédar Senghor, was one of several current or former heads of state who were members, as well as Gough Whitlam of Australia, Lazar Mojsov of Yugoslavia, and Luis Echeverría Álvarez of Mexico. Robert McNamara, then president of the World Bank, was the only US member of the commission. Out of some thirty members, only three were women, but they were extraordinary women—Susanna Agnelli of Italy, Simone Veil of France, and Sadako Ogota of Japan, who later became the UN High Commissioner for Refugees. I was able to meet all the commissioners at their three-day meeting held at Peace Palace, where the World Court was located at The Hague in the Netherlands, in December 1984.

I stayed on at The Hague after the meeting to talk with the Nicaraguan

delegation that was there to present a case against the United States before
the World Court. Early in 1984, the United States had over a period of months
blown up oil storage tanks at Puerto Corinto, Nicaragua, and had mined the
harbor, causing the explosion of several foreign ships. Soon afterward, Nicaragua brought a case for reparations and an end to US funding of the Contras before the World Court. After twenty-six months of litigation, the court
found in favor of Nicaragua on June 27, 1986, ordering the United States to
stop "arming and training" the Contras and to pay reparations. From the beginning, the United States had boycotted the court hearings, and refused to
recognize authority of the court in the matter.

Because Zia knew everyone at the UN High Commission for Refugees
(UNHCR), and because its sprawling compound was located across the street
from the ICIHI offices, I was able to meet the refugee officials who dealt with
Central America. That would lead to a new phase of my work against the
Contra war, dealing with the Nicaraguan Miskitu refugees in Honduras. The
officials in charge of Central American refugees at the UNHCR encouraged
me to visit the Honduran refugee camps for the Miskitus. They wanted my
view of the situation, and in November arranged for the UNHCR official in
Honduras to facilitate my travel to the camps. Almost simultaneously, I was
able to obtain a Honduran government invitation through its ambassador
to the UN in Geneva, José Mario Maldonado. I had begun a dialog with the
ambassador in August, and by September he had written a letter of introduction to the Honduran foreign minister, Dr. Leo Valladares. By November, I
had a formal invitation to speak with government officials and permission to
travel to Mokorón, the UNHCR refugee center for the Nicaraguan Miskitus
in Honduran Miskitu territory.

Ambassador Maldonado had grave misgivings that he shared with me
about the US military presence in Honduras. He had been the Honduran Air
Force chief in the 1960s under General López Arellano's progressive military
government, which had been intent on land reform. Land conflicts near the
border with El Salvador led to a brief war in 1967, called the "Soccer War"
because it was the Honduran military's response to the abusive treatment
of the Honduran team during a World Cup game in San Salvador. Maldonado's air force was badly defeated, and he became agriculture minister in
the early 1970s, developing a radical reform of creating peasant cooperatives

and a state forestry corporation. Unfortunately for the Honduran peasantry, the late 1970s saw changes in international lending agencies that prohibited public spending and allowed only privatization. Honduras was way over its head in debt and therefore vulnerable to US pressure to host the Contra war. Maldonado blamed General Álvarez, who would be deposed by Honduran officers in August 1985.

I scheduled the trip to Honduras to coincide with the annual meeting of the American Society for Ethnohistory (ASE) in New Orleans, stopping there first, then going on to Honduras. My paper for a panel on the Miskitus had been accepted earlier in the year when I assumed I would be in the United States. I had never participated in an ASE meeting, but I knew that its membership was primarily anthropologists and historians. The other members of the panel on the Miskitus were three US anthropologists—Mary Helms, Michael Olien, and Philip Dennis—who had done fieldwork, research, and written on the Miskitus during the Somoza era.

Mary Helms was the senior scholar and the dean of Central American lowlands work. Her book, *Asang: Adaptations to Culture in a Miskito Community*, published in 1971, was the only existing in-depth study over time of a Miskitu community. Helms had created a term to describe Miskitu contemporary culture: "purchase society." It referred to what I would call the transition from a subsistence economy to a cash economy after the occupations by the US Marines and the installation of the Somoza family dictatorship, nearly a century in time. I found the book interesting and insightful, but lacking a grasp of the processes of capitalism and imperialism, or of the pernicious and overwhelming dominance of US Christian missionaries in the area, led by the Moravians. As, of course, it would not have, since Helms herself was Moravian.

I expected to clash with her and did, because my paper was about the influence of the Moravians on the Miskitu. I showed how the Moravians worked closely with the US Marines and US fruit companies to turn the Miskitus into a cheap labor force, dependent on imported goods as they abandoned subsistence farming and fishing for purchasing Spam, Wonder Bread, Vienna sausages, and Ipana toothpaste from the company stores to which they became indebted—an example of what development theorists called "the development of underdevelopment."

The other two anthropologists did not wish to get on the bad side of Helms, because the Moravian archives in Bethlehem, Pennsylvania, were essential for any ethnographic research on the Miskitus. Phil Dennis, who specialized in medical anthropology, had followed in Helms's footsteps by focusing on one Miskitu community, Awastara, and soon returned to Nicaragua to continue his research. Michael Olien had completed a masterful, nearly obsessive work on the role of the Miskitu king, a ceremonial position created by the British colonizers in the eighteenth century through which to rule. Olien documented the fact that Creoles, not Miskitus, dominated the office of king. Yet, the king and the "Mosquito Kingdom" created by the British continued to define modern Miskitu aspirations for self-determination. Brooklyn Rivera, Steadman Fagoth, and other contenders for autocratic leadership of the Miskitus exploited this colonized mentality to establish themselves. The Moravian hierarchy supported Brooklyn, but their main man was Armstrong Wiggins, Brooklyn's Washington lobbyist, who had been groomed by the Moravians from youth to be a Moravian Miskitu leader.

The ASE panel provided me with useful background for understanding the Miskitu situation in the Honduran refugee camps—but as it turned out perhaps I should have attended a *Soldier of Fortune* convention as well.

14

Missionaries and Mercenaries

The minute I sat down beside the man, I regretted it. He began talking instantly, in that friendly way certain travelers have of addressing their fellow passengers. I looked around the crowded Tan Sahsa airliner leaving Miami, bound for Honduras. Every seat was taken.

As things turned out, meeting John Kennett was a bit of luck. He told me everything about himself on the plane ride and gave me his card. Kennett was a Canadian citizen who had retired from the Toronto police force, where he served for fourteen years. His card said that he was the "Pilot-President of Missionary Air, Inc." His address was La Ceiba, Honduras, but he said that he actually worked out of Tampa, Florida, where his guru, a missionary named Jean Isabel, lived. At first, he told me his company was a transport and storage firm to serve the swelling ranks of missionaries in Honduras. But he could not stop himself from talking, and eventually whispered, confidentially, that the transport company was actually a setup to assist MISURA. His goal was to get a small airplane with water-landing gear to be able to land on the rivers to supply the "warriors" and to bring in medical supplies to treat battle injuries.

Kennett did not seem like the missionary type. He did not talk about God or try to convert me. In fact, he asked me no questions at all, apparently assuming that my mission was similar to his. He said that the woman who worked in the air traffic control tower at Tegucigalpa was a friend of his and helped him, he did not say how or with what.

As the plane descended into its daredevil landing at the mountain-enclosed Tegucigalpa airport—"just like cleaning a salad bowl," Kennett said—he asked me where I was staying. I told him I had reservations at the Hotel Alameda, which was the charming hotel where our Women's Alternative group had stayed the year before.

Kennett looked shocked and asked, "Why would you stay there? It's no place for a lady."

I told him I had stayed there before.

"Well, it has changed—now it's full of Yanks, soldiers. They probably won't even let you check in there."

At the baggage claim, passengers from another plane that had landed were collecting their bags. They were all English-speaking men, many with southern accents. The bags they were grabbing were army duffels and rifle cases.

"Mercenaries," Kennett whispered in my ear. He said that they were from a private paramilitary group based in Decatur, Alabama, and called themselves "Civilian Military Assistance" (CMA). But there were other, older white men as well, their hands clasping Bibles rather than rifle cases, clearly missionaries. Missionaries and mercenaries, a regular crusade. I knew that US Senator Jeremiah Denton from Alabama was behind the CMA. The most active organization allied with the Contras, especially with the Miskitus, was "Friends of the Americas," the brainchild of Woody and Diane Jenkins from Louisiana, whose patrons in Congress were Louisiana representatives Robert Livingston and Hamilton Fish. They were trying to get "humanitarian aid" to the Miskitu Contra camp at Rus Rus, right on the border across the river from Nicaragua.

Kennett insisted on riding in the taxi with me to the Hotel Alameda. The sky was growing dark. I stared out the window and watched the crowds of people walking along the highway, mostly street vendors pushing their carts home. A few had mangy ponies or burros pulling the carts. Many were women with stair steps of small children straggling along behind them. Their forms were silhouetted against a mango-colored sky that turned soft pink, and then suddenly brightened to pure fuchsia, an opaque blue barely bleeding through the vivid sunset. One day, I thought, I will visit a Central America without war, without the grinding poverty of the many and the gluttonous wealth of the few—what a paradise it would be. The taxi driver had hesitated to take us to the Alameda, and when we arrived he would not pull into the hotel's entrance but insisted on stopping on the highway to let us out. Kennett told him to wait, but he sped away.

The semi-circle driveway in front of the hotel, lit by a bright spotlight, was jammed with US Army jeeps and unmarked SUVs with dark windows, most with their engines running. The thick mahogany entry door was askew, off one iron hinge. That would take some doing, I thought, maybe an earthquake. The small stained-glass window in the door was shattered. I entered the lobby, which had been an elegant tiled room adorned with Mayan pottery and masks, furnished with hand-carved mahogany furniture. Now everything was smashed and scattered. On first sight, it looked like a fraternity party out of control. Dozens of uniformed and armed GIs in various stages of intoxication were draped around dark, teenaged local girls. The noise was deafening. Bodies, some naked, streaked through the hallway that skirted the courtyard off the lobby. Drunken fistfights were in progress, and within seconds, before I could take another step, several glasses and beer bottles had sailed through the air, crashing on a tile floor that was already covered with shards of glass.

I froze, bewildered. No one paid attention to me. Then I felt the towering presence of Kennett beside me. "See what I mean?"

But I stayed the night. The door to the room I was given was broken, so I went out to get another one. Kennett was still there. The man at the desk took us to the conference room, which was apparently the only room in the hotel that was not in shambles and had a working lock. There were army cots there, so I took one and Kennett took another. The noise continued all night.

When I woke, Kennett was gone. I called the UNHCR office and an official came for me, scolding me for staying there. The small four-seater World Relief plane was waiting for me at the airport, so we went directly there. World Relief was funded mainly by the US Agency for International Development. It was a branch of the National Evangelical Association, based in Wheaton, Illinois, and its current operational director in Honduras was Tom Hawk. Hawk's father had been the first regional director, but he had died suddenly in 1982, and Tom took over. He had no higher education or preparation for the role. He was a religious zealot who hired others of his kind for work in the refugee camps.

The plane was full, with three other passengers: two World Relief staffers and Dr. Kenneth Dale Wells, a Mormon elder from Pennsylvania. He told me all about himself and even gave me a copy of his résumé. When I told him I was a native of Oklahoma, he said that his son lived there and invited me to accompany him on his visits to several refugee camps before going to UN-HCR offices in Mokorón. I did and was thus able to see much more and talk to more people than I would have otherwise. The other two young men were World Relief staffers, Wilmer Dagen and Duke Miller. Duke said that he had worked with the Hmong in 1981. Wilmer was the development coordinator for World Relief's funds from the US Agency for International Development. The head of World Relief at the Miskitu refugee center in Mokorón was the son of World Gospel Service missionaries in Bolivia. In one camp we visited, this one for Sumus, a young woman who grew up in Ecuador where her parents were missionaries was in charge. The first thing all of them did was to gather in a circle to pray. I stood to the side of that ceremony. They called themselves "missionary kids," or "MKs" for short.

My first thought, when I finally visited the camps, was that the situation was nearly out of control. The Honduran government—even the military—seemed to be overwhelmed due to the armed force of MISURA, with its 3,000 heavily armed Miskitus under the command of Steadman Fagoth. MISURA was probably the single largest presence in the region and exerted control over the camps through intimidation and even terror. I was told of forced recruitment of Miskitus into MISURA, clandestine prisons, and executions.

Most of the actual aid to the Miskitus seemed to be funneled through World Relief, which administered the Miskitu and Sumu refugee camps in the region. Though World Relief condemned MISURA, they appeared to have some level of cooperation with them, certainly enough to allow WR to work in the area. The staffers of World Relief were the young, blond children of protestant evangelical missionaries in Latin America. They seemed profoundly incompetent, more adept at prayer circles than delivering services. Clearly, however, they wanted to move beyond refugee aid to development, taking over the region and remaking it in their image. Here the UN High Commission on Refugees was able to act as a kind of check on World Relief, making sure that no aid went within fifty miles of the border, and that no funds were committed to development aid. Otherwise the UNHCR itself seemed to have little control over the camps and had no representatives there.

As far as day-to-day living went, the Miskitus themselves were all right— they knew how to take care of themselves and they knew the region. They simply took whatever aid was forthcoming from World Relief and used it to run their own communities.

In my report on the situation, I recommended that the Honduran government move as quickly as possible to get World Relief out of the region completely. I suggested instead that it bring in the UN Food and Agricultural Organization or the UN Development Program for development work. For the long term, I argued that the Hondurans would have to study the Miskitu indigenous question, especially land tenure. If the Honduran government did not consider Honduran Miskitu claims, MISURA would only grow stronger in the region. To help prevent that from happening in the short term, I suggested that the Hondurans put authority for assisting the Nicaraguan Miskitus in the hands of the Honduran Miskitu organization, MASTA. To my sponsors, the UN High Commission on Refugees, I suggested that they more closely supervise the activities of World Relief. I suggested that they too work on the indigenous question to better understand the Miskitu/Sumu refugee situation, perhaps to advise the Honduran government. Finally, I cautioned that they should be prepared to provide a prolonged presence in the region, even if they were pressured to phase the work out. Until the land tenure question was resolved, the situation would remain volatile.

The following week, UNHCR held a conference on Central American refugees in Colombia. By the time I returned in January, it had endorsed my recommendations and decided to place a UNHCR official at Mokorón to oversee World Relief. Similarly, the Honduran government began an investigation of World Relief.

My return Tan Sahsa flight from Tegucigalpa on my way back to Geneva stopped for passengers at the civilian airport in San Pedro, Honduras, on the Caribbean north coast. We were delayed leaving there while another plane landed. That plane was a United States SR-71 spy plane, clearly marked "US Air Force." Then, at a stop in Belize City, a C-120 cargo plane landed, painted camouflage but clearly marked "USAF." British Royal Air Force dollies rolled up to the plane to unload a Jeep Cherokee. Despite their protestations, the US military was clearly supplying counterinsurgencies throughout Central America.

The last two weeks of January, I returned to Honduras, after a stay in Managua to finalize plans with INIES, the Jesuit research center based there, to return in the spring. At a two-day conference on Nicaragua held in Geneva in October, I was asked to speak on the Miskitu issue. Andres Dubois from INIES was there, and invited me to go work at INIES to help develop some ideas on autonomy for the eastern region that could be presented to the Sandinistas. I told him I would be there in January. Xavier Gorostiaga and Andres met me at the airport and took me to the house where I would be staying. They were also cooperating with INCINE (the Nicaraguan film institute) in making a film in the Miskitia. The filmmakers invited me to go with them to the Miskitu assembly that took place over two days at Tasba Pri. Miskitus ran the entire meeting in the Miskitu language, with Spanish translation for the guests (which they often forgot). It was exciting to see their enthusiasm for autonomy and to hear the long debates. I was disappointed to learn that Comandante William Ramírez had been reassigned as minister of transportation in Managua. Comandante Luis Carrión, a member of the Sandinista Directorate, was in charge of the Atlantic Coast and negotiations with the exiled Miskitu organizations and the return of refugees.

I was pleased to find that the Sandinistas were planning to send a large, high-level delegation to the UN Commission on Human Rights in Geneva the following month, headed by their former UN representative, Alejandro Bendeña, now in the Foreign Ministry. Several indigenous representatives from the Miskitia would be part of the delegation. Also, Oscar Hodgson of MISITAN had been selected by the World Council of Indigenous Peoples to represent the organization at the Commission.

I was able to meet with the Honduran ambassador to Nicaragua on recommendation from Ambassador Maldonado in Geneva, who was his good friend. The ambassador made calls to Tegucigalpa and set up an appointment for me with the chairman of the Honduran refugee committee, Colonel Garcia Turcios. To my surprise, he said that my November report had led to the relocation of the Big Pine III Honduran-US war games, scheduled for March 1985, from the Miskitu region to the Gulf of Fonseca on the Pacific side. He also said that, due to my report, the government had expelled Steadman Fagoth, and that World Relief was under investigation.

In Tegucigalpa, I also met with Dr. Ramon Custodia, the main civilian critic of the Honduran military, whom I had met on the women's delegation tour. Like me, Dr. Custodia was preparing to go to the February 1985 meeting of the UN Commission on Human Rights, and I wanted to obtain the most recent information for lobbying there. He planned to share precise information he had on the disappearance of nearly two hundred Honduran civilians during the past three years of US military presence in Honduras. Dr. Custodia urged me to meet Danira Miralda as she was also planning to go to Geneva.

Danira Miralda Bulnes was a thirty-seven-year-old Honduran anthropologist and president of a development program in the eastern region of Honduras, working closely with MASTA, the Honduran Miskitu organization, and with the Garífunos on the north coast. The Honduran military and the United States, as well as World Relief's Tom Hawk, denounced MASTA as communist-controlled. In November, I had met Professor Smelling Wood, the president of MASTA, and the MASTA leader, Walsted Miller, in Puerto Lempira, the capitol of the Honduran Miskitia. They impressed me as being devoted to indigenous rights, but they were clearly opposed both to the heavy presence of the Honduran and US military on their native lands and to the three thousand armed Nicaraguan Miskitus linked with the Contras who likewise were encamped in their territory. The Honduran Miskitus were particularly upset that the Nicaraguan Miskitu refugees were receiving ample aid and good homes while the Honduran Miskitus were impoverished and were not compensated for the use of their territory.

Danira had worked for several years with Catholic Relief Services (CRS) both with Salvadoran and Nicaraguan refugees in Honduras. CRS had a long reputation for being politically neutral; however, she noted that CRS had increasingly taken on the US point of view since Lawrence Pezzulo, the former Carter-appointed ambassador to Nicaragua whom I had met in 1981, had become president of the organization. Danira affirmed that Moravian pastors in the Miskitu refugee camps made up the ideological infrastructure of MISURA, and that they remained closely tied to the Moravian church.

Ted Wilde, international director of Moravian missions, visited often. A Paraguayan lawyer had told me that Wilde had been asked by the Paraguayan Guaraní Indian organization in 1978 to leave their area because they believed him to be working for the CIA.

On his own request, I met with Tom Hawk, who was furious with the report I had made to UNHCR and the Honduran government detailing my negative views of World Relief's role controlling the refugee camps. He gave me a proposal that outlined WR's project to establish a development agency, very similar to the US Agency for International Development, from which he expected operational funds. Although WR's official line, required by the UNHCR, was for timely repatriation of the Nicaraguan Miskitus, the development plan sought to "integrate" the Honduran and Nicaraguan Miskitus—a plan that signaled a protracted Contra war against the northeastern zone of Nicaragua.

The person in charge of World Relief's development project was Dr. Florence Eggen, a French citizen and medical doctor. She had first gone to Honduras in early 1982 representing Medicins sans Frontiers (Doctors without Borders), soon becoming director of World Relief's UN refugee operation in Mokorón. US embassy reports from Honduras to George Schultz, US secretary of state, during the 1982 "Red Christmas" exodus of Miskitus from the Río Coco border villages refer to Dr. Eggen as being key to that operation, including her frequent interviews with the US and European press in which she alluded to Sandinista genocide. I wrote in my notebook, after meeting her: "Dr. Eggen is very intelligent and a very dangerous person, almost certainly directly connected with the CIA plan. She seems to have a profound influence on Tom Hawk, who is not very intelligent."

World Relief, it seemed, was assuming the role of its masters, for I soon discovered that the CIA was in the process of tightening its grip on the Miskitu combatants. I learned that the Miskitu Moravian pastors Wycliffe Diego and Roger Herman had replaced Steadman Fagoth. Under this new leadership, MISURA would soon be reorganized as KISAN (United Indigenous Peoples of Nicaragua). Meanwhile, the CIA, the Moravian Church, and Brooklyn Rivera's associate, Armstrong Wiggins, were having talks with KISAN and the CIA to allow MISURASATA to operate in Honduras, which began a few months later. Soon, Ambassador Negroponte was reassigned, and the Miskitu combatants would be controlled almost entirely from the White House through Oliver North and the National Security Council.

D anira Miralda, Chockie Cottier, and I took a room together in Geneva. We made a good team, linking up with the other large nongovernmental delegations from Central America. In the process of paying attention to Central American refugees, it was becoming increasingly clear that the UN refugee agency needed to develop specific programs for indigenous refugees. Danira had been aware of that for some time and welcomed having us as allies. We spent many hours in meetings with refugee officials and with delegates of the International Committee for the Red Cross, which oversees the Geneva Conventions. Chockie and Danira left after two weeks, and I moved to my friend Julia Messina's apartment for the final four weeks of the Commission. Julia, who worked for UNHCR, had wise advice for me: "Watch out. It's seductive, working with refugees. You get a terrible and ecstatic feeling of the power of life or death over so many people. It's addictive."

Planning meetings took place for the NGO conference at the third UN Conference on the Rights of Women, which was scheduled for September 1985 in Nairobi. Genevieve Vaughn, whom I had met in Houston and who had paid for the *New York Times* ad, arrived with the women we had met with in Rome the previous November—I had gone there from Geneva at Thanksgiving where Gen had a villa and invited a dozen or so women. None of them had been to a UN meeting before. UN conferences are meant to have that effect, getting civil society involved. The UN women's conferences in 1975 in Mexico, 1980 in Copenhagen, 1985 in Nairobi, and 1995 in Beijing, were remarkably successful in both getting women from all over the world involved in international human rights and in pressuring governments and the UN itself to appoint women to important positions. In those brainstorming sessions in Geneva, we came up with the idea for a "peace tent" at the upcoming Nairobi NGO conference. Although I was unable to go because of my work with the Miskitu and Sumu refugees in Honduras, the Peace Tent was the star of the conference, bringing together women from countries in conflict: Palestinian and Israeli women, Ethiopian and Eritrean women, Indian and Pakistani women. The tent idea was carried to the Beijing conference in 1995, with dozens of tents representing various issues and the Peace Tent still the center of the conference.

I was also on the organizing committee for a world conference on Nicaragua to be held in May 1985. This was an initiative of the Geneva nongovernmental organizations, headed by Edith Ballantyne and Romesh Chandra, who had organized our indigenous UN conferences. I was able to solicit a sizeable contribution from Gen Vaughn for expenses. Edith and I flew to Lisbon to meet with the local organizing committee, most of them from the Portuguese Communist Party, which had considerable power in parliament. I would return two months later for the conference.

After the UN Human Rights Commission meeting in Geneva, I flew to meet Chockie Cottier in New York, where the UN NGO Committee was finally ready to take up our application to gain official NGO status for the Indigenous World Association. The committee had a rotating membership, and the United States was a member. The committee made decisions by consensus, so that if any one country objected, the organization's application failed. Fortunately, the Swedish ambassador for human rights, Bernt Carlsson, was head of the Swedish delegation to the committee. I had met and talked with Bernt in Geneva in October when he was there with the Swedish prime minister, Olaf Palme, and Bernt had agreed to support the IWA application. I also had obtained a commitment from Yugoslavia and, thanks to AAPSO, from the nonaligned-country members of the committee. In those days, getting Sweden, Yugoslavia, and the nonaligned countries together was a dream combination for winning in the UN (except for the Security Council) because the socialist bloc would never oppose anything supported by the nonaligned countries, and the European states would support Sweden and Yugoslavia, both of which were considered neutral. But the Reagan administration opposed nearly everything, including the existence of the UN. All we could hope for was that their lack of attention to detail would allow us to slip through—and that seems to have been what happened, since the IWA was accepted without objection.

In May, I returned to Nicaragua to work at INIES. It was great to have an office again in Nicaragua, especially one in a nongovernmental institute. Xavier Gorastiaga, the director, was nearly sixty years old, a Jesuit from the Basque country of Spain. He was brilliant and congenial, and I learned a great deal from him. The people he had gathered consisted of exiles—Edwige from Baby Doc Duvalier's dictatorship in Haiti, Amilcar Turcios from Guatemala—as well as internationalists from Belgium, Spain, Mexico, and the United States. The only Nicaraguan was the director, Daisy Zamora. Daisy, a well-known poet, had been the voice of the Sandinistas on their clandestine radio during the insurgency, and I treasured the friendship we developed. The physical site was a bit decrepit but charming, an old stone building on a rise with a panoramic view of the lake, across from the Hotel Intercontinental. My office space was in a room with all the other researchers, each with a small desk, a manual typewriter, and a telephone that only occasionally functioned.

My task at the institute was to write a book summarizing Miskitu history and the current crisis. Not just a history, the book was to function as a kind of jumping-off point for a solution to the land tenure problem. As such, it was also to include a review of existing international law on the right to self-determination, as well as an account of existing autonomy arrangements in other nations, such as that of Greenland in relation to Denmark and the Indian reserves in the United States and Canada. When I finished, the book was translated at INIES and published as *La Cuestión Miskitu en la Revolución Nicaragüense*. I also developed another paper, "A Proposal for International Symposium on Autonomy for the Atlantic Coast of Nicaragua," which I proposed be held on October 12, 1985, during which the Sandinistas would declare that Columbus Day to be instead the "International Day of Solidarity with the Indigenous Peoples of the Americas." The conference was postponed to June 1986, although October 12 was named a national holiday for Atlantic Coast autonomy.

Writing the book, for the first time I felt that my knowledge gained from the UN work had been of use. The Sandinistas had been struggling to develop an autonomy plan, but there were no international lawyers in the country free to work on it. Poverty does not just mean a lack of things, but also a lack of the most basic skills and access to ideas. And when a country must spend all its skinny resources to defend itself against a dirty war, there is nothing left for questions like land tenure, autonomy, or self-determination.

My lodging was in a private home of an elderly widow from one of the wealthy families of the Somoza era, the Icaza. Stripped of the family income that had come from Somoza's largesse, Amanda Icaza took in boarders. Señora Icaza hated the Sandinistas, calling them bandits and bank robbers, jail-birds. She believed that they were bringing shame to the beloved republic, and she hoped the United States would invade and drive them out. Despite my politics, I was her favorite among the boarders because I was from the United States. She was nasty to the other boarders—two Cubans and an Argentine—all economists working in the agricultural ministry.

I hadn't lived in Managua since 1981, and it had changed a great deal in four years. It seemed as if half the women wore black for mourning loved ones killed by the Contras. Most of the fine restaurants had closed, and the cordoba, Nicaragua's currency, was nearly worthless with the black market booming. Electricity and water were rationed and off half the time. On the other hand, there was a new literary café halfway between my office and where I lived, where I stopped most evenings to drink mojitos, talk with young Sandinistas, and read.

This was my eighth trip to Nicaragua in four years. The more time I spent there, the more I admired the resilience of its people. Citizens in the United States tend to be cynical—we believe in nothing, have confidence in nothing. In this way, we are our own worst victims, bereft even of a belief in the basic goodness of human beings and the just society we are capable of building. When I had first arrived in Nicaragua after the Sandinista victory, that sense of possibility was palpable. The spirit of the place was absolute joy, the air filled with electrical energy. Hopes and dreams—feeding the poor, doctoring the people, teaching literacy, organizing poetry workshops, women's freedom, indigenous self-determination—all things had seemed possible. I recall thinking to myself that the feeling of excitement was in a way almost erotic in its air of creativity. Sexy. After four years of dirty war, that feeling was gone. The people had become war-weary.

I had planned to work at INIES until I had to return to my teaching job at Hayward in late September 1985, but in May, Mirna Cunningham, the Miskitu physician who was now governor of the northeastern region, requested of INIES that I go to Puerto Cabezas (now Bilwi, the original Miskitu name) to work with her. The book was done, and, as usual, I felt restless and wanted to get back into the action. In Puerto Cabezas, Mirna put me to work doing various things, but mainly sitting in on her meetings and taking me along to Miskitu communities. I stayed in a different boarding house, one owned by a Chinese couple. On May Day, which on the Atlantic Coast was a celebration involving the maypole, not the labor holiday, we flew on a small plane to Bluefields to party with Lumberto Campbell and others. To my surprise, Tomás Borge was there as well as Eduardo Galeano, the Uruguayan writer whose *Open Veins of Latin America* I much admired. I was the only US citizen there.

Peace was coming to the Río Coco, allowing the former residents to leave the Tasba Pri settlements and return to their communities to rebuild. However, negotiations with Brooklyn Rivera of MISURASATA went nowhere, and eventually Rivera, accompanied by his arrogant US advisers, Bernard Nietschmann and lawyers from the Indian Law Resource Center, walked out of the talks. In a way, that created an opportunity, because the Sandinistas on the ground began negotiating directly with individual Miskitu commanders. Especially after their leader, the charismatic Steadman Fagoth, had been removed from MISURA and the organization changed to KISAN, the local MISURA commanders were ready to deal; they now called themselves KISAN por la Paz. In June 1985, a cease-fire between key commanders and the Sandinista government was announced. With the cease-fire, the Río Coco Miskitus who had been relocated to Tasba Pri were able to go back home to their beloved river.

Mirna took me along to visit the people who had returned. For two days, we traveled in her jeep in a convoy of army trucks with about two hundred soldiers, going along the river border all the way to Cabo Gracias a Diós, the farthermost town at the mouth of the Río Coco as it spilled into the Caribbean, the only spot on the continent touched by Columbus on one of his voyages. The people were ragged and without much until the troops arrived bearing food and supplies. Mirna was received like a queen. The women took her away to bathe her and give her a place to rest. She had doctored nearly every living Miskitu in the region and was well loved. We spent the night there, where I slept in an army truck.

With little or no fighting now between Miskitu insurgents and the Sandinistas, there was no reason the Nicaraguan Miskitu who had fled to Honduras could not go home. For the rest of the summer, I shuttled back and forth between Honduras and Nicaragua, taking photographs of people and carrying letters back and forth, working to convince the refugees that they could now return.

15

Refugees

In late August of 1985, I was in Mokorón, Honduras, the administrative center for dozens of Miskitu and Sumu Indian refugee camps, preparing to conduct another round of shuttle diplomacy to bring the refugees back home. The tropical rain forest along the Nicaraguan–Honduran border marked by the Río Coco suddenly stops about ten miles outside Mokorón, replaced by a pine-dotted plain that continues for forty miles to the Caribbean coast.

Mokorón had been a sleepy Honduran Miskitu town, I was told, before it was overwhelmed by a flood of US and Honduran soldiers, mercenaries, US missionaries, and Contras, and by fifteen thousand Nicaraguan Miskitu and Sumu Indian refugees. With urging from the United States, Honduras had been generous in dispensing land to those Nicaraguan refugees, land appropriated from Honduran Miskitus who had no say in the matter. Most of the land, however, was being appropriated by the Honduran authorities for their development plans, since they saw the situation as an opportunity to "open the frontier," as they put it, for Spanish-speaking settlers from the western part of the country. The Contra war gave Honduras the excuse to challenge Indian control of the precious tropical hardwoods and pine, to look for possible oil and gold, and to clear the tropical rain forests for cattle grazing. Spanish-speaking cowboys arrived daily with their cattle, traversing the rain-proofed road that had been cut out of the jungle by the US Army Corps of Engineers during the US war games there, the first land connection between western and eastern Honduras. The Honduran newspapers were filled with excitement over the boom in the Miskitia. It was being treated like a mini gold rush.

Local Indians remained in the background of the refugee center, avoiding confrontations, even conversation. The refugees taking over their land were, after all, their relatives. If the Hondurans had believed the tales of woe and horror the refugees told—tales mainly fed to them by the Moravian pastors and Contra leaders—then perhaps they would have been more eager to join with the Contras themselves. But the Honduran Miskitus had their doubts about what was really going on across the border. The Honduran Miskitus, like the Nicaraguan Indians, were not happy at being separated from their relatives by the Río Coco. Nor did they feel that the Honduran central government had their best interests at heart. So, when the Sandinistas first gained power, the Honduran Miskitus had wanted to believe that the Sandinistas were liberators. In particular, they had heard rumors that the Sandinistas supported reunification of the Miskitia, which had been cut in two, and autonomy, an old dream of the Indians.

For nearly four years, Nicaraguan Miskitus were coming over the border telling their cousins that the Sandinistas were not liberators. Yet the Honduran Miskitus did not believe everything they were hearing from their Nicaraguan relatives, not after they had seen them surrounded by "Yanqui mercenaries," or so Mattie Love told me as she prepared my breakfast. Mattie was a Honduran Miskitu and housekeeper for Vladimiro Huaroc (Vladi), a newly appointed UNHCR officer who was a Quechua Indian from Peru and head of the refugee center. It was six in the morning and Mattie and I were alone in the house, where I had spent the night. Mattie was pleased to hear what I told her about Nicaragua, that the Sandinistas were not monsters and that they supported Miskitu autonomy.

By seven in the morning, I was waiting on the east bank of the Mokorón River for a boat Vladi had arranged to take me up river to visit some of the refugee camps. The river trip would take several hours. Two other women, both Honduran, had arrived on the morning flight from Tegucigalpa and joined us for the trip. Carolina Gómez was a woman in her twenties, employed by the International Committee of the Red Cross (ICRC) to deliver mail to the refugees from relatives in Nicaragua, and to collect mail from them to go to Nicaragua. ICRC did not allow sealed letters, and it seemed that the refugees had been told by their pastors that these letters would be turned over to Sandinista security, so Carolina found the task difficult. Carla was only eighteen; her mother, Meneca de Mencía, was president of the Honduran Red Cross and this was her first trip to the camps. Carla had been a Girl Scout, so she was a real trooper, also providing us with snacks and medicines she had thought to bring.

I did not expect a yacht, but I was surprised when a crude wooden dugout, what the Miskitus call a *pipante*, pulled up to the Mokorón riverbank. A five-horsepower motor, bearing a miniature blue UN flag, was attached to the boat's tail. Three men stood on the boat as if it were a surfboard. One stepped out to help me climb onboard, introducing himself as José Blanco. José in turn introduced me to the Honduran Miskitus—Elmer the rower and Jake the pilot, who wore a black patch over one eye and a bandana around his head, looking like a pirate out of central casting.

Our first hour on the river was uneventful, smooth sailing between riverbanks lined with a postcard jungle. Red, blue, and yellow parrots flitted through the trees, and we could hear monkeys chattering and catch glimpses of them swinging from branch to branch. José was a talker, a former schoolteacher. He spoke Miskitu to the boatmen, Spanish to Carolina and Carla, and English to me, to practice, he said, since he had applied for political asylum in Canada. He could have been from anywhere in Latin America, more Latino than Indian or Black in appearance—tall, athletic, light-skinned, with dark hair and eyes. He was fussy about his appearance and wore Levis and a red tee shirt that advertised Budweiser in black.

I said, "Funny, you wear the Sandinista red and black."

He threw his head back in laughter, apparently not having considered the colors before: "It is true, but I do not mind. I am sympathetic."

"Why did you leave Nicaragua then?"

"I left with Brooklyn, the MISURASATA."

"And Canada, why do you want to go there?"

"It is the only way I can see how to get back to Nicaragua alive." He laughed again, but with a bitter edge in his voice. Like many others I would meet, he was afraid, not of the Sandinistas, but of the Contras.

The river abruptly widened and rain began to fall, softly at first, but quickly harder, hitting us like dull knives. The placid stream was suddenly broad and deep, steep, churning, rocky as the river ran through mountain rapids a half-mile wide. I had no reference point for my terror. The scary river runs in Nicaragua did not compare—I had never been on one upstream during rainy season.

For nearly an hour the *pipante* slammed in every direction, going backward much of the time. All the while Jake stood in front and balanced the boat, probing with a long stick for rocks and depth, throwing hand signals to Elmer and José, who crouched, working the oars and the motor. I burrowed into the bottom of the boat, my heels dug in, knuckles white from clutching the sides. I was on automatic survival mode.

When we finally reached a plateau, perhaps a thousand feet higher than Mokorón, the river was even wider but relatively smooth. Branches of monstrously gnarled, giant trees formed a tunnel, straining the light. Monkeys scampered through the branches chattering, swinging from vines and dive-bombing us. Scarlet, chartreuse, turquoise feathers fluttered in the green dimness. The soundtrack was from *Tarzan*.

The rain increased to a deluge as we stopped at three refugee camps on the banks of that wild river. We climbed steep, muddy cliffs to reach each one, the last one containing the refugees from José's village in Nicaragua. He introduced us to his wife and baby, and we stayed to rest awhile and ate the canned Vienna sausage and crackers that Carla had brought. I had a message for the refugees: "Return to Nicaragua in safety with amnesty, no reprisals from the Sandinista; the UN guarantees safe passage."

The refugees asked, "What about the Contras? They will kill us if we try to return."

I explained that there was now a cease-fire with many of the KISAN commanders committed to a cease-fire on the Nicaraguan side. I had pictures to show them and a few letters for people there. No one minded that I took pictures, which I promised to take to their relatives in Nicaragua, whom they assumed were most likely dead. They scribbled letters for me to take back, but would not give any to Carolina.

The village elder told me, "No one from our village joined the Contras. MISURA kidnapped us, they forced the whole village to march to Honduras, and that is why the UN placed us up this river, so the Contras cannot reach us, but for all of us to leave here at one time is another matter, too dangerous. José will go first, alone, and find out if it is safe for us to leave this place."

When we returned to the riverside to leave, we found that the water had risen to the level of the village. Within an hour, the river had swollen fifteen feet, and we had only to step into the *pipante*. I was pleased not to have to climb down the muddy cliff I had struggled up, but Elmer the boatman doused my enthusiasm and warned of grave danger, for the whole river would have changed form, and the rapids would be even more dangerous than before. José and the boatmen took us a rough five miles up the river and left us there before returning to Mokorón. In that camp, despite their difficulties, the refugees were becoming self-sufficient in food and gave us delicious roasted fresh corn to eat.

We had to walk several miles to Musawas, the new camp for the Sumu Indians I had visited at another location the year before, and there I found a remarkable change. All the missionary kids were gone, and Peter Gaechter, a Swiss UNHCR official, was in charge. And the Sumus had decided to return to their villages in Nicaragua. I spent an afternoon and evening listening to their stories. They told me that they originally settled in Tapalwas where I had visited, near the border, two hours by automobile or boat from Mokorón. Many young Sumu men were forced into MISURA by Steadman Fagoth, with a few reaching high positions in the fighting force. But Sumu fighters were used by MISURA as shock troops and suffered proportionally more casualties than the Miskitus. They also complained about World Relief allowing US evangelicals to control the camp and appoint their leadership, something I had observed. That led to a reappraisal by many of the younger Sumus of their participation in the armed opposition to the Sandinistas, and they demanded to be relocated away from the border area and away from the older-generation Moravian Sumus, who remained convinced that the Sandinistas were in league with the devil. They named the new camp Nuevo Musawas, after their village of origin in Nicaragua. The move also coincided with the withdrawal of Sumus from MISURA, which henceforth could count on only the moral support of some of the elder Sumus in Tapalwas, who had been given vague promises of lands and opportunities once the Sandinista regime had fallen.

We spent the night in Peter's thatched-roof cabin that he had built himself, and the next morning rode a small plane to the Río Patuca refugee camps.

The first refugee village we visited there was where the people taken from Francia Sirpe in the 1983 Christmas "exodus" lived. It was obvious to all of us that Contras tightly controlled the camp, and the people were reluctant to talk. Pastor Hitler—his actual name—was the spiritual leader/ruler of the camp, a Moravian Nicaraguan-Miskitu minister. Standing right in front of us, he had exhorted the refugees, "Pay no attention to the Sandinista lies brought by these foreigners." But the former Francia Sirpe schoolteacher, whom I had met in Nicaragua on my first trip, was able to pass me a note saying they had all been kidnapped by Steadman Fagoth's Contra fighters and were being prevented from going back to Nicaragua by threats from KISAN.

I was still trembling from riding the Mokorón rapids two days before, and was reluctant to board another boat. But here we used a bigger boat, contracted to UNHCR—aluminum, with a twenty-five-horsepower engine—for our journey up the Río Patuca. The Patuca was a wide, muddy river, and was not wild until it reached the mountains; fortunately, we would not be going that far. I had never seen the Amazon, but the Patuca in Honduras was the widest river I could even imagine. The Patuca once formed the border between Honduras and Nicaragua until 1960, when the border was moved a hundred miles south to the Río Coco, and the Patuca still marked the northernmost edge of the Miskitia.

We were traveling on that river to visit the half-dozen refugee camps on its banks. The boatman, a Spanish-speaking Honduran, was paid by UNHCR to carry people and supplies in his privately owned boat up and down the Patuca to the refugee camps that had been built there during the past year. He was not a talkative man. I stared at an object in the water ahead, a log, I thought. We were traveling at high speed and I feared that our boat would crash into it. I looked back and forth from the object to the boatman, thinking he must see it, too. I could tell by instinct that he was not a man who would appreciate being told what to do, least of all by a woman. I was well trained as a child to keep my mouth shut in the company of such men, men like my father. The man was tense, rigid, and permanently angry. Cat eyes, steel-wool hair, and thick dark skin. A Smith & Wesson revolver lay within his reach.

Just as I could no longer bear to remain silent and was about to warn him of the log in our path, he swerved to the left, and in the same instant grabbed the pistol and fired, a cracking pop lost in the noise of wind, water, and motor. The object thrashed, he shot again, and I saw it was a crocodile as long as the boat, eight feet at least. The boatman looped braided hemp into a lasso and roped the dying creature, tying it to the side of the boat.

The killing had happened quickly, and it felt like a cold, surgical routine. That cowboy had become a real frontiersman. He reminded me so much of my father, especially the chilly anger just under the surface. I had thought that breed of men was unique to the US West, but I realized they were the same on any frontier, the foot soldiers of colonization. Maybe that was why the cowboy types from home, the US mercenaries I ran into everywhere, loved this place so much—frontiers to move, wild animals to kill, natives to exterminate.

I yelled out what one is supposed to say to such men: "Good shot, clean kill," and he smiled proudly.

Honduran Miskitu villages dotted the south bank of the river. Nicaraguan Miskitu refugee camps had been built between them. We passed motorless *pipantes*, local Honduran Miskitus fishing or returning from market, whole families, and the inevitable spotted mongrel that looked like Little Orphan Annie's dog. Our high-speed boat tossed them in its wake; one *pipante* capsized, and I was embarrassed. My boatman did not bat an eye—just as soon shoot them as look at them, I thought. Cowboys and Indians.

We docked on a bank. The boatman pointed up the embankment, and I saw children peering over the side down at us. As I climbed the steep, muddy cliff, I glanced back and saw the boatman already skinning the crocodile. It would make a lot of shoes and belts.

At the final refugee settlement we visited, one where the Miskitus from the Río Coco village of San Jeronimo lived, an elderly man spoke for the group to me as we prepared to leave: "How beautiful that you have come from so far away to visit us. You must really care. But more beautiful is the message you have brought us. Many strangers have come through here, but none came with such a wonderful message as yours."

That made my day.

A UNHCR-contracted plane took us back to Mokorón, where I visited one more refugee camp, this one the UNHCR-controlled camp closest to the border with Nicaragua. It was off the road to Puerto Lempira and near the base of the Honduran 5th Battalion. I wanted to find Margarita Corbella, who had enrolled as a UNHCR-protected refugee from Sandy Bay and was living in the Tapanlaya refugee camp. I had met her in Panamá with Brooklyn Rivera's MISURASATA delegation and wanted to find out why she was no longer a combatant, or if indeed she was. It was not hard to find Margarita, who welcomed me and took me to her tent—structures had not yet been built, so the camp was a sea of tents. There I showed her photographs, and she had me take her picture and wrote a letter. I said that I would return in December after going to the Nicaraguan Miskitia. Margarita was hopeful for a peace agreement, and although she was still loyal to Brooklyn Rivera, she was no longer a combatant. She wanted to help people from her village in the camp, teaching literacy and other classes. Either she was a sincere organizer, which I thought she was, or planted by Brooklyn to organize on behalf of MISURASATA. She asked me to bring a tape recorder when I returned, so she could send an audio message back to Puerto Cabezas.

In September, I returned to Nicaragua, where Maya Miller, who was helping fund projects in the region, joined me. With her was Stephen Quesenberry, an Indian rights lawyer from the Bay Area. Mirna and José Gonzales, the local Interior Ministry commander, arranged for us to drive to Waspám. Our driver, Rafael Dixon, an elderly Miskitu merchant, drove us there in his pickup truck filled with bags of rice and beans, plastic sheeting, clothing, household goods, and other aid items for the returned residents who were rebuilding their homes.

About halfway to Waspám, Rafael turned left off the road and drove along a narrow trail into a wooded area. Without explaining, he got out of the vehicle and invited us to do the same. From the woods appeared a dozen young men wearing mix-and-match military garb, crisscrossed with bandoliers, and toting automatic weapons. I had heard countless horror stories of people being kidnapped by the Contras, but I was so shocked I did not panic. Maya and Stephen appeared equally stunned. Rafael called them *nuestra muchachos* ("our boys") and spoke with them at length in Miskitu. He unloaded a few items from the truck to give to them. Then he turned to us, and in English explained that these were KISAN combatants whom the Sandinistas allowed to patrol certain areas with their weapons, a part of the cease-fire agreements hammered out during the past six months between the Sandinistas and a majority of the KISAN commanders. I had been speaking of the cease-fire that whole summer to the refugees in Honduras, but here was proof that the cease-fire held.

We talked for an hour with them, Rafael translating into English. I had a pack of photographs I had taken in the Honduran refugee camps, and I showed them to the KISAN soldiers. They were excited to see family members and thanked me for visiting them. I said I would be returning the following week and they asked me to take their picture to show there. Each wrote notes to relatives and friends on paper from my notebook.

Farther along the road to Waspám, a small band of KISAN boys stopped us to check who we were and what we were carrying. Of course, they knew and respected Rafael, as did everyone else. Under the terms of the cease-fire, they were allowed to serve as sentries on the highway. Again, Rafael gave them some food, and we continued, picking up people who were walking until the small truck was covered with people on top of the cab, the bumpers, hanging off the end and sides of the truck bed. A bunch of kids were piled on top of the bags of rice and beans.

Rafael shared with us his theory of why the United States wanted to control the Miskitia—bananas. The United States, in his view, wanted cheap Nicaraguan bananas because they were the most succulent in the world.

Entering Waspám—which had been a bustling market center with 3,000 permanent residents and with large public buildings and nice homes—we saw nothing except for the foundations of former buildings. The returnees, clustered by the river, camped out in makeshift huts and tents while they were rebuilding their homes. They had carried their tin roofs and lumber from their Tasba Pri houses and had created makeshift dwellings from these and other salvaged materials. It was lunchtime, and the people had come from various sites of reconstruction to eat and rest. They gathered around the truck to receive their rice and beans, orderly but in a din of bargaining. Rafael quieted the throng and announced that I had just returned from the Honduran camps with pictures and letters. The joy they expressed and the handshakes with me brought tears to my eyes. I had thought this would be a one-time thing, but soon realized that it would be useful to keep it up. All wanted their pictures taken for me to give to relatives in the refugee camps, and they busied themselves writing letters for me to carry.

We walked northwest along the river for a few miles, stopping where there had been smaller communities and residents were rebuilding. I showed pictures as well, and delivered letters along the way.

On the return trip to Puerto Cabezas, Rafael took us to the Miskitu village of Yulu, which was now homebase to the KISAN por la Paz fighters. I never got exact figures of how many—between a hundred and five hundred, depending on whom I talked to. Some, but not all, were from Yulu, and Yulu had supported them when they had moved clandestinely with the Contras. The townspeople expressed pride in their being based there. The fighters and civilians gathered around us to hear about who we were and what we were doing, thanking us. Many wrote letters, and I took pictures.

Finally, before leaving, it was time to try to find people in Puerto Cabezas for whom I had letters and pictures. One woman with two children, rifling through the photographs, came upon a picture of José Blanco with his wife and child and his wife's family. He had not written a letter or told me to find anyone to show the photograph to, so I was surprised when the young woman shrieked with joy. She said José was her husband and father of her children, and then asked who the other people were. I had to give her the news that they were his new family. But she was so overjoyed to see that José was still alive that the news did not shake her. She had long thought that he had been killed by the Sandinistas during Red Christmas.

M eanwhile, I was going back to Tegucigalpa to work on the cease-fire and repatriation of refugees. I had only one week, since I was due back in the Bay Area to teach a full load at my university on September 28. My goal for that week was to meet and talk with Roger Herman, Henry's brother, who was now a chief officer for KISAN in Honduras. I had photographs and letters for him from his parents and from Henry, and I wanted him to see the pictures of people returning to the river from the Sandinista resettlement camp of Tasba Pri, to see their hope and happiness. Perhaps if he truly wanted to do what was best for his people, he might rethink his position.

When I arrived at Tegucigalpa, a letter was waiting for me from Peter— the UNHCR official in the Sumu camp. "All of a sudden repatriations have stepped up," Peter wrote. "I have a suspicion it has something to do with your trip here. I know the Patuca has always been incredibly 'potential' material for refugees. I think your presence helped, as did the literature you sent afterwards." This letter encouraged me immensely.

I stayed in the Hotel Maya, then the only luxury hotel in Tegucigalpa, located across the street from the UNHCR offices, where I had long meetings with the program officer. The Hotel Maya was where US military brass and the CIA stayed, but also mercenaries looking for work, US journalists, Christian missionaries, drug dealers, and Contra leaders. I was able to contact Roger at the number his family had for him and invited him over to pick up the letters from his family. He was there in a short time and he was rather uncomfortable, but he did sit down to talk.

Roger handed me a sheet of paper that listed the officials of the new Miskitu Contra organization that replaced MISURA. KISAN was structured around a seven-member executive committee, with a command structure made up of eleven *comandantes*, and a four-member "Buro Politico," of which Roger was the chief. The whole setup smelled of CIA design, and, of course, for them the Political Bureau would be in charge, taking orders from the CIA. My hopes for changing Roger's mind sank as I realized he was the CIA's man.

After a trip to deliver the letters and photographs to Mokorón from Nicaragua, I left Honduras concerned about the apparently renewed CIA effort.

Peter wrote me in San Francisco in the fall of 1985. He and Carolina were planning to meet me at the UN Human Rights Commission in Geneva, since they were both leaving their posts to return to teach and would be available to talk to Commission members about their experiences with the Contras. In October, he wrote, "Tapamlaya [the refugee camp for Miskitus from Sandy Bay in Nicaragua where Margarita was located] has decided to repatriate almost in its entirety. We interviewed some 600 persons this week, and the problem now is getting Tegucigalpa to back us up on the logistics."

Two weeks later, Peter wrote with the good news that they had been flying the Sandy Bay Miskitus out for several days, and about 240 were back already in Puerto Cabezas in Nicaragua:

Massive, expensive operation, but well worth it. Though we have almost the entire camp registered, it looks as though KISAN is forcing the men to stay and allowing old people, women, and children to repatriate. We may not be so lucky next time. But it has made a great impact in the area, and by next year, repatriation should be in full swing. We're trying to convince the Honduran gov't to allow direct flights from Puerto Lempira to Puerto Cabezas (80 miles), but they haven't gone for it so far.

He said he was also making hundreds of copies of some of my photographs from Nicaragua to distribute in the camps.

But by late November Peter was pessimistic, warning me not to come there as planned on my Christmas break:

Here, mostly bad news. I'm afraid that our friends up north have conceived a simple but effective plan to rev up the war, wreck any chances of peace, and autonomy may be the saddest victim of all. Lately, KISAN has been stepping things up. They have scheduled "seminars" for 1–15 Dec., at which no doubt repatriation, *lucha*, etc. will be discussed—recruitment as well. KISAN and FDN [Somocista Contras] are firm allies . . . also EPS [the Sandinista military] has begun to respond to attacks from KISAN in the border area; people have begun coming into Honduras, because they're hungry and presumably in danger—1981 all over again. Roger says that CIA is making one last-ditch effort to bring Steadman back as a comandante (with US Indian mercenaries—can this be?). So the next few months will be hairy, and I think both the Nicaraguan government and the Miskitos lose. Steadman's return may be the weak link in this plan, because many may not accept him.

Radio 15 de Septiembre [FDN Contra radio] has been doing some broadcasts in Miskito, naming Centero as a spy for UNHCR, and generally inciting people to violence. He was scared off, naturally, and as soon as I informed Tegucigalpa about it they started talking to the Honduran authorities to get it stopped. They also mentioned YOU as a principal in repatriation efforts. I don't think it would be wise to come to the Mosquitia until this has clarified itself somewhat more, or died down. Because of this offensive, we have to try to get people out of the country (i.e., José Blanco). I will keep you posted.

Peter warned me not to go. But go I did.

First, I went to Managua, then to Puerto Cabezas, to travel around gathering letters and taking photographs for the Miskitu camps in Honduras. I arrived in Puerto Cabezas on Christmas Day. The hopeful mood I found in September had changed to nervousness. There had been KISAN attacks from Honduras, and they had blown up the bridge on the road to Waspám. I was disappointed that I would not be able to visit Waspám to gather letters and to take pictures to show in the Honduran camps, but I did take photographs and letters from Miskitus who had taken refuge in Puerto Cabezas to take back with me. Mirna was clearly exhausted and worried, as was everyone in Puerto Cabezas. I had Christmas dinner at her home with her children and her mother. She took me along to visit people in their homes, where each family offered us special Christmas cake and rum, Eddy Arnold's country Christmas album playing on a loudspeaker.

Mirna had a letter for me to take to the refugee camp at Tapamlaya, where Miskitus were being prevented from repatriating. The letter was signed by Comandante Tomás Borge, assuring them of their safety in returning to their homes, and pledging that the Sandinista government would grant the region autonomy.

I arrived in Tegucigalpa three days after Christmas. Peter and Vladi had both left UNHCR to continue their graduate studies, and the UNHCR main program officer for the Miskitia, Arturo Mengotti, had moved from the UNHCR Tegucigalpa office to Mokorón to replace Vladi. He was expecting me there. José Azcona Hoya had just been elected president of Honduras after winning with 30 percent of the vote, and I was invited to a party being held in his honor. Señora de Mercía, the mother of Carla, the girl who had accompanied me in August, was hosting the party. I had met her for lunch in August after returning with Carla, who had raved about the adventure, and about me.

I walked a thin line between knowing and being trusted by the Honduran authorities, who could help me, and remaining relatively invisible. I did not want to become well known. The Hondurans themselves were not the problem; the problem was that they were owned and controlled by my own country's government. The next day I was to fly to Mokorón. I had a letter from the Honduran ambassador in Geneva that I had requested, addressed to the Honduran military command, vouching for my trustworthiness. And

I had the letter from Comandante Tomás Borge. I had brought Nicaraguan Miskitu letters and photos. I thought it best to go to the party.

I walked to the plaza to hail a taxi. Tegucigalpa had the feel of a mountain town. The air was drier and cooler than the rest of Central America, more like Mexico City, but without the smog. I had grown fond of the city and the whole country, partly out of pity for their role as reluctant host to the US military and their Contras. But the city also had a charm, something mysterious about it, as if it held secrets, perhaps because it was occupied by a foreign military, and I had never before been in an occupied city. I imagined Honduran patriots seething in quiet anger, talking in the privacy of their homes and in the dark corners of bars about revolt, stockpiling rifles and ammunition, waiting for the right time to strike, and feeling their helplessness in the presence of the giant from the north.

The Mencía home was in the same neighborhood (a wealthy one) as the US Embassy. As the cab passed the fortress-like embassy, a black Ford Bronco with darkened windows pulled out in front of us and took the same turns as we did, stopping in front of the house. I was tempted to return to the hotel. If I was uncomfortable meeting Honduran officials, I avoided the US officials altogether. I did not want to call attention to myself or draw their interest, for they were sure to pressure the Hondurans to prevent my travel to the refugee camps, or worse. A man climbed out of the embassy car, a man perhaps in his forties, with a boyish face. He was not the ambassador, who was older. There were supposed to be a hundred or more people at the party, so I thought I could avoid this embassy staffer. I delayed my entrance by asking the driver to take me to pick up cigarettes. When we returned, the packed house buzzed with conversation and laughter.

The Mencía family were lined up inside the door greeting guests. Each member of the family hugged me, then Señora de Mencía took my arm and said: "I want to introduce you to a fellow countryman of yours." The nuns in San Antonio, Texas, had taught her to speak perfect English. She was dressed almost exactly as I was, in a white cotton dress. About my age, she reached only to my shoulder. She was round all over and always cheerful, an older version of her daughter, Carla.

Clusters of jabbering guests parted to let us through. The men tipped their champagne glasses. I racked my brain for any excuses to not meet the "fellow countryman," but we stopped in front of the man I had seen getting out of that Ford Bronco. She said, "You two have something in common besides being *Norteamericanos*—your love for the Miskitu." And then she abandoned me.

The man glared down at me with cold, green eyes. I felt I had seen him before. Challenge was written on his face. He looked older up close, with deep frown wrinkles, graying hair in a hammerhead cut. His white *guayabera* was starched, his black slacks creased perfectly, and his black pennyloafers were polished to a mirror. His shoulders were squared, neck and head rigid. A military officer, I figured—probably CIA.

"What do you do with the Miskitus?" he asked in a boyish voice, surprisingly squeaky. Spaces between his front teeth, like my own, gave him a hillbilly appearance when he opened his mouth.

"I'm writing a book."

"You're a reporter?" The veins of his neck protruded and pulsated.

"No, no, just an academic, a linguist," I lied.

"I work with the Miskitus, too. I train them in underwater sabotage to combat the Sandinista communists," he said.

"Oh?" I was at a loss for words.

"They're the best I've ever seen, grow up deep-sea diving for lobsters, turtle, so they develop an extraordinary capacity for underwater work, without tanks or snorkel. They're fish." His face glowed with admiration and pride.

"It sounds like dangerous work." I tried to suppress my revulsion, and my voice came out giddy sounding.

"They love it, four hundred dollars a month is more money than they see in a lifetime in Nicaragua," he said.

He stared over my head, his eyes glazed. I searched for words, but I realized he was not interested in a response from me.

"Hey, did you hear about our Shoeboxes for Liberty campaign two years ago?" His eyes sparkled.

"I don't believe so," I said, although I had.

"Well, that's the kind of thing you should organize when you get back stateside, if you care about the Miskitus. Good people all over America packed shoeboxes with Christmas goodies for the poor Miskitu refugees here in Honduras. It was a neat idea. That way, the Miskitus know Americans are behind them and projects such as that involve folks at home at the grassroots level. Here's my card—call me if you can help out."

He walked away. I stared at the card: Lt. Col. Oliver North, USMC Retired, National Security Council, The White House.

It was not so easy now to reach Mokorón. UNHCR could not find a pilot to fly me out—it was New Year's Eve. The Tegucigalpa office radioed Arturo Mengotti at Mokorón (there were no telephones, and radio was the only means of direct communication), and he said I should try to get on the SETCO flight to Puerto Lempira and they could pick me up there. SETCO, dubbed the "CIA airline," was owned by Honduran drug king and billionaire Juan Ramón Matta Ballesteros. It was contracted by the CIA to supply Rus Rus, the Honduran Miskitu town on the Río Coco border that had been taken over by Nicaraguan Miskitu combatants. The plane stopped there to drop supplies and continued to Puerto Lempira on the coast. Less officially, SETCO was also used to drop supplies to Contras inside Nicaragua. It also, famously, made drug runs.

I was lucky that the plane was at the airport with the propellers turning when I arrived in a taxi. The interior of the decrepit cargoliner had no seats, only a narrow bench along one side. Two passengers were clearly Miskitu combatants; another was a US evangelical missionary. The four of us were nearly surrounded by burlap bags. The plane landed at Rus Rus in hard rain on a muddy landing strip. My three fellow travelers left the plane there and several Miskitu women boarded.

Young men dressed in the blue uniforms of the Contras, weighted down by rifles and grenades, abruptly appeared out of the dark, close jungle. Without a word they routinely began unloading the burlap bags of rice, stamped with the official US emblem and marked: "A Gift from the People of the United States of America." Blue-uniformed and armed Miskitus surrounded the plane. As far as I could see, there were no weapons in the cargo.

While the unloading was in process, the pilot appeared from the cockpit smoking a cigarette with the engine still running. The lit cigarette in the running airplane on the ground scared me more than the heavily armed Contras peering in the loading door. I asked the pilot how long it would be before we took off again, and he assured me that it would be quickly. His accent was pure Texas. Great company to be in: a mercenary pilot, an evangelical missionary, and Contras. Sioux spiritual leaders had once told me that one is stuck forever with the people one dies with, so it was important to be careful. I did not believe it, but the thought always crossed my mind when I was in bad company.

There was no UNHCR vehicle in sight at the tiny, sandy Puerto Lempira airstrip, so I walked the short distance to the town center. I felt at home in Puerto Lempira, having met nearly every permanent resident in the town, all Miskitus. There were always foreigners—preachers, aid workers, mercenaries—mostly from the United States, and there were shiny metal storage facilities said to be filled with weapons that the CIA stashed there for KISAN. Puerto Lempira was for me the most beautiful of all Miskitu villages I had visited, a mostly untouched Caribbean paradise with clear water and phosphorescent fish that glowed in the water at night, a white powderlike sand beach with fish drying, the unpaved streets also white with sand.

I went to a *comedor* I knew, one of several eating places in people's homes. There I found the Mennonite doctor from the United States, whom I had met in August. That was lucky because I was suffering with a fever and ached all over, probably from something I caught in Puerto Cabezas. After I ate a delicious fish stew, the doc took me to his small clinic and gave me antibiotics.

The UNHCR vehicle showed up, with Walsted Miller, the Honduran Miskitu leader of MASTA, driving. We visited Mayor Smelling Wood, a revered Miskitu elder, and then drove the twenty miles to Mokorón, where Arturo and his Salvadoran wife were waiting for me. They gave me my old room, and I slept for hours. I told Arturo about my desire to visit Tapanlaya again and he agreed. We talked and drank rum until midnight, celebrating the new year.

Before noon on New Year's Day, Walsted and I left for Tapanlaya in a UNHCR-marked jeep. It was off the road to Puerto Lempira, and we had to pass the 5th Battalion army base. They often stopped vehicles for identification checks, but never official UNHCR ones, since there was an agreement with the Honduran government. But they stopped us that day. The two guards seemed to know exactly what they wanted: me. They ordered me out of the vehicle and told Walsted that he could drive on. I told Walsted in English to wait for me and to radio Arturo in Mokorón. He looked terrified, as if he wanted to get out of there fast, but he stayed.

The guards took me past the gate and inside the base, then ordered me to sit on a sandy rise to the side of the sentry post. The sun was broiling by then and the heat bored into the top of my head. I was surprised that they did not inspect my bag or take it from me. I regretted not having left it with Walsted. Inside were the two letters, written in Spanish, from Comandante Borge and from Ambassador Maldonado, plus a stack of letters and photographs. I also had the official UNHCR letter of invitation and my own UN identity badge.

An hour passed, and the young soldiers began taking aim at me, pretending to shoot me. It dawned on me that I very well might not leave that place alive. I called out to the soldiers, holding out the UNHCR letter and my UN badge. One approached me cautiously and looked at them, but obviously he couldn't read. He shook his head and started to walk away. "Espera!" I called out for him to wait. He turned and I took out Maldonado's letter. The letterhead seal of the Honduran Republic caught his eye, and he showed it to his compatriots. I saw one pick up a telephone, which was surely for internal base communications only, and after what seemed another hour a soldier beckoned me to follow him.

We walked down a paved walkway in between barracks and offices. A tall, blond man in civilian clothes walked across the path in front of us, giving me a long stare. I suspected that this was the CIA man who had ordered my detention. Clearly, he wanted me to see him. I was taken to the office of the base commander where his subcommander was on duty, the commander away. The man held Maldonado's letter, staring at it. He looked up to greet me and was exaggeratedly hospitable, offering me a glass of water, which I welcomed. He asked if I needed to "wash up," meaning go to the bathroom, and I did. When I returned, the man profusely apologized and went on and on about how much he admired his dear friend Maldonado. He did not ask to search my bag and told me I was free to go, but that I must return to Mokorón and not go on to Tapanlaya. I did not object.

Arturo was disturbed at my being detained. To him it was a major diplomatic crisis, since I was in Honduras as an official representative of UNHCR. It was hard for me, as it is for anyone outside it, to grasp the nuances of the diplomatic world, but I knew very well that diplomatic faux pas could mean life or death. Arturo feared that the Honduran military was being pressured by the United States to get rid of UNHCR, the only barrier to full Contra recruiting. He also feared for my life and wanted to get me back to Tegucigalpa and out of the country.

There was no plane available at Mokorón, so he radioed all over the area and found a pilot who agreed to fly us. Arturo, his wife, and I crowded into the tiny one-engine Beechcraft. A storm was heading toward us from the west, and the pilot did not want to fly into it to take us to Tegucigalpa, so he flew north and landed at the Miskitu town of Ahuas, refusing to go on. He and Arturo got into a yelling fight, but the man would not budge. I did not like being stuck in Ahuas, but I did not want to fly if it was unsafe, which the pilot claimed. Finally, he agreed to fly us to Olancho, where we could hire a taxi to drive us the five hours to Tegucigalpa. The drive was exhausting, the three of us jammed together in the back of a small car that had no springs.

We arrived in Tegucigalpa after midnight. I slept on the Mengottis' couch for a few hours before going to the airport to get out of the country. The only flight available was Challenge Airlines to Miami—another CIA operation, it was said. The airline had only one passenger jet, leased from KLM. It made two nonstop round trips daily between Tegucigalpa and Miami, filled with US citizens who were CIA and diplomatic officials, and USAID workers.

Arturo's face was drawn and tired when we said good-bye. He said, "You know we cannot allow you to come to Mokorón again?" Yes, I said. I had figured that out.

16

Quemada

Roxanne Dunbar Ortiz has consistently misrepresented the Miskito position to the US left and, in the words of one Indian leader, "has done more damage to the Miskito cause—and the Sandinistas—than any other person." Her letter is typical of the half-truths and untruths she peddles. . . .

—Penny Lernoux, *The Nation*, January 11, 1986

Beginning in the spring of 1982, when Russell Means unilaterally expelled me from the International Indian Treaty Council and linked up with Brooklyn Rivera, I had been excoriated by a number of individuals and organizations. These included Tim Coulter and his non-Indian lawyers with the Indian Law Resource Center in Washington, D.C., who were Rivera's advisers; Survival International, an organization of mainly anthropologists based in London; and Cultural Survival in Cambridge, a group of anthropologists originally founded to provide the US State Department with information and insights about the "hill tribes" of Southeast Asia. In the November 1985 issue of the Survival International newsletter, British anthropologist Stephen Corry published a nasty review of my *Indians of the Americas*, calling me "Orwellian," engaged in "doublespeak," and a "vulgar materialist." I was also attacked in more academic publications; for example, that same fall the *Journal of Ethnic Studies*, of which I was a "corresponding Associate," published a nauseatingly negative response to my spring 1984 essay in the journal, "The Fourth World and Indigenism: Politics of Isolation and Alternatives," by anthropologists Shelton Davis of the Anthropology Resource Center and Richard Chase Smith of Cultural Survival.

Registered letters, three and four single-spaced pages long, frequently arrived at my home from the Indian Law Resource Center's most obnoxious white lawyer, Steven Tullberg, questioning my Indian identity. At a conference on refugees in Washington, D.C., to which I had been invited to speak on the Miskitu refugees in Honduras, Tullberg sat directly in front of me with a tape recorder, and he continued to stalk me. I was also attacked repeatedly by Rivera's adviser Bernard Nietschmann, a U.C. Berkeley geography professor and frequent correspondent to the Moonie-owned *Washington Times*.

These attacks did not hurt as much as the underhanded actions of Native American veteran activist Hank Adams, who joined Russell Means in the fray late in 1985. I had never met Adams but had regarded him as a hero for his militant fight in the early 1960s on behalf of Northwest Indian fishing rights in Washington State. In 1972, Adams was one of the main organizers of the "Trail of Broken Treaties" caravan across the United States to Washington, D.C., and author of the Twenty Points presented to the Nixon administration. The following year, he was a negotiator between that administration and the AIM militants trapped in the Wounded Knee siege. By 1985, Adams was associated with Dr. Rudolph C. Ryser, also a Native American from Washington State, and Canadian Chief George Manuel, creator of the term "Fourth World" to describe tribal peoples around the world and founder of the World Council of Indigenous Peoples (WCIP) in 1975. Ryser and Manuel established in 1984 the Center for World Indigenous Studies (CWIS) in Olympia, Washington, apparently, at first, for the sole purpose of supporting the Miskitu insurgency against the Sandinistas. Bernard Nietschmann and Armstrong Wiggins were on the organization's Board of Directors.

Adams widely circulated a dossier of "documents" along with a cover letter—eleven single-spaced pages—dated November 30, 1985, addressed to "The Honorable Ronald Reagan," and cc'd to a list that included Secretary of State George Schultz, the US attorney general, and twenty-nine US representatives and senators, plus "National Indian Organizations" and "Selected News Media." The letter mainly condemned me, though it also excoriated several others, including AIM activists Vernon and Clyde Bellecourt and the mainstream Democratic Party activist LaDonna Harris, a Comanche from Oklahoma and wife of former Senator Fred Harris—for our work with the Sandinistas.

The upshot of the letter was that I should be investigated for fraud for claiming to be Indian, and for treason for giving aid and comfort to the enemy—the enemy being Nicaragua, but also Cuba. Included in the thick packet was "evidence" that I had been to Cuba, which of course was no secret. The "evidence" consisted of a paper I had presented in 1981 in Havana that was subsequently published in the Cuban journal *Tricontinental*. Other "evidence" of treason was a copy of a 1972 red-hunting report by the US Congressional Committee on Internal Security, titled "America's Maoists," as well as excerpts from books I had published in which I had cited Karl Marx or other Marxist writers. They also dug up the "secret" that I had been a prominent leader in the late 1960s women's liberation movement.

The dossier included my mother's death certificate (filed by my brother) and my own birth certificate, in which "White" was designated as our race. Additionally, my birth certificate was used to question that I was even from Oklahoma (I was born in San Antonio, where my parents had gone for work, returning to Oklahoma when I was six weeks old). I had never claimed to be registered with the federal government as an Indian, nor did I claim to have grown up in an Indian community, although the rural Oklahoma county where I did grow up had many Indian towns and was part of the Cheyenne and Arapaho territory that had been partitioned and sold to white settlers, such as my father's family. I had been invited to join the American Indian Movement, like many other unacknowledged part-Indians, during the mid-1970s period of "recovering the Indian" in the Western Hemisphere. Our aim then was to create a large pan-Indian movement without borders, and to challenge precisely the sort of self-appointed authorities who tried to define who was an Indian.

Jimmie Durham in New York handed me a copy of the dossier in the spring of 1986, five months after it had been circulated; it was in a manila envelope with the return address of Ward Churchill in Boulder, Colorado. By then, Jimmie was writing and doing art, having recently married a Brazilian artist. I had visited him in the apartment in a building on the Upper West Side in New York that he and others were occupying so it wouldn't be torn down. We apologized to each other for our previous conflicts. He had meanwhile written a good op-ed piece in the *New York Times* on Russell Means's antics in traveling with armed MISURASATA combatants to Nicaragua.

The attacks on me by Hank Adams and Russell Means, and his scribe, Churchill, who supported Miskitu insurgency against the "communist" Sandinistas, were ironic, because the Miskitu people/nation were identified principally by the fact that they spoke Miskitu (if not, they were considered Creole). Most US Indians, thanks to federal boarding schools, did not speak a word of their tribal languages. The Miskitus were mixed culturally and by skin color and did not identify as tribes or clans, and nearly every one was a devout Christian, many identifying first with the Moravian Church. They were a people, a nation, but not a tribe that desired Indian reservations such as those in the United States, which were being promoted by Rivera's US advisers.

For me, the most heartbreaking attack came from Gerald Wilkinson, president of the National Indian Youth Council, based in Albuquerque. I had met him through my husband Simon Ortiz in 1975, and regarded him as a close friend and colleague. During my two years at the University of New Mexico, we had often met, and I had encouraged him to get involved with international indigenous work. He never talked to me or wrote me about his disagreements about the Miskitus, but simply refused to speak to me. Gerald was a close friend of the Kennedy family, having begun his work with Indians during the John F. Kennedy presidency. Through Gerald, Senator Edward Kennedy was sucked into supporting Brooklyn Rivera's organization, even gaining CIA funds for it.

The attacks at some point bundled into a critical mass. As one anthropologist, Jim Stephens, who worked for the American Friends Service Committee's (AFSC) project on the Miskitus, told my friend Armando Rojas Smith, the Miskitu lawyer in Puerto Cabezas, "Roxanne está quemada" (burned), adding that Armando should not associate with me because it might rub off on him. Armando was outraged and told me about it, but who knows how many people Stephens told that to? He was in charge of Native American groups organized by the AFSC visiting the Miskitia.

There were partial truths in the allegations. I was Marxist, anti-imperialist, and feminist. I supported the Sandinista and Cuban revolutions, but I wasn't uncritical or idealistic about them. I believed they had the right to develop as they wished without US intervention. And I had not been raised as an Indian, nor did I possess federal status as an Indian. It became hard for me to keep the situation in perspective, to remember that my attackers were few and my friends and supporters many, as Chockie constantly reminded me. In fact, she too was being attacked because of the association between the American Indian Center, which received federal funds for some programs, and the Indigenous World Association, mainly by Ward Churchill, who spread the rumor that IWA was federally funded, which hardly fit the accusations that we were communist. At any rate, IWA did not receive any funds from the American Indian Center; like many other civil society organizations, we made use of the facilities. The attacks on Chockie grew to the point that she was ousted as director, and soon after, the American Indian Center closed down.

I felt that I was walking around with a bull's-eye on my back. I had swum through similar waters before, in the early 1970s when J. Edgar Hoover's FBI COINTELPRO program was in high gear. But it was a struggle to ignore the letters, packets, and rebuffs from strangers, and especially from people I had considered friends. My only recourse had been to keep doing the work, particularly the work I had begun in November 1984, traveling to the Honduran refugee camps and doing what I could to help with cease-fires and repatriation. Now that work was blocked.

I returned home to San Francisco on January 3, 1986, not only exhausted and nearly hopeless, but also in fear for my life. I wrote in my notebook: "Feeling battered—psychologically, physically, and from all quarters. How does it work? In concert? Is someone in charge of discrediting me in the CIA or FBI? Is there a Roxanne desk assignment? They drive people crazy—that is what happens. I am nearly exhausted, and still sick. Must recover. Quit smoking, quit drinking. There is something so peculiar about this time, something chaotic. Operation Chaos was the name of the anti-left campaign in the 1960s."

Waiting in my mail on my return was perhaps the most vicious attack on me yet, because it appeared in the pages of the left-liberal weekly magazine *The Nation. The Nation* had railed in almost every issue against the US sponsorship of the Contras. I had thought it a friend. Now, suddenly, *The Nation*, which had never in its century of publication ever published anything on the

Miskitus, published a long two-part series denouncing the Sandinistas and repeating every piece of propaganda promoted by the Moravian Church and the US State Department's Office of Public Diplomacy. The author, Penny Lernoux, the magazine's Latin American correspondent, likewise had never before written about Indians in Latin America. She was a practicing Catholic and her journalism specialized in liberation theology in Latin America, which was passionately and eloquently summed up in her 1980 book, *Cry of the People: The Struggle for Human Rights in Latin America and the Catholic Church in Conflict with US Policy.*

The series on the Miskitus did not mention me personally. In fact, the article did not reference any view of the Miskitus other than those of Brooklyn Rivera and Margaret Wilde of the Moravian Church. In late September, I sent a fourteen-page manuscript to *The Nation*, asking them to publish it as an article in response to Lernoux's. I truly believed they would publish the full text, because it was such a sensitive issue and because we were in the midst of congressional debates on Contra military funding. Instead, they insisted on publishing only a "letter to the editor" from me, limited to eight hundred words. I reduced my critique, figuring something would be better than nothing. I did not expect the result. They published my letter with a reply of equal length from Lernoux, in which she questioned my credibility, my representation, and my character, rather than answer the corrections I had made to her "facts" or my questions about her unattributed quotes. It was obvious to me that Lernoux had never been in the Miskitu region, although I did not doubt her claim to have visited Managua. I wrote in my letter that that was one of her problems: "Her failure to provide an objective account seems rooted in her lack of experience and knowledge of the region and the people, never having visited the Mosquitia of Nicaragua or Honduras."

In her reply, Lernoux angrily asserted, "Contrary to her assertions, I have traveled extensively in the Indian territories of Zelaya." This was a lie, as I discovered when I was in New York at the international law consultation with the Sandinistas on their draft constitution. I had prepared a paper on constitutional autonomy that was supportive of Sandinista intentions and initiative on the subject, but critical of many of the provisions. Margaret Wilde, the wife of Ted Wilde, a Moravian missionary and pastor—they had spent most of their lives doing missionary work in Latin America—introduced herself to me, commending me for my paper. We had dinner together and became real pals as we consumed several bottles of wine. She admitted to me that she and Lernoux were longtime friends, and that it was she who wrote the article and response in *The Nation*, and that Penny Lernoux had tweaked her text and submitted it in her own name. At the time, drunk, I found this hilarious, as did Margaret, as, apparently, had she and Penny while doing it. It seems that they were longtime friends and Lernoux did the piece as a favor to Margaret. I did not find it amusing when I awoke the next day. Unfortunately, Penny Lernoux died of breast cancer in 1989, and I never had the opportunity to discuss the matter with her. However, Victor Navasky, the publisher of *The Nation*, did apologize to me and explained the magazine's editorial policy granting absolute autonomy to its correspondents. However, that doesn't explain why they didn't give me a full opportunity to reply. I've never felt quite the same about *The Nation* since.

M aya, Chockie, and I had hatched a humanitarian aid project that would deliver some aid, particularly fishhooks, but would mainly serve to publicize the cease-fire and repatriation, which was receiving little media attention in the United States. We hoped to build a small engine that could ignite more extensive humanitarian aid as well as prevent the reinstatement of congressional support for the Contras. In the months ahead, this aid took the form of Project Renewal, a direct-mail effort that Maya funded with Mal Warwick, a Berkeley progressive who had done a number of successful direct-mail fundraising drives. Staughton and Alice Lynd joined us as organizers. We were able to compile a strong list of co-sponsors for the appeal, each of whom then received a letter from William Lay, the vice president of Causa International, the Moonie organization, urging the sponsors to withdraw and arguing that the Miskitus from Nicaragua were not refugees in Honduras:

> In the opinion of many of my Miskito and American Indian friends, there is nothing particularly complicated or complex about the plight of these Indians today. They are not caught in the midst of a dispute between the Sandinistas and the contras. They *are* [original emphasis] the contras. . . .
>
> I can provide you with an excellent video-tape of the Miskito Indian

situation today and I will be happy to send you a transcript of a recent interview I conducted with Mr. Russell Means regarding his experiences in Miskitia. . . .

In February 1986, Chockie and I went to Geneva for the UN Commission on Human Rights, although I was able to stay only a week because of my class schedule. Peter Gaechter, formerly with UNHCR, and Carolina Gómez, now studying in Geneva, met us there, as well as Danira Miralda, the Honduran aid worker. We worked well as a group, meeting with the International Committee for the Red Cross and with UNHCR officials and briefing them on our observations of the Miskitu refugee situation in Honduras. We also met with government delegations and other NGOs attending the Commission meetings. My friend Sidni Lamb, who had been with the UNHCR in Tegucigalpa, was now at the Geneva headquarters, as one of the editors of the UNHCR magazine, *Refugees*. I began writing a series for the magazine on indigenous refugees, such as Sitting Bull in Canada, Chief Joseph and the Nez Perce, and the Mayans of Lacadonia.

In July, the autonomy symposium I had proposed when I was working at INIES finally took place, and Chockie and I went together. It was scheduled to coincide with the seventh anniversary of the Sandinista revolution. At the end of the four-day meeting, all the participants were guests for the July 19 anniversary celebration, which, for the first time, took place outside Managua. As a display of defiance of the Contras, it was held in the north, where Contra attacks were common. A number of foreign dignitaries from the Non-Aligned Movement countries' embassies were bused up to stand with the Sandinistas. Our bus was one of hundreds of buses, accompanied by truckloads of armed troops in front and behind the snaking caravan.

On the two-hour drive, I sat beside Miguel Alfonso Martinez, a Cuban professor of international law, who was also a member of the UN Sub-Commission and one of the five members of the Working Group on Indigenous Peoples. He had been appointed by the Sub-Commission to conduct a study of treaties between nations and indigenous peoples, which infuriated the Reagan administration, as well as Canada, because the majority of such treaties existed in North America. Miguel had earned the respect of the indigenous participants in the Working Group. I had met Miguel on my first trip to Cuba in 1970, as a member of the Venceremos Brigade, a project that put US citizens to work chopping sugar cane, or, in the case of my brigade, to plant, fertilize, and pick citrus on the Isle of Youth. Miguel was one of two Cuban interpreters for our evening meetings. He had also been one of the Cuban government's representatives at UN headquarters in New York.

Miguel had witnessed the campaign against me during the Sub-Commission in 1984, when my book came out. Now, on this dusty drive, I confessed to him that two years of unrelenting attacks had worn me down. He said, "Join the honorable community of those attacked by the United States. Now you know a little of what it is like to be a Cuban loyal to the revolution." That talk and his comment—turning setbacks into victories, as the Cubans would say—helped me gain perspective.

The symposium on autonomy was held at the largest conference center in Managua, and the participants were lodged in the Intercontinental Hotel and treated like diplomats. Nearly all the participants were Indians from all over the Americas, including a large delegation of Miskitus, Sumus, Ramas, and Creoles from the eastern region. I was delighted to see the KISAN commanders Juan Salgado and Reynaldo Reyes, who were involved in cease-fire agreements. Foreign guests included the Uruguayan writer Eduardo Galeano. Except for the opening and closing assemblies—presided over by Comandante Tomás Borge, flanked by members of the Autonomy Commission—we worked in committees on various issues involved in autonomy, with each committee presenting recommendations for improving the Nicaraguan draft autonomy plan. On the evening of the last day the Nicaraguan government hosted a sumptuous banquet and reception. The nine *comandantes* who made up the FSLN Directorate mingled with the guests. I was not surprised, but many of the Indians were amazed at being received at such a high level.

I did not travel to the eastern zone as many others did because I had to go to Geneva for the meetings of the Working Group on Indigenous Peoples and the Sub-Commission. Actually, because of budget deficits and pressure from the United States, the official meetings of the Sub-Commission and all its working groups were canceled that year. The NGOs were determined to hold the meetings anyway, and we did so, with most of the Sub-Commission members attending at their own expense. It was a mass act of civil disobedience that forced the United States to back off from dissolving the bodies.

The International Labor Organization (ILO) had organized a weeklong seminar to follow the Sub-Commission. The ILO preceded the formation of the United Nations and dates back to 1919. It is also unique in its tripartite organizational structure, which includes state members, labor organizations, and employers. In 1957, the ILO had created a treaty for the protection of indigenous and tribal peoples and their integration into unitary nation-states. ILO officials had participated in the 1977 NGO conference on Indians and presented the treaty calling on Indian organizations to promote the treaty and pressure governments that had not signed the treaty to do so. Unanimously, the Indian representatives rejected the treaty because of its paternalistic language of protection and assimilation. For several years, the ILO tried to peddle the treaty, without success, so it decided to revise it. The seminar was a consultation with indigenous groups in that process. Petuuche Gilbert, from Acoma Indian Pueblo in New Mexico, and I represented the Indigenous World Association at the seminar. Within two years, the ILO had a new, improved treaty, the first international instrument that refers to indigenous *peoples* rather than populations. This is significant, because in UN parlance *peoples* is synonymous with the right to self-determination. The seminar ended on September 10, my birthday. Lorraine Ruffing, with whom Petuuche and I were staying, organized a dinner party at a Geneva restaurant. Dozens of people showed up, including some who had shunned me during the campaign against me two years earlier—a return of some old friends that I greatly appreciated.

A s US/Contra credibility plummeted, some of the pressure on me subsided. A series of events in 1986 knocked the Humpty-Dumpty Contra war off the wall, shattering it into so many pieces that it could not be put back together again, at least not in the "neat" (Oliver North's adjective for describing the operation) form it was before.

The Contra war continued, of course, but the United States had an increasingly difficult time hiding its direct involvement. However, the situation on the ground had gotten bad again, as KISAN operatives in Honduras agreed to come under FDN (UNO) Somocista command in order to receive

$300,000 in US Contra funds. KISAN used this money to renew its attacks inside Nicaragua, cutting off food supply lines to the northern Nicaraguan Miskitu villages. Terrified of KISAN warnings that fighting would return to the villages unless they fled, Nicaraguan Miskitus again began crossing the river into Honduras.

In April of 1986, Otto Reich and Oliver North tried, but failed, to stage another refugee flight like Francia Sirpe. On April 8, 1986, Joanne Omang reported in the *Washington Post*: "The Reagan Administration considered sending Vice President Bush to Honduras last week to call attention to the Indians' flight, according to the State Department." The plan was for the US embassy in Tegucigalpa to fly sixty journalists to the Honduran Miskitia. Because of high winds, that flight was not possible. However, three journalists made their own way there. In stories in the *Philadelphia Inquirer* on April 6 and the *Boston Globe* on April 7, coaching of the Miskitu refugees was reported. *Globe* reporter Julia Preston wrote: "'It was the worst public relations job I've ever seen,' said one foreign relief official. He said exile leaders told him they had delayed refugees at the border so they could 'make them politically conscious' before facing questioners in the camp." Andrew Maykuth of the *Inquirer* reported: "About 9:45 a.m. Thursday a team of US military personnel—five doctors, five nurses, two dentists and four veterinarians—were flown in Chinook helicopters to Auka as planned. They brought about 20 trunkloads of medical supplies, apparently expecting to see as many as 800 refugees. . . . Only about 50 refugees were there. 'The colonel was very angry,' the refugee official said. 'He said, where are the refugees?'"

Yet the apex of Otto Reich's propaganda career came with the June 17, 1986, nationwide PBS broadcast of *Nicaragua Was Our Home*, portraying the "exodus" of all the Miskitus from Francia Sirpe in Nicaragua to Honduras. The film's director, Lee Shapiro, had told me in 1984 that the film was funded by the United States Information Agency, which should have barred its domestic use. However, the real coup for Reich was its appearance on PBS's nonprofit, publicly funded stations across the country. It was also a victory for the Reverend Moon's Unification Church in gaining mainstream credibility, as its newspaper, the *Washington Times*, was also doing. Some called the PBS broadcast "the browning of public television"—an example of killing two birds with one stone.

That was Reich's last propaganda triumph. Soon, a more decisive blow to the Contra supply effort came. On October 5, 1986, a teenaged Sandinista militiaman in the south central Nicaraguan jungle spotted an unmarked cargo plane flying low and dropping bundles. With one well-placed shot, he brought down the clunky aircraft. Hanging in the sky was a man at the end of a parachute who drifted down near the young militiaman, who took him prisoner. The pilot had been killed in the crash. Other Sandinistas in the area gathered around, and one took a photograph of the dark, skinny little militia marksman leading the tall blond prisoner at the end of a rope tied to his wrists. That photo would appear on major magazine covers and front pages of newspapers around the world and even in many local papers in the United States, a living symbol of David and Goliath, more powerful than Reich's staged propaganda.

Eugene Hasenfus, a Special Forces Vietnam veteran from Minnesota, was the prisoner. In his pocket was found the business card of Donald Gregg, Vice President George H. W. Bush's assistant. The Sandinistas presented Hasenfus at a press conference in Managua, in which he was forthcoming about what he had been doing and why. Jobless, he had been recruited by a mercenary organization "to do what I did in Vietnam," that is, work as a "kicker" on clandestine CIA cargo planes delivering weapons and supplies to CIA-organized tribesmen enlisted in counterinsurgency against Vietnam and Laos. He said that he was not supposed to survive if shot down, but before that particular mission, his brother, also a vet, had pressed a parachute on him. He said that he was being treated well by his captors and showed no signs of abuse. Soon he was released by the Sandinistas and free to go home.

Vice President Bush's office denied any knowledge of the supply flight. The White House claimed that it must have been a rogue operation, not linked with its own Contra support program. But a month later, the plot thickened. An Arabic-language magazine in Beirut revealed information about US arms-for-hostages sales to US archenemy Iran. Since 1982, when Israel invaded Lebanon and drove the PLO out of Beirut, various Islamic militias had been taking US citizens as hostages, making demands for Israeli withdrawal from Lebanon, among others. Interestingly, the White House National Security Council that had been running the Contra war for more than two years was also implicated in the Iran-hostage deal. I read the familiar names: John Poindexter, who had recently replaced Robert McFarlane as national security adviser; Lt. Colonel Oliver North, the errand boy; and Under Secretary of State Elliott Abrams, whose charge was Latin America.

Finally, US journalists, who had appeared hypnotized or bought off by the Reagan administration, perked up and began asking questions, turning up new clues and links. The daily White House press briefings were consumed with one subject only. Otto Reich and his band of glib and wildly successful propagandists—including Robert Kagan and Linda Chavez—were unable to change the subject, rather only deny, deny. To top it off, Democrats won control of the Senate in the November elections, the day after the Iran-hostage deal was exposed.

After fifty days of denial, which garnered further bad press and congressional hounding, the White House came clean. On November 25, 1986, Attorney General Edwin Meese held a live televised news conference in which he explained in detail the sale—for grossly inflated prices—of missiles to Iran, using Israel as the middleman to deliver them, and the way the profits were then deposited into a secret Swiss bank account accessible to Oliver North to divert the funds to the Nicaraguan Contras. He announced that Oliver North had been fired and that Poindexter had resigned earlier that day. Conveniently, the CIA director, William Casey, the Dr. Strangelove behind the whole affair, had been disabled by a stroke.

Now it was the Iran-Contra scandal, rather than Iran-hostage deal.

The following week, on Thanksgiving 1986 break, I accompanied our Peace Ship delegation to Managua. Indigenous World had collaborated for a year with Nicaragua support groups on organizing the project: the Peace Ship/Peace House. One of the organizations on the steering committee was MADRE, an organization of women, which provided aid to women in Central America. I was on MADRE's advisory board. Also, the War Resisters League and the Office of the Americas joined, as well as Burlington, Vermont, which had recently chosen Puerto Cabezas as a sister city. Both the International Indian Treaty Council and the Indigenous World Association were steering committee members. Our task was to raise funds to fill a ship to send to Puerto Cabezas with aid for the Miskitus and Sumus together with construction supplies to build a "Peace House" in Puerto Cabezas.

The Thanksgiving delegation was made up of several International Indian

Treaty Council representatives, two of whom were also Vietnam War veterans. Other delegates were Muskogee poet Joy Harjo, Chicano poet and activist Raul Salinas, and Vietnam veteran and peace activist Brian Willson. Brian had fasted on the steps of the Capitol in Washington earlier in the fall, demanding an end to support for the Contras. His fast drew attention to the war and attracted Vietnam and other war veterans, who formed an organization, Veterans for Peace. After spending three days in Managua, the delegation flew to Puerto Cabezas and Waspám, while I stayed in Managua another day with Hazel Lau and then returned for my university classes.

With the Iran-Contra scandal invigorating hopes for an end to war, Managua was alive with excitement and energy—people who had been exhausted from six years of being attacked by the largest military machine in world history were now celebrating. The US economic blockade had made the simplest items impossible to obtain, while the canned fruit and vegetables, soap, and tissue donated by socialist bloc countries were of poor quality. Cuba and Mexico provided pharmaceuticals, which they produced domestically, but clinics and hospitals were overwhelmed and medical clinics and doctors were scarce. It was good to see that glimmer of hope. But as William Walker, who with a band of mercenaries invaded and conquered Nicaragua and declared himself president, said when captured and executed in 1860: "The United States will never leave Nicaragua alone."

My personal life, my person, was falling apart, my drinking out of control. My notebook at that time was filled with concern about drinking, knowing that I must stop, but still not seeking help. And, finally, the inevitable happened: I was stopped for drunken driving. Unfortunately, my lawyer talked the judge out of sentencing me to an alcohol recovery program, only lifting my driver's license for six months and imposing a fine. The DUI did not stop my drinking. It only stopped me from driving for a time, which was good.

Before my license was suspended, I drove to Oklahoma for Christmas break, the first time I had been home for seven years. I stayed with my father and stepmother (my mother had died in 1968) in their tiny house in southwest Oklahoma City, near the Stockyards, the part of town poor whites and

Indians, rural transplants like my father, lived in. For days I listened to my father's stories, which I had heard hundreds of times before, about his Wobbly father fighting the KKK, and about all the farms we had sharecropped in Canadian County while I was growing up. We drove to all the old home places and visited the rural cemetery where most of our relatives are buried, including my mother. My brother, two years older than I, accompanied us, along with our cousin Gene, a shell-shocked Vietnam vet. All of them were drinking and so did I. My older sister visited for a few days on her way to see her daughters. She had been in China teaching English for nearly two years and would return for three more. The long trip to Oklahoma and back along the "Mother Road," old Route 66, was restorative. I longed to drive on, all over the continent, escaping myself.

Rather, I found another way to escape. I accepted an invitation to be a visiting fellow at the Refugee Studies Centre at St. Antony's College, part of Oxford University in England, for Trinity Term in the spring of 1987.

Had I stayed home, I would have been glued to a television screen watching the Congressional Iran-Contra hearings, which were broadcast gavel to gavel in the United States. As it was, in Oxford I had no television other than the one in the common lounge, where I watched the BBC evening news and caught a brief recap of the hearings. During my third week there, on April 28, 1987, news came that a young hydraulic engineer from Oregon, Ben Lindner, had been killed by the Contras, shot execution style in northern Nicaragua near the border. He had built a water system that produced electricity for the first time in the region, and for that he died. The war was not over.

Most of the fellows in the Refugee Studies Program (RSP) were African and Asian refugees, many of them from the Sudan, South Africa, Ethiopia, Sri Lanka, Cambodia, and Afghanistan. The founder and director of RSP was Dr. Barbara Harrell-Bond, an "American," as everyone in England refers to US citizens. (It always grates on me, knowing that Latin Americans are insulted by being required to specify to what part of the Americas they belong while the United States appropriates the whole hemisphere for itself. When asked, "Are you American?" I always answered, "I am from the United States." Of course, the term would not rankle so much were it not for US dominance and constant intervention in Latin America.)

My charge in the RSP was Central America, my subject the Miskitu and

Guatemalan Mayan refugee repatriations. Most of the lectures I gave were well attended; however, my third lecture, on Nicaragua versus the United States in the World Court case, was uniquely packed, forcing us to move from the seminar room to the auditorium of Queen Elizabeth House. The city of Oxford had a sister-city relationship with León, the great university town of Nicaragua, so the mayor of Oxford and a number of citizens attended, along with practically all the international relations specialists at Oxford University, including Ian Brownlee of All Souls College, who had been on the legal team of the Nicaraguan government for the World Court case. He and other dons then invited me to "high table" in their colleges. I was treated very well while at Oxford, meeting nearly everyone in England who was involved in human rights and humanitarian issues.

During my stay at Oxford, I flew to Geneva twice to meet with Zia Rizvi at the Independent Commission, where I had worked as a consultant three years before. The report on indigenous peoples would be launched for the tenth anniversary of the 1977 Geneva conference on Indians of the Americas, which I had helped organize. Zia had asked me to read the draft report when I had been in Geneva in February for meetings of the UN Commission on Human Rights. I had taken it back with me to San Francisco to read and make recommendations, agreeing to work at ICIHI after I finished the term at Oxford. Prince Sadrudhin Aga Khan and World Court judge Manfred Lachs had agreed to present the final report to the UN Sub-Commission in August, and to host a reception for the indigenous representatives. I finished my stay at Oxford, and on June 15 decamped for Geneva, where I would stay until September 6. Once again, I was in my studio at the Hotel Mon Repos and had an office at ICIHI. It was good to be back.

The author of the indigenous report, which we titled "Indigenous Peoples: A Global Quest for Justice," was Julian Burger, a British anthropologist, who later became the UN officer in charge of indigenous issues. We had met many times at UN human rights meetings when he represented the British Antislavery Society. I liked Julian immensely, but we disagreed about nearly everything regarding indigenous peoples. I regarded his views as typically anthropological, but also colonialist and paternalistic—"the white man's burden" mentality. He was interested in the innocent, endangered, and exotic tribal peoples in much the same way that environmentalists were interested in endangered species. He had little interest in militant indigenous organizations, calling them "urbanized Indians," although he sympathized with the Miskitus "resisting" the Sandinistas and the armed hill tribes of Burma. It seemed to me that he longed for the time of what he saw as benevolent British colonialism in Africa and Asia.

I saw in Julian's approach a parallel to the US and Canadian governments' attempts to drown the 5 million Indians of North America in a sea of 200 million minority ethnic groups in Asia and Africa, thereby shifting attention and responsibility from the rich countries of North America to the poor countries of the Third World. The text of the report he had written practically ignored Indians of the Americas and omitted the origins of the international work, which had been initiated by the International Indian Treaty Council following the Wounded Knee uprising. Not only did our views differ, but as a historian, I thought Julian was rewriting history. In a documentary he and Zia had commissioned to accompany the book, most of the narrative focused on the Polynesian people of Western Samoa, which was an independent country with membership in the UN, controlled fully by the Samoans, rather than American Samoa, which was a colony of the United States. Zia relished putting together two individuals with opposing views and having them duke it out in front of him so that he could determine who was right. He mostly chose my version, to Julian's dismay. The report was published in book form.

My daughter, Michelle, who had visited me in Geneva three times before for brief periods, came for the book launch. By 1987, the Sub-Commission, which had been suspended the year before, had grown so large in participation that its meetings were moved to the spacious auditorium of the UNCTAD building, a modern annex to the Palais. The hall was packed the day of the ceremonial presentation of the book by Prince Sadrudhin and Judge Lachs. For me, a dream had come true. I was deliriously happy and felt vindicated in that hard decade of struggle. Those who had previously turned on me during the campaign against me now shook my hand and congratulated me for work well done. The lawyers of the Indian Law Resource Center and the National Indian Youth Council, along with Brooklyn Rivera, had tried to dominate the Working Group on Indigenous Peoples before the Sub-Commission, but without success, and they were now absent. The Iran-Contra hearings had revealed their ties with the illegal operations of the National Security Council.

On the last day of the Sub-Commission, I received the news that Brian Willson had been run over by a US Navy weapons train loaded with arms destined for the Salvadoran military. I had become very close to Brian and his wife, Holley Rauen, after the Thanksgiving Peace Ship delegation the year before. He had been among the many protesters at the Concord Naval Base, across the bay from San Francisco, who sat on the tracks to stop the trains on their way to the port. On this day, the train not only did not stop but rather speeded up. Brian did not make it off the tracks, and both his legs were severed above the knees. It was a sad reminder that the war was not over. Brian saw himself as one among hundreds of thousands of maimed Nicaraguans, casualties of a dirty war in which 38,000 Nicaraguans were killed. Although my wounds were nothing compared to Brian's, I felt the same way.

My time in Europe that spring had begun with Ben Lindner's execution by the Contras in Nicaragua, and now it was ending with Brian having been marked for death because of his high-profile activism. But earlier in August there had been good news that the Central American presidents, including Nicaragua's Daniel Ortega, had agreed to a peace plan drafted by President Oscar Arias of Costa Rica. Soon negotiations would begin between the Sandinistas and the Contras, much to the Reagan administration's displeasure. Nicaragua would lift its state of emergency, followed by Congress killing the Contra aid program. The Iran-Contra actors would be indicted on criminal charges.

In Geneva, I had begun to black out after drinking a small amount of alcohol, a condition that I had experienced in 1975 that led me to quit drinking and enter a recovery program. When I returned to San Francisco in mid-September, I was able to reclaim my driver's license, but another DUI would mean jail time. I became hyperconscious of abusing alcohol and with great discipline was able to cut down, counting my drinks daily in my notebook. I also quit smoking, because I knew that the two went together. Several times that fall I drank too much, again blacking out. I did drink alone too much and began to suffer depression. But I enjoyed being home and back to teaching.

For several years, I had been aching to write, and that required solitude and time. I kept a separate journal that I called "Miskitu stories," which were autobiographical short stories. I began thinking of turning them into a novel I would call *Norther.*

Finishing classes and exams in mid-December, for the first time in years I was in San Francisco for the holiday season and enjoyed shopping and spending time with Michelle, who loves all holidays and gift giving. I had spent a great deal of time with Brian and Holley since returning from Geneva. They had become celebrities and much in demand. One event was held at the huge Masonic Auditorium. I later drove Brian to Maya Miller's ranch outside Reno, Nevada. I wanted them to meet each other. Holley, who was a midwife and had a baby to deliver, flew in to join us. It was a magical four days, snowbound, restful. Like most alcoholics, I spent too much of the Christmas season drinking. On the drive back, Brian, who did not drink, lectured me on drinking too much and about my responsibility to be alert and contribute to the struggle. Of course, he was right, but I resented his self-righteousness.

I ended 1987 in Washington, D.C., at the annual meeting of the American Historical Association. I had not participated in a history conference since 1980, just when my academic career was taking off, and I planned to return to the University of New Mexico with an appointment in history amid a number of job offers available to me. Now I felt like a Martian, nearly forgetting how to speak the language of historian. I realized that I could not just pick up where I'd left off: I had chosen a different path.

17

The Final Chapter: Rednecks and Indian Country, Again

The last time I traveled to Nicaragua was in June 1988, at the invitation of the Nicaraguan government and the UN High Commissioner for Refugees. I was invited to be an official observer of the "land bridge" repatriation of Miskitu refugees from Honduras to Nicaragua. There was also the celebration of the completion of the Peace House in Puerto Cabezas. Chockie Cottier and I traveled together along with Reynaldo Reyes—once called Comandante Ráfaga, the former insurgent Miskitu commander for MISURA/KISAN, since he had been staying with us in San Francisco.

I interviewed Ráfaga before we left, and his explanation of why he and others became insurgents against the Sandinistas was clear and honest, as was his evaluation of the Miskitu resistance. (Ráfaga's autobiography, written with J. K. Wilson, *Ráfaga: The Life Story of a Nicaraguan Miskito Comandante*, was published in 1992 by the University of Oklahoma Press.)

The Sandinistas did not understand us, didn't respect our language and customs. It's not that they were repressive in the beginning, just insensitive. My people thought they were rude and arrogant. Their experts came in and tried to tell us how to use our land, how to farm, how to fish, when we have been surviving by our own ways for centuries. They didn't understand how we use our land communally, and they tried to divide it up and give us land titles—imagine the arrogance of "giving" us our own land! It became embarrassing, as an Indian, to be associated with the Sandinistas. So I followed Steadman Fagoth and joined the counterrevolution in 1981.

When I look back now, I realize many things I didn't know then. We expected a lot of the Sandinistas, and they did a lot that was overshadowed by their lack of understanding of our culture, our lifestyle, our language. In fact, we in MISURASATA were given a lot of power, resources, and autonomy. We had offices in every part of the Atlantic Coast, and a big house in Managua. We were free to organize and really do whatever we wanted. When the literacy project began in 1980, we demanded to control it on the Atlantic Coast, and we won that demand. We carried out a Miskitu and Sumu language literacy drive and cut illiteracy among our Indian people from 75 percent to 20 percent. Roads were built; electricity and sanitation facilities were installed; health centers were established, and campaigns against malaria, polio, measles, intestinal infections, and other prevalent diseases among us were carried out very successfully. Our people had suffered a lot from the bad conditions working in the gold mines, and the men died very young from black lung disease, leaving many young widows with children. The Sandinistas immediately provided life pensions to all widows of miners and began to improve the conditions in the mines.

We expected all that and much more of the Sandinistas even though we had never expected anything good from Managua before. Still, the old resentments and fears of the "Spanish," as we call the Pacific zone Nicaraguans, were still there. A lot of rumors were heard about a counterrevolution forming and bad things about the Sandinistas. I believed some of the rumors that I now think were probably untrue—rumors about Sandinista repression against the Miskitus. Now it is clear that Steadman Fagoth was using MISURASATA to organize for the counterrevolution, and no credit for any of the improvements in the region went to the Sandinistas, but rather to Fagoth. When the Sandinistas began to realize toward the end of 1980 what was happening, they became suspicious of all of us, that is, of all Miskitus. Among their own people they could tell who was a Contra and who wasn't, but with us, they didn't know how to judge, so for a while they treated us all like enemies. They began arresting MISURASATA organizers, and all this built up to bloodshed in the Miskitu town of Prinzapolka in February 1981, when the Sandinista police tried to arrest some of our people in the church, and eight men were killed in the fighting—four of them and four of us. By that time, the whole leadership of MISURASATA, about thirty, were in jail, including Steadman Fagoth. Our people protested, and the Sandinistas freed all of us except for Fagoth. But they even freed him in May 1981, knowing he had worked for the Somoza secret police. He promised to calm the people down and to leave the country to study abroad on a fellowship, but once he got out to the border, he crossed over into Honduras and joined the FDN, the Somocistas.

The reaction of the Sandinistas to all this was to suspect all Miskitus. No, they didn't kill or massacre us as Fagoth alleged, but we were closely controlled and watched. Many Miskitus were arrested on suspicion of being Contras. The Miskitus began to hate the Sandinistas, which made it easy for us who were fighting them to get the support of our people.

The Sandinistas recognized that they overreacted and drove our people to take up arms. We did not think in terms of overthrowing the Sandinistas, and we did not know about the Reagan administration program for that purpose. We just wanted to get the Sandinistas off our backs and to regain our traditional freedoms.

Maya joined us for the Peace House celebration, along with dozens of local officials and Miskitu leaders. The house was plain on the outside, constructed of concrete blocks with a metal roof, but quite beautiful inside with floors and walls made of local wood and with wooden fans hanging from a beamed ceiling. Eight small rooms with twin beds in each opened to a large central room. The house perched on the bluff above the Caribbean, with a covered patio dining room overlooking the sea. When Maya and Chockie returned to the US, I stayed on to observe the repatriation. For the first time, the refugees were able to cross the Río Coco border in boats, and I spent three days crossing with them back and forth.

Hope was palpable in Nicaragua, although everyone was war-weary, including me. The Reagan administration was distracted by its Iran-Contra scandal; and since Reagan could not run for another term we were all hopeful about the presidential elections that year. At first, I even hoped

Jesse Jackson might win the Democratic nomination, since he got off to a strong start in the early primaries. But it was not the will of the Democratic Party bosses that a radical like Jesse win. He was tarred with accusations of anti-Semitism because of his support for Palestinian self-determination, and branded a radical leftist for his denunciation of the Reagan administration's intervention in Central America. Former Massachusetts governor Michael Dukakis was anointed as the candidate.

Through most of the campaign Dukakis led in the polls while the Republican candidate, Vice President George H.W. Bush, ducked questions about his role in running the Contras. Even though his aide's business card had been in the pocket of a mercenary who had been captured in Nicaragua, Bush insisted that he was not "in the loop." Kitty Dukakis, the possible first lady, was well known and loved by UNHCR because she had long been involved in supporting refugee rights. I doubted that Nicaragua would be allowed to survive if Bush were elected.

As it turned out, Dukakis took only ten states in the election. He was no match for the dirty tricks and propaganda crafted by Bush's con man, Lee Atwater, who was able to define Dukakis as a cold New England liberal, soft on crime, opposed to the death penalty, and a coward, perhaps even un-American (he was from a Greek immigrant family), who had never served in the military. Bush opened his campaign in a factory that made US flags and pretended to be a Texan, although he was a son of an old-money New England family.

That year, the Soviets pulled out of Afghanistan, which Reagan and Bush proclaimed as a great victory over communism. Prince Sadrudhin had been appointed by the UN secretary-general to oversee the Afghan situation, and Zia Rizvi was working with him. I had talked with them when I went to Geneva for the UN Commission on Human Rights in February 1988, and it was clear to them that the Soviet withdrawal had been Gorbachev's initiative despite, not because of, the Reagan administration.

The Reagan administration's strategy, continued by Bush, was to turn attention away from Iran-Contra by demonizing the elected president of Panama, Manuel Noriega, beginning in January 1988. The CIA rounded up a few Panamanian businessmen to form an "opposition" that called for Noriega to resign. All of us who knew the geopolitics of Central America were aware that Noriega had been in the pay of the CIA to assist the Contras and very likely had been involved in the death of General Omar Torrijos in a plane crash in 1981. The Reagan-Bush administration charged Noriega with drug dealing, which was certainly the case, but in reality they were trying to wipe away their own fingerprints.

They did the same thing in Honduras, targeting Juan Ramón Matta Ballesteros, a drug king who had helped the Contras and owned SETCO, the Contra supply airline in Honduras that also transported drugs. In April 1988, Matta Ballesteros was kidnapped from his home in Tegucigalpa by US forces and taken to the US, where he was tried and later sentenced to life in prison. Two days later, as the news spread, a crowd of angry Hondurans demonstrated in front of the US Embassy in Tegucigalpa—angry because on top of US domination of Honduras during the past seven years, US agents now had violated Honduran sovereignty by illegally extraditing a Honduran citizen. They torched the annex to the embassy that housed the Agency for International Development, which all Hondurans knew was a front for the CIA. Honduran soldiers and police stood by and watched as it burned.

In 1987–88, Massachusetts Democratic Senator John Kerry chaired a Senate Foreign Relations Committee hearing investigating charges of Nicaraguan Contra–connected cocaine trafficking. He found plenty, which was documented in the committee's 1989 report "Drugs, Law Enforcement and Foreign Policy," but no legislation followed and the report received little attention. However, the committee found that the CIA had known about Matta Ballesteros and SETCO's drug operations since 1983.

I returned home from Nicaragua with a respiratory lung infection that was diagnosed as pneumonia. I was treated with antibiotics and felt well enough to make a trip to Amsterdam to give a paper on Miskitu repatriation. On landing, I learned that a US Navy cruiser had shot down an Iranian jetliner, killing all aboard. It was the Fourth of July, 1988.

That entire week, however, I suffered debilitating spasms of coughing. When I got back home I was diagnosed with bronchial asthma, the return of my childhood nemesis. Asthma is a life-threatening disease—the biggest killer next to heart disease in adults and the biggest killer of children—not because asthmatics cannot breathe in, but because we cannot exhale, which creates a toxic time bomb in the lungs and causes wheezing and coughing attacks. I wondered how I had survived it as a child without medication. Now the cure my doctors sold me on was prednisone. Without informing me of its severe side effects, the emergency room doctor prescribed a heavy dose for the month of August. My wheezing and coughing stopped after two days, so I decided to go ahead and attend the UN Sub-Commission in Geneva.

I gave testimony at the Sub-Commission about the effects of the US-backed Contra war against Nicaragua, particularly US manipulation of the Miskitus on the border and the refugees in Honduras. I recounted my detention in January 1986 by the Honduran army, and my exclusion from the refugee camps, accusing the United States of being behind it. One of the US staffers at the Sub-Commission afterward asked me for a copy of my presentation, and invited me to the US reception, an event to which I had never before received an invitation. I decided to go. There the guy told me that the US was not going to reply to my statement because he had cabled the State Department in Washington to run a check on me, and had received the information that I paid my taxes. That seemed a weird reason to stamp me okay. Two months later, I received my first notice from the Internal Revenue Service for a tax audit of the Indigenous World Association; the American Indian Center and Chockie were also being audited.

In Geneva, I began experiencing insomnia, agitation, paranoia, and unpleasant hallucinations, as well as pain in every bone of my body. I later learned that all these symptoms were side effects of prednisone. By the time I returned home in early September, I had finished the medication regimen—and found that it had done me little good, since I collapsed in a major asthma attack. Rushed to an emergency room in an ambulance, I barely escaped a tracheotomy. No beds were available in the San Francisco hospital, so I was transported by ambulance to South San Francisco, where I was hospitalized for two weeks, pumped with prednisone intravenously for ten days.

My new doctor, a pulmonary specialist, told me I had to continue prednisone indefinitely as well as give myself treatments of abuterol, a drug that was forced into my lungs by a portable home nebulizer. Kaiser Permanente, the health maintenance organization I belonged to, had at one time touted preventive care rather than medicating sick people. That was before the Reagan era. Now, with the defeat of national health care plans, pharmaceuti-

cal giants dominated the health care system as lobbyists with the ear of the
White House and Congress. Anticommunism was used to neutralize campaigns for national health care ("socialized medicine") as it existed in Canada
and Europe. Kaiser's goal had morphed from preventive care to keeping pa-
tients out of the emergency room and out of the hospital by using powerful drugs. Prednisone, a cortisone steroid, can cause all the same bad effects
as anabolic steroids—paranoia, insomnia, aggression, depression, dramatic
mood swings, destruction of bone density—but offers none of the positive effects of building muscle and increasing strength. On the contrary, prednisone
destroys muscle tissue, causing ballooning of the body, particularly notice-
able in the "moon face" that results. The bone aches I suffered, the excruciat-
ing pain, were due to the prednisone eating away at all the bones in my body
from the inside.

I could function, but just barely. I continued to teach in the fall 1988 term,
and I flew to Mexico, Colorado, Atlanta, and Virginia to present papers at
academic conferences, toting my nebulizer, in those days the size of a toaster
oven. At that time, smoking was allowed everywhere, including airplanes.
Ironically, after having been a heavy smoker for years, I now could not tolerate being among smokers, or even in a room with a fireplace. On each of
these trips I could barely function, and at the conference in Mexico I suffered
a severe asthma attack and was unable to give my paper. Yet I kept traveling,
as if it were an addiction. And I kept drinking, which *was* an addiction.

That Christmas, I flew to Oklahoma City to spend time with my father
and two older brothers. My father was eighty-one years old, and we had become close since my last visit two years before, after a lifelong contentious
relationship. I wanted to hear his stories again, the stories of his youth as a
young cowboy and about his Wobbly father in Canadian County.

The day I arrived in Oklahoma coincided with the December 21, 1988,
explosion of a Pan Am jumbo jet over Lockerbie, Scotland. The following
morning, the passenger list was published in the newspaper. As I had feared,
Bernt Carlsson, the Swedish diplomat, was among the dead. I knew that he,
as head of the UN Council on Namibia, had flown to South Africa for negotiations with the apartheid regime about ending apartheid, reinstating the
African National Congress, and, in the short term, stopping its illegal occupation of Namibia. Bernt had called me in early December, before the trip, and

said that he would visit San Francisco for New Year's celebrations with me. I had scheduled my return home so that I would be there to meet him.

I was overcome with grief, for Bernt, but also for the possible setback for southern Africa freedom. I was certain that the South African regime, assisted by the United States and possibly Israel, had sabotaged the airplane—a possibility that was never raised during the investigation. My father and brothers could not comprehend why I was so distraught by the death of someone who was not a relative or a boyfriend. They too were sad about the death of so many people, as well as the possibility of terrorism, but my grief for one person they did not know was unfathomable. I could not bear it there, and I am certain that the effects of the prednisone made me more volatile than the situation called for, and I was drinking.

I rented a car and drove east, stopping in small towns, staying in motels, crying most of the time. I called Judy Wilson in Muskogee, and she invited me to Christmas with her family. Judy understood, having mourned for "strangers" killed in Nicaragua. Also visiting her was Reynaldo Reyes, "Comandante Ráfaga." Judy was taping Ráfaga's story, for his autobiography. I was closer to them, nearly strangers, than to my own family, because of the common experience that was still so raw for the three of us.

I returned to San Francisco to learn that Holley and Brian Willson had split up, the celebrity and public visibility taking its toll on their private life. I visited each of them, separately, and was relieved to see that the split was not going to affect my relationship with either of them. Holley and I met for lunch and a matinee movie, during which I suffered a serious asthma attack. Holley drove me to the emergency room, and again the trauma doctors were able to save my life without a tracheotomy. I was in San Francisco's Kaiser hospital for a week and had to cancel my classes for winter quarter.

Fortunately, I had enough medical leave to take off the next two quarters with full pay, scheduled to return for the fall 1989 term. I emerged from the hospital barely able to walk. A thrush infection had developed in my mouth and throat from the heavy doses of prednisone. It was like one enormous canker sore, extremely painful, especially when I swallowed. The infection indicated that my immune system was shot, one of the effects of prednisone. I became determined to find another way to treat asthma, and I read every book I could find. For one thing, it was clear that the change in air pressure while flying provoked asthma. What I gleaned from my study was that I had to change my lifestyle. I put myself on a strict vegetarian diet and took yoga classes. I lifted free weights and aimed at walking five miles each day, building up to it slowly. I rebuilt my strength. I restricted my drinking to two drinks a day, only rarely abusing alcohol. I tapered off the prednisone, but continued the nebulizer treatments. By May 1989, I felt better than I had even before asthma had struck the year before.

When an invitation arrived from UNHCR inviting me as a special guest to their conference on Central American refugees to be held in Guatemala City, I felt well enough to go, and I did—with my nebulizer. Many old friends were there from Nicaragua, as well as from Oxfam, Amnesty International, and other NGOs I had met while at Oxford two years before. I was disappointed that no refugees had been invited, only concerned governments, including the United States, with NGOs participating as observers. That was one of the Oxford Refugee Studies program complaints about UNHCR, that it did not involve refugees themselves. There were twenty-seven special guests like me, all of them far better known. I was unable to remain long in any meeting because people smoked everywhere. But I was glad to be there to experience what I thought then was the certainty that the Sandinistas would prevail, and that the combatants in El Salvador and Guatemala had been vindicated—both countries' militaries had been put under fragile civilian control. The Central American countries had taken the first step to forming a Central American parliament, harking back to their initial independence from Spain in 1821, as the Central American Republic, which the British and the United States managed to break up into tiny countries with unclear and disputed borders.

Congress had renewed funding to the Contras in order to continue to keep them together until after the Nicaraguan elections scheduled for February 1990, which the US had insisted on—a sword hanging over the country. The idea that the Sandinistas could be ousted from power only eight months after winning their war, this time by an electoral coup, was then unfathomable to me. Yet the Sandinistas were reeling from the long war and really did not have time to develop the infrastructure needed for national elections.

The San Francisco Bay Area earthquake of October 17, 1989, seemed to foreshadow the political earthquakes that changed the course of history. The whole socialist bloc collapsed, beginning with Berliners tearing down the wall that divided their city on November 9, 1989, and ending with the August 1991 collapse of the USSR into its fifteen separate republics—interestingly, as provided for in the Constitution of the Soviet Union. Cuba, 75 percent dependent on socialist bloc trade and subsidies, including all its oil, and still under US economic boycott, was predicted to implode. Of course, the collapse had started long before the iconic dismantling of the Berlin Wall, back in 1985 when Mikhail Gorbachev became president of the Soviet Union. Gorbachev's policies of building an open society and restructuring the economy along capitalistic lines unleashed forces beyond his control, especially since those forces were assisted by funding from the Reagan and Bush administrations.

Under pressure and threats from the Bush administration, the Sandinistas held their national elections a year earlier than they had planned, in February 1990. Just to make sure that the people of Nicaragua understood the consequences of making a choice the United States did not like, President Bush sent 25,000 US troops to Panama on December 19, 1989, two months before the Nicaraguan election. The goal of the Panamanian operation, codenamed "Just Cause," was regime change. The new government of Panama, handpicked by the Bush administration, was installed before Manuel Noriega surrendered on January 3, 1990. Noriega was whisked to a cell in Miami, tried, convicted, and sentenced to forty years in prison. It was the first direct military act of regime replacement in US history (not counting the many covert operations that led to regime replacement in Iran, Guatemala, Chile, and many others), foreshadowing the preemptive strategy the junior Bush would implement a decade later in Afghanistan and Iraq. The Panama invasion was dubbed "Operation Just 'Cuz" by those who could see no point in the operation, but I was sure it was meant to terrify Nicaraguans into voting the Sandinistas out, because they knew that the US would never leave them alone until they did so. The bloody drama in Panama City was a demonstration to the Nicaraguan population of what would happen. The United States also made it clear that the economic boycott of Nicaragua would continue if the Sandinistas won, and that it would continue to support the Contras, threatening perpetual low-level war.

Sure enough, in the February 25 elections the FSLN gained only 46 percent of the vote, which, when I thought about the no-win choice offered the Nicaraguans, was amazingly high. The Contra war had cost 50,000 Nicaraguan deaths out of a population of 3.5 million, with whole communities wiped out, leaving 100,000 homeless and the country's infrastructure, such as it was, wrecked. Now the wealthy again took the reins of power. Elliott Abrams, the former State Department official in charge of the Contra war who had been indicted for crimes related to the Iran-Contra affair, crowed: "When history is written the Contras will be folk heroes."

That was a lame prediction. No one remembers the Contras as anything but mercenaries of the United States, except perhaps for Abrams and his small circle of neoconservatives. There is no way a government can create a people's resistance. Only the people can do that. The Miskitu people remember and honor the young men and women who fought for them, even those who attached themselves to the Contras. After the Sandinistas were voted out of power, some Miskitus allied with the Sandinistas, some with other parties, while the majority remained independent. What they have that they did not have before the Sandinistas came to power is the legally recognized platform of autonomy from which to struggle for their rights, or even independence one day. The Míkitus had fought the Sandinistas for their rights, and had earned their respect.

As Kris Kristofferson's "Sandinista" on his 1990 album, *Third World War*, proclaims, "Sandinista, you can hold your head up high / You have given back their freedom / You have lived up to your name."

Spring 1990. I am in Portland, Oregon, for a public rally to honor Ben Lindner, who had been killed by the Contras in Nicaragua two years earlier. Portland was a hotbed of protest against US policy in Central America throughout the 1980's, and Ben was from Portland. His still grieving parents will speak. In part, this gathering is an act of solidarity among those of us involved in that struggle.

I find Pioneer Square, where the rally is to take place. It is a cold, rainy day, and from under my umbrella I look out over a sea of umbrellas, slickers, and placards. I enter the crowd and strain to hear the speaker, but people are talking around me. The crowd is energetic, the atmosphere charged with anger and outrage. I look up into the face next to me, a vaguely familiar face, a white man in jeans and a plaid wool shirt, short graying blond hair, cowboy boots and a cowboy hat, no umbrella. The woman next to him looks like a smaller version of himself.

Something is wrong, I realize. There is nothing about this crowd that is similar to the other Central American events I have participated in for the past nine years. Yet I feel like a fish in water, so at home. I hear voices, soft but twangy. Then I realize these are Okies and I am stunned: Okies aligned with someone who died supporting the Sandinistas? No, impossible—something is definitely wrong.

I edge to the front of the crowd and see a banner draped behind the speaker, another cowboy-booted man speaking in that same familiar voice. The banner shouts: SPOTTED OWL OR HUMAN JOBS? These are out-of-work loggers protesting their fate. These are descendants of the Dust Bowl Okies, the people I come from. Some may even be my cousins who came to Oregon for logging jobs.

I scan the rest of Pioneer Square and at the far end I see a knot of mostly young people, along with the more formally dressed men and women who will be church people and aging leftists like me. I walk away from the loggers toward the other group, and something in me screams at having to make that choice, that says stay and fight, argue with the loggers, tell them about Central America; and then I think, at least tell the Central American rally about those loggers. But the gap is too wide. There is no communication. I come from one but choose the other. Traitor, I accuse myself.

I spot the organizer whom I know, a college student.

"Sorry about this. We didn't know we'd have to share the square with a bunch of rednecks," she says.

And my neck burns red.

Then came the Gulf War. In early August 1990, Saddam Hussein ordered his army to invade Kuwait. The Bush administration immediately launched Operation Desert Shield, supposedly to prevent Iraq from invading Saudi Arabia. The United Nations Security Council called for the immediate withdrawal of Iraqi forces, followed by an ultimatum, in late November, giving Iraq until January 15, 1991 to withdraw, at which time a US-led coalition was authorized to force them out.

When the war started, I was at a month-long writer's retreat at Port Townsend on an island off the Washington coast. I was partway through a year-long paid sabbatical from my university. My retreat was on a long-closed military base, Fort Worden, which had been featured in the movie *An Officer and a Gentleman*. My abode was a former officer's house—a plain, wooden three-bedroom house overlooking the angry ocean. There was no telephone or other means of communications outside a pay telephone booth a mile away, and no television. I arrived on January 2, stocked up on groceries that I thought would last the month, and, surrounded by snowbanks, planned to hole up in my cozy cabin to write—my first attempt to write a book about the Miskitus and the Contra war. However, during the first week I went into Port Townsend to do a reading at the local bookstore and learned that demonstrations and a vigil against the looming war were planned. Local high school students who also organized meetings at the school led the demonstrations, and I attended them nearly every day. I volunteered to spend two hours a day at the twenty-four-hour vigil in a small church, my hours being the unpopular 4–6 a.m. stint. I bought a radio, and when I was not out demonstrating I listened to it compulsively. I was able to get the excellent NPR FM station out of Seattle, which aired the Senate debates on approving the use of force to remove Iraqi armed forces from their occupation of Kuwait. I need not mention that my newly purchased Mac portable was not put to much use.

On January 17, I awoke to the news that US planes were bombing sites all over Iraq. I cried until my face was puffy and swollen, and I cried for the next two months. I could not stop crying. The local demonstrations shrank to only a few of us in a clutch downtown being yelled at and nearly run over by the local "patriots." Now the chants and picket signs said "Support Our Troops." The vigil against the war continued, and I stayed at the church more than my volunteered two hours, since few people were now participating in the vigil. I felt transported back to 1964, when so few of us were demonstrating against the Vietnam War. The grounds upon which I temporarily was living seemed to scoff at war. Fort Worden was a museum, making it appear that war was no longer conceivable.

I left my retreat at the end of January and drove to Portland, where I spent the night in a hotel. For the first time, I saw the television images, CNN around the clock, the military's pictures of precision bombing with guided missiles, a "clean" war, with no people killed, lies and more lies, vivid pictures of lies that people were accepting as a game, an elaborate video game. There were frequent news conferences featuring General Colin Powell, Bush's chairman of the joint chiefs of staff, and Dick Cheney, secretary of defense. They both twisted and leered at the cameras in such a way that it suggested pornography, as if they were getting off on the bombing. Reporters lobbed softball questions. There were jokes and laughter, as if it were a sports event instead of a war. There was a lot of talk about the "Vietnam Syndrome," or rather, about its end, hailing the public's positive response to this large-scale war and its fabulous success in overwhelming "the enemy."

In San Francisco, I spent only two days, one of them at a huge demonstration against the war, where for a few hours I felt part of something larger and more confident that the war would gather popular opposition. Then I drove across country and learned differently. I learned that the "Vietnam Syndrome" of anti-intervention had been dissolved, and that was what the war was about, not Kuwait, but post–Cold War US militarism. Obviously, from the amazing advanced weaponry on display, the Reagan and Bush administrations had been busy rebuilding the US armed forces, and the public was dazzled.

I had accepted an invitation offered a year before to spend a semester as a "visiting distinguished professor" at Western College, a part of Miami University in Oxford, Ohio, a few miles from Cincinnati and Louisville. I drove the southern route in case of winter storms to the north, and I drove alone. In every town where I stopped, streets and homes were adorned with yellow ribbons and candles in the windows, large signs declaring "Support Our Troops," and various others equating Saddam Hussein with Hitler. Driving across Texas, I realized that had I stuck on a bumper sticker opposing the war, I would have been killed, or my car demolished if I was not in it. I stopped in New Orleans, where I had lived in the early 1970s, for Mardi Gras. I stayed in a hotel room in the French Quarter so I could watch from the balcony, but the joyful event had turned into a pro-war parade and rally. The same for the Grand Ole Opry in Nashville. I had reserved a ticket so I could see the favorites of my radio childhood in person. The hall was packed, and I had a front-row seat. It too was a rally, and every song was a war song, or turned into one. I arrived in Oxford, Ohio, deeply distressed, crying.

Western College was more like a British college than a US university, even though it sat on the grounds of Miami University. I lived in a faculty apartment in the single building where all the students lived and where the classrooms were located. The students were mostly white and well off, because the tuition was high. But it was good to be where nearly all the faculty and students in the Western program opposed the war (unlike the town and Miami University). Again I joined a vigil at a church every morning and got to know all the local peace activists, a couple of dozen people. When I heard a retired military officer on the news call Iraq "Indian Country," the military term for "behind enemy lines," I realized that indeed the US was engaged in another Indian war, and I wrote an essay titled "Indian Country."

One weekend, I drove from southern Ohio to upstate New York to visit Brian Willson, who had moved back to his family home after his parents died. In talking to him on the phone, I'd felt he might consider suicide, as had several Vietnam vets when the US began bombing Baghdad. Brian had told me that only permanent peace could vindicate 58,000 dead American soldiers in Vietnam, and all the misery suffered by those who returned; only if Vietnam was truly the war to end all wars, revealing as it did the brutality and senselessness of war in general, and the wrongness of US imperialism; only permanent peace, he said, could allow the Vietnam vet self-forgiveness and significance; that another genocidal war against a brown people would make him and other Vietnam vets murderers, not fallen innocents or victims of history. There was a plea in his voice, a heartbreaking crack. I thought of what he had said when I heard a soldier say to a reporter on National Public Radio, regarding waiting in the desert for the ground war to begin: "I'm so tired of just sitting around here that if I don't get to kill somebody soon, I'm going to kill somebody."

But Brian survived, and I survived. Not everyone did.

Epilogue

I do not regret my involvement in that decade of the Contra war that nearly destroyed me. I learned hard truths about myself and about politics, but especially about the United States. I'm proudest of the early organizing, lobbying, and writing I did on international indigenous issues. Representatives of indigenous nations have continued to struggle for their right to self-determination under international law, achieving a remarkable institutional presence within the ongoing UN Working Group on Indigenous Peoples, as well as in the Permanent Forum on Indigenous Issues based at UN headquarters in New York. There is now a UN Special Representative for Indigenous Peoples, and a UN working group is drafting a Declaration on the Rights of Indigenous Peoples, which one day will become a treaty. In 2003, a UN expert seminar was convened to review the extensive Sub-Commission study on treaties between states and indigenous peoples, authored by Miguel Alfonso Martínez, professor of international law at Havana University. (The expert presentations and other UN documents related to indigenous peoples are available at www.unhchr.ch/indigenous/main.html.)

The combination of the UN decades against racism, for women's rights, and for the world's indigenous peoples brought to the foreground the emerging leadership of indigenous women. Now, even in the farthermost communities of indigenous peoples, there is knowledge of their rights under international law, a tool of survival in the face of states that would rather they just disappear. They will not disappear; nor will they remain quietly in the background.

During the 1990s, Nicaragua, sadly, fell back into the economic conditions of the Somoza era; it is now the second poorest country in the hemisphere next to Haiti. The traditional tiny oligarchy is back in power. But the Sandinistas, against all odds, had left the legacy of democracy and a constitution. The FSLN has retained 40 percent or so of the seats in parliament, making it impossible for the oligarchy that controls the presidency to return to brutality and dictatorship. In the northeastern autonomous zone, the people, led by the Miskitus, are developing self-government and institutions. Dr. Mirna Cunningham is president of the autonomous University of the Atlantic Coast that has gone from a dream in the 1980s to a reality. She continues to participate in international indigenous meetings, as do many of the others. Brooklyn Rivera and Steadman Fagoth, rival exile leaders, are back home. A completely new generation of Miskitus has grown up taking for granted that autonomy is their birthright.

The United States, under both Democrat Bill Clinton's administration and Republican George W. Bush's administration, continued intervening in Nicaraguan and Salvadoran affairs, threatening to cut off aid and trade if the FSLN or FMLN returned to power, managing to throw elections out of their grip. The February 2004 US-manipulated regime change in Haiti, removing left-leaning President Aristide, served as a continued warning to other small nations of the Caribbean and Central America that only governments acceptable to the United States would be allowed in the region. That old Monroe Doctrine, asserting United States' right—no, *duty*—to dominate Latin America and the Caribbean, lives on. However, Cuba has survived, and Latin American resistance to US domination was rising again in the new century.

On September 10, 2001, I celebrated my birthday—sober, for nearly four years—in flight from the Indian Ocean to Florida, seventeen hours nonstop aboard a South Africa Air jumbo jet. The plane was filled with people I had long known and others I recently met, all of us returning from the same conference, the World Conference against Racism (WCAR) held in Durban, South Africa, which had ended the day before. Everyone was too excited to sleep much or watch the movies. In clusters representing different cities, regions, or constituencies in the United States, we brainstormed and shared our plans for follow-up work and meetings. In the San Francisco Bay Area, we already had conferences planned and venues reserved to report back to our communities. I felt—as did many—that I was a messenger returning with the good news: that we were part of a worldwide force that could bring down the citadel of militarism, imperialism, white supremacy, and patriarchy.

Many times before during my nearly three decades of international work, I had experienced the energy that comes from meeting soulmates from other parts of the world, particularly from the Third World. Most of the activists who attended the WCAR had not yet had that experience. They were grass-roots activists organizing in their own communities: immigrants, women of color, indigenous peoples, members of the African American community organizing to win reparations for slavery, sweatshop workers, and janitors. But it was the participation of women, mostly women of color from the United States, that most thrilled me. In the previous two UN conferences on racism in 1978 and 1983, I had been one of a handful of women present. The UN Conference on Women, held in Beijing in 1995, had mobilized women who also realized that there was no such thing as simply women's issues, that women would have to take leadership in the struggles against poverty, militarism, and racism. The timing of the Beijing conference was just right for women to take the lead in planning the WCAR conference in Durban. For me, this was a dream come true, one that I had begun to work on in 1967 as a pioneer in the women's liberation movement, but had not imagined possible in my lifetime. And I was proud to have played a part in the preceding UN decades and conferences against racism that culminated in Durban.

The location of the conference, South Africa, was itself proof of the triumph of the international movement to combat racism in its most deadly and dehumanizing form—the apartheid system. On February 2, 1990, the recently elected president of South Africa, F. W. de Klerk, announced the dismantling of apartheid and lifted the thirty-year-old ban on the African National Congress and all other anti-apartheid organizations. He made a commitment to release Nelson Mandela from prison, which he did a few months later. Without the communist boogeyman, apartheid had no justification for existence. But had it not been for the Cuban troops trouncing South Africa in

Namibia and Angola, the white supremacist National Party would have tried to hang on. The South African Communist Party and the workers movement remained a powerful force in South Africa, despite the collapse of Eastern European and Soviet socialist regimes.

Preparations for the Durban conference had taken place during the second Clinton administration. For the first time, a US administration was participating in the twenty-five-year-old United Nations program against racism. Clinton established a seven-person advisory board for the President's Initiative on Race, which was called "One America" and chaired by African American historian John Hope Franklin. The board met in many parts of the country, holding hearings and recording testimony. The final report was submitted at the end of Clinton's term in 2000, with the assumption that Al Gore as president would implement the report and send a high-level delegation to the World Conference Against Racism the following year.

The surprise Supreme Court decision to give the election to George W. Bush, no friend of the United Nations, did not bode well for US participation in the conference. However, the appointment of African American Colin Powell, also an advocate of affirmative action, as secretary of state gave hope that he would insist on leading a delegation to Durban. The suspense dragged out until the last minute, when the Bush administration announced that Powell would not go, sending instead a low-level delegation of State Department civil servants, two white men. This was more insulting to conference supporters than an outright boycott, even more so when the White House pulled them out of the government conference on the third day. The reason given was the inclusion of a condemnation of the Israeli occupation of Palestinian territories in the nongovernmental conference document that was completed during the NGO conference that started the week before the official governmental one. It was the first time in memory that the United States had ever acknowledged the conclusions and recommendations from an NGO conference.

But the heart of the NGO document dealt with the transatlantic slave trade, slavery, and its legacy, with demands for reparations to Africans in the diaspora as well as in Africa. It dealt with the xenophobic racism in North America and Western Europe that manifested in immigrant bashing and deportations. Indigenous representatives, old hands at UN work as well as at

combating racism, provided strong leadership. The Dalits ("Untouchables")
of India were present in great numbers, educating other NGO representatives
about their long struggle for equal status. The South African hosts, mostly
student volunteers, heirs to the struggle against apartheid, were not that well
organized but made up for it in warmth and hospitality, as well as their clear
political views. Many South Africans, who called themselves the "poors,"
staged large demonstrations pressuring their own government to not cave in
to the international lending agencies by eliminating public services.

All of this energy for change, plus the well-received five-hour speech by
Fidel Castro at the closing of the NGO conference—not the inclusion of Israeli occupation—led the Bush administration to vacate the conference, as
had been done under two earlier administrations, Carter's and Reagan's. I
expect that a Gore administration, under right-wing pressure, likely would
have behaved in a similar fashion: Democratic Congressman Tom Lantos,
a Gore ally, was present, holding press conferences and demanding that the
Bush administration pull out of the government conference.

The official UN conference went very well after the US delegation left.
The NGO representatives who stayed, mostly those of us with UN status,
were given conference buildings near the official conference site, and there
we caucused and planned lobbying strategies while a tribunal took place in
which victims of racism testified. I was with the indigenous caucus of over a
hundred representatives, which met every morning and then fanned out to
lobby, regrouping for evening reports. It was the most unified and cooperative
indigenous gathering on record.

Despite attempts by the Bush administration to sabotage the conference,
it inspired great hope of international cooperation to end racism. That hope
was dimmed eight hours after I arrived home and watched on television the
destruction of the World Trade Center. I knew right away that the former
Islamist Mujahadeen that the CIA had mobilized to fight the Soviets in Afghanistan during the 1980s had committed the terrorist acts. In a classic case
of what the CIA calls "blowback," the monster created to fight the USSR had
turned on its former master. These forces had made their presence known as
early as 1988, when they opened fire on the CIA building in Langley, Virginia,
after the Soviets agreed to withdraw in Afghanistan. The same forces had
been responsible for the first bombing of the World Trade Center in 1993.

The killers of nearly three thousand civilians on September 11, 2001, were Reagan's freak children, his beloved "freedom fighters" against the "evil empire." Since the Eisenhower administration, the Central Intelligence Agency has been directed to form covert actions and covert armies to overthrow governments, and in the aftermath, those mercenaries have been given homes and jobs in the United States, particularly the Cubans who carried out actions against Fidel Castro. Besides Cubans, there were Laotian Hmong, Nicaraguan Contras, fascist Croatians, and various African mercenaries, along with deposed military men who had supported US interests from Vietnam, Cambodia, Argentina, Uruguay, El Salvador, Guatemala, Iran, the Philippines, and a long list of other countries. But none of them had ever turned on the United States. With the CIA's internationalization of localized Islamist fanatics from the Arab countries and from Indonesia and the Philippines, they consolidated a force that would never have formed on its own. The United States gave arms, credibility, and power to marginalized Islamicists.

On April 7, 1998, I quit drinking and entered an intensive recovery program. For five years after asthma struck me down in 1988, I had controlled my drinking—very rarely drinking more than two drinks a day and often none. But I was still an untreated alcoholic. After I moved to a new loft in San Francisco and obtained a publishing contract for a book in 1996, my drinking increased to a bottle of wine a day, then two, sometimes more, sometimes tequila. In my much larger place and with an oversized dining table, I hosted frequent dinner parties as well as big parties featuring cooking and drinking. I also drank alone. Yet somehow I maintained my exercise schedule, joining a nearby gym, and continued my full-time teaching. On free days and on summer breaks, I wrote every day, at first without drinking while writing, but soon drinking while writing, as long as I could before blacking out. There was hardly a day in those last three years of drinking that I did not black out, sometimes more than once. The final year was the worst. My book, *Red Dirt: Growing Up Okie*, was published in May 1997, and I traveled around the country promoting it during that summer and fall, drinking heavily.

When I quit drinking a few months later, I talked to friends and relatives, apologizing for my bad behavior, and wrote others. I was shocked when nearly everyone responded with surprise, saying that they had not been aware that I had a drinking problem. Even worse, they had thought my behavior—much of which I did not remember—was normal or reflected my personality. A planned April 1998 trip on Brian Willson's delegation to visit the Zapatista villages of Chiapas was the immediate reason I went into recovery. Another was my daughter, Michelle, who had come to live with me during the first two years of my sobriety, without which I could not have continued. And, not least, I was unable to write while drinking and I had come to regard myself primarily as a writer. My next book, *Outlaw Woman: Memoir of the War Years, 1960–1975*, was written cold sober and published in 2002.

I quit just in time to be able to withstand and deal with the political trauma to come: war without end, the most blatant manifestations of racism, militarism, and imperialism since nineteenth-century colonialism. What I had observed and experienced in Nicaragua seemed particularly relevant since many of the same characters had emerged in the Bush administration. In March 2002, when I heard University of Virginia professor Larry Sabato say, in reference to Bush's appointment of Reagan's national security advisor John Poindexter: "I doubt you could find one American in 100,000 who could explain what the Iran-Contra scandal was all about," I decided I had to get back to my book about the Contra war.

In 1990, John Poindexter had been convicted on five felony charges for his role in the Iran-Contra arms-for-hostage deal and sentenced to six months in prison, but the decision was overturned on appeal. In 2002, George W. Bush appointed Poindexter, a retired admiral, to head the Pentagon's Defense Advanced Research Projects Agency (DARPA), which had created a spooky project called "Total Information Awareness." In early 2003, when information leaked to the press that the Total Information Awareness outfit was planning to sell futures in predictions of terror, the resulting outcry from the public and Congress led to Poindexter's resignation. Not so for others of the Bush appointees who had run the Contra war.

Former Iran-Contra defendant Elliott Abrams served first as George W. Bush's special White House assistant for democracy and human rights, then as National Security Council point man on the Middle East. Abrams had been Reagan's assistant secretary of state for Latin America. He pleaded guilty to withholding information from Congress, but was pardoned by George H. W.

Bush in 1992. Otto Reich, the master propagandist for whom the Office of Public Diplomacy was created by the Reagan administration, received George W. Bush's nod as a top State Department official for Latin America. Reagan's political director, Mitch Daniels, who helped do damage control during the Iran-Contra scandal, was made George W. Bush's budget director. George W. Bush's deputy secretary of state, Richard Armitage, was a Pentagon official under Reagan and involved in contacts with Israel to supply missiles to Iran, the profits going to the Contra war.

No less a cleanup man than Colin Powell, Reagan's last national security adviser, who managed the Iran-Contra scandal, became George W. Bush's secretary of state. In his 1995 autobiography, *My American Journey*, Powell recounts that he supported Contra funding and even claims that he was "the chief administration advocate" lobbying Congress to continue that funding. He used his Vietnam War experience to make his advocacy more convincing. He recalled how in Vietnam he had waited for supplies that could mean life or death, saying, "It's no different for the Contras today."

George W. Bush's vice president, Dick Cheney, had been the sole US representative from Wyoming during the Reagan administration and an indispensable ally in pushing through Contra aid as chair of the Republican Policy Committee from 1981 to 1987. He was elected House minority whip in 1988. Cheney segued into the first Bush administration as secretary of defense and helped direct the illegal invasion of Panama, which preceded the Nicaraguan elections that ousted the Sandinistas, and, of course, the Gulf War that followed in 1991.

And with complete disregard for the ramifications to international diplomacy, George W. Bush appointed John Negroponte, the former US ambassador to Honduras who managed and delivered funds to the Contras, as his ambassador to the United Nations. Frankly, I was only surprised that George W. had not managed to find a place for Oliver North, although he was given a program, "War Stories," on the Fox News cable channel. Later, Negroponte would be the US ambassador to Iraq, proconsul of the war there as he had been in Honduras; then in 2005, he was appointed director of national intelligence. John Bolton, another Reagan operative during the Contra war, was nominated as ambassador to the UN.

Democratic Party officials and most party members, as well as liberals in general, viewed the Bush administration's seemingly reckless and unilateral preemptive foreign policy as something historically unprecedented. Short memories, a whiteout of history. They had forgotten Nicaragua, or repressed it completely. There was no excuse for the forgetting. In 1995, the *Baltimore Sun* published a series by Gary Cohn and Ginger Thompson, documenting John Negroponte's role as US ambassador to Honduras in creating the Contras, as well as provoking a crackdown on Hondurans who resisted.

A tragic case of the establishment rewriting history was that of Gary Webb, a *San Jose Mercury News* reporter whose 1996 three-part series exposed how the Contra–cocaine connection led to a crack cocaine crisis in South Central Los Angeles. The *New York Times*, *Washington Post*, and *Los Angeles Times* unrelentingly attacked Webb's series in editorials and articles until the *Mercury News* withdrew its support for Webb's exposé and downgraded his status, forcing his resignation. Why did the major newspapers do this? Among other reasons, they otherwise would have had to admit that their own reportage during the 1980s was profoundly lacking. Their reporters were witnessing, as I did (just an activist and human rights specialist), the drug trafficking taking place out of the Honduran airports. The airline the CIA used to supply the Contras was SETCO, owned by one of Latin America's biggest drug kings, Honduran Juan Ramón Matta Ballesteros. I heard reporters call SETCO "the CIA airline," and everyone knew who the owner was. They saw everything I did in Honduras, but they didn't write about it—or if they did, it wasn't published. Webb quit his job to write *Dark Alliance: The CIA, the Contras, and the Crack Cocaine Explosion*, published in 1998 by a small press, Seven Stories. But his reputation and credibility as a journalist had been destroyed; in 2004 he committed suicide.

The retrenchment of the hard right wing, linked with the Christian Coalition, emerged from the twelve-year Reagan-Bush reign, creating a kind of right-wing populism that, even during the eight years of the Clinton administration, managed to sustain right-wing hegemony. The collapse of socialism gave a certain popular credibility to their extremism, and liberal politicians decided that they could not risk challenging their claims. This retreat was not limited to domestic politics. When I attended the UN Sub-Commission in August 1991 after a two-year absence from UN meetings, and only a few months after the UN had buckled and endorsed the war on Iraq at US insistence, I was shocked at the docility and the deference given to the United States. Only the Cubans stood tall, despite the fact that their main source of trade and aid—the Soviet Union—had disappeared. It struck me that all the other diplomats behaved as if they were rape victims. I do believe that the UN would have withered and died had it not been for the new Decade for Women and the UN Decade for Indigenous Peoples.

The proof of renewed resistance came in the fall of 2002 and winter of 2003 when, as the US mobilized for the invasion of Iraq, the UN Security Council and the General Assembly refused to give its stamp of approval. The South African government, as head of the Non-Aligned Nations Movement, led its membership in a solid bloc of opposition to war. France, Russia, and Germany received the credit, but they would have caved had not the majority of the world opposed the war. This stance was confirmed on February 15, 2003, when more than 30 million people marched worldwide, in every capital and many smaller cities, saying no to US plans to invade Iraq—protests that the US ignored.

March 19, 2003: NEAR THE IRAQI DESERT, KUWAIT
Ellen Knickmeyer (AP)
Tank crews from the Alpha Company 4th Battalion, 64 Armor Regiment, perform a "Seminole Indian war dance" before convoying to a position near the Iraqi border Wednesday, March 19, 2003.

Capt. Phillip Wolford's men leaped into the air and waved empty rifles in an impromptu desert war dance. Troops of the 101st Airborne Division ate a special precombat meal of lobster and steak. Soldiers sent e-mails to loved ones and savored what could be a last good shower for a long while.

To the ever-louder drone of warplanes, American soldiers in the northern desert that will serve as a launch pad for attacking Iraq engaged Wednesday in some final rituals before a war that seemed inevitable. . . .

Upon hearing of the attack, Marine Lance Cpl. Chad Borgmann, 23, of Sydney, Neb., said: "It's about time. Today we've been here a month and a week. We're ready to go."

"It's the right thing to do. We are going to be part of the liberation of Iraq," said a fellow member of the 15th Marine Expeditionary Unit, Lance Cpl. Daymond Geer, 20, of Sacramento, Calif.

With no sign that Saddam and his sons would heed Bush's order to go into exile, the 20,000 men of the Army's 3rd Infantry Division had received some of the first orders Wednesday to line up near Iraq.

With thousands of M1A1 Abrams tanks, Bradley Fighting Vehicles, Humvees and trucks, the mechanized infantry unit known as the "Iron Fist" would be the only US armored division in the fight, and would likely meet any Iraqi defenses head on.

"We will be entering Iraq as an army of liberation, not domination," said Wolford [the commander], of Marysville, Ohio, directing the men of his 4th Battalion, 64th Armor Regiment to take down the US flags fluttering from their sand-colored tanks.

After a brief prayer, Wolford leaped into an impromptu desert war dance. Camouflaged soldiers joined him, jumping up and down in the sand, chanting and brandishing rifles carefully emptied of their rounds. . . . About 300,000 troops—most of them from the United States, about 40,000 from Britain—were waiting Wednesday within striking distance of Iraq. . . .

Another Indian war.

Nicaragua was the last great hope for national liberation movements to succeed in breaking free from imperialism. That window of opportunity for national-democratic transitions from Western colonialism and imperialism has closed. More than that, the nation-state as such has failed to make a transition to peaceful international relations. A formation that is the product of capitalism and imperialism, the nation-state was once thought to have the possibility of transcending its history. Establishment pundits speak of "failed states," referring to countries like Somalia and Haiti, or preach about preventing Iraq or Palestine from becoming a "failed state" to justify foreign occupation. But they are only examples that appear to prove that there is such a thing in the world as an unfailed nation-state, supposedly a natural, rather than a historical entity. The historical process of nation building that occurred with the rise of capitalism in Western Europe has reached its limits. Had the West, particularly the United States, nourished the struggles of peoples for the development of authentically independent nations out of the ruins of colonialism in Africa and imperialism in Asia, the Pacific, Latin America, and the Caribbean, perhaps the dream of a United Nations could have become a reality. Today, that dream does not appear possible, making indigenous movements ever more fundamental to humanity in reaching a different conclusion than a nuclear war or environmental disaster.